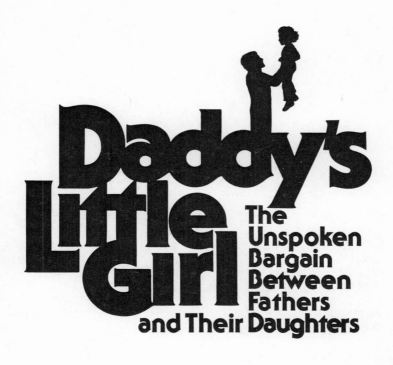

Daddy's Little Girl

The Unspoken Bargain Between Fathers and Their Daughters

William Woolfolk
with Donna Woolfolk Cross

PRENTICE-HALL, INC., Englewood Cliffs, N.J. 07632

*DADDY'S LITTLE GIRL: The Lifetime Bargain
Between Father and Daughter,*
by Wm. Woolfolk with Donna Woolfolk Cross
Copyright © 1982 by William Woolfolk
and Donna Woolfolk Cross
Copyright under International and Pan American
Copyright Conventions
Printed in the United States of America
Prentice-Hall International, Inc., London
Prentice-Hall of Australia, Pty. Ltd., Sydney
Prentice-Hall of Canada, Ltd., New Delhi
Prentice-Hall of Japan, Inc., Tokyo
Prentice-Hall of Southeast Asia Pt. Ltd., Singapore
Whitehall Books Limited, Wellington, New Zealand

10 9 8 7 6 5 4 3 2 1

Library of Congress Cataloging in Publication Data
Woolfolk, William.
    Daddy's little girl.
    Includes index.
    1. Fathers and daughters—United States.
I. Cross, Donna Woolfolk. II. Title.
HQ755.85.W66   306.8'7   81-12012
ISBN 0-13-196345-7

This book is dedicated to my daughter.

William Woolfolk

This book is dedicated to my father.

Donna Woolfolk Cross

CONTENTS

The most important journey of any woman's life is from her father's to her own home.

Thomas Uzzell

INTRODUCTION

When my daughter and I began to write this book we intended our personal account to be supported by research on the subject. We quickly discovered that the literature on the father-daughter relationship is comparatively scant, a small fraction of what has been written and published on mothers and daughters. Nevertheless, we painstakingly went through the available books, pamphlets, magazine articles and doctoral theses.

We finally decided that we were on the wrong track. We did not need to know how many "paternally deprived" daughters suffered from poor peer relationships, nor how many who were hostile to their fathers later had their marriages end in divorce, nor what percentage of "father-absent" daughters eventually became delinquent or homosexual. External data did not interest us as much as the truth about inner problems that is harder to come by, but constitutes the reality of all human relationships. For these answers we could not rely on statistics. We had to interview people who were actually caught up in the net of emotional relationships.

This method does not provide the kind of hard data needed by public-spirited citizens interested in passing laws or forming organizations to grapple with social problems. Personal accounts are subjective, and to that degree unreliable. Nevertheless, a pattern emerged from our interviews. We did not impose it; life imposed it. We have not embellished or rearranged anything. We did excerpt, often only a few minutes from an interview that took several hours. If we had not done so, the book would have sprawled to an unmanageable length.

In a further attempt to get at hidden truths, we relied on the services of three well-known psychoanalysts, all of whom live and work in New York City. They prefer to remain anonymous. Their identities are therefore concealed under a single pseudonym, a doctor we have chosen to call Dr. C. B. Pollard. These psychoanalytic interpretations will be offered whenever appropriate.

My daughter Donna interviewed most of the young women because it seemed a reasonable presumption that she would be able to establish a closer rapport. Interviews with the fathers were conducted mostly by me, for the same reason. There is, of course, some overlapping. In pursuit of a further insight or a new

1

perspective, Donna and I interviewed the same persons at different times, and sometimes interviewed the same persons together. Follow-up interviews to correct or amplify or confirm were conducted by whoever was free to do so.

The great majority of subjects are drawn from the middle- and upper-middle-income classes. We spoke to few persons who could be classified as very rich or very poor. This was a deliberate choice. A book that concentrates on the underprivileged is better done by a social worker, and a book restricted to the greatly privileged would not yield much insight to the majority of our readers. The poor and the rich may not be different from you and me, but they do live differently.

Our hope is that the reader will find in this book an honest account of what many people think is important to know about the relationship of fathers and daughters. Their truths may be partial truths, the evidence they offer far from absolute, but the sum of their insights is the nearest equivalent to reality. These insights would not be available or would not receive the proper emphasis in more systematic methods of observation or more sophisticated statistical analysis. The idiosyncratic, intuitive, impressionistic method comes closer to the truth about human beings than any rigid mathematical framework.

"So far as mathematics refer to reality, they are not precise, and so far as they are precise they do not refer to reality." The man who wrote that understood the limits of the purely scientific method. His name is Albert Einstein.

The kinds of answers we uncovered by our method I would not have been able to predict. Writing this book has changed my perceptions. Both Donna and I have made a sometimes painful exploration of our growing up together, and what we have learned about our relationship confirms what other fathers and daughters have told us about their lives. I wish I had understood my relationship to my young daughter half as well as I do now. I would not have in the name of love placed as many obstacles in her path.

WILLIAM WOOLFOLK

ONE

DAUGHTERS
AND DADS

FATHER HAS A BABY

Recently I came face to face with the possibility of losing my daughter. That brief encounter with the unthinkable became the genesis of this book.

On two previous occasions I had reason to be concerned about Donna's safety. Some years ago she was in a railroad accident in which passengers were killed and injured. Donna had to climb to safety across the roof of the overturned railroad car, through smoke and fire and twisted wreckage. At three o'clock in the morning she called me to say she was safe and there was nothing to worry about.

I didn't know what she was talking about. The report of the train wreck had been on the late news but I hadn't watched it. The danger through which she had passed was not quite real to me, the end being known.

On the other occasion, Donna was living in an apartment house on the Upper West Side of Manhattan. As she entered the elevator one afternoon, a man quickly followed her inside. He drew a knife and demanded that she take him into her apartment.

Donna has unusual presence of mind. When the elevator discharged them at her floor she stood in the corridor, trying to reason with him and hoping someone would open the door from another apartment on the floor. He became angry and threatened to kill her if she didn't do as he ordered. Still she refused to let him into her apartment. She knew her chances were better outside in the corridor.

Someone on another floor signaled for the elevator. The man was holding the door open with his foot. While his attention was momentarily distracted, Donna ran to the door of her apartment, opened the door, got inside and slammed the door in his face as he came racing after her.

When the police arrived there was no sign of the knife wielder.

Once again I was insulated from the reality of her danger because I did not hear about it until days afterward. I had been on

5

vacation in Mexico, and my concern was all in retrospect. There was none of the force of a lived-through event.

On June 6, 1976, however, my wife Joanna and I were staying with Donna and her husband Richard in Syracuse, New York, awaiting an event that had no premonition of misadventure. Donna was pregnant, expecting to give birth at any time.

At five o'clock in the morning a knock on our bedroom door wakened us. Richard informed us that Donna's labor had begun earlier that night and he was taking her to the hospital.

On a dark misty morning we stood in the driveway to wave them off in their Volvo. Then we had breakfast and settled down to wait for news. I had no reason to worry. Donna was healthy, her pregnancy had been uneventful. She and Richard had decided on natural childbirth; he would be with her in the delivery room to assist in the birth of the baby. They had attended classes in this technique, were well prepared for any contingency and had complete faith in the competence of their doctor.

At noon I began to will the telephone to ring. Richard had promised to call as soon as he could.

At four o'clock Donna had been in labor for twelve hours. I told myself there was no reason to be alarmed. Labor lasting twenty to thirty hours was not too uncommon. I called the hospital but they had no information to give me. At five o'clock tension began to tighten. I grappled for the first time with the possibility of misadventure. I thought of Donna or the baby in real danger. I had time for the kind of reflection that establishes priorities of feeling, weighs consequences, assays risks and discovers who we are.

At six o'clock there was no outcome I had not imagined—my daughter dying, the baby born dead, Richard wandering the street in shock, unable to call with the grim news. I telephoned the hospital again. They still had no information to give me.

I had been fortunate in not losing people important to me. Death had always struck at the periphery of those I loved. My parents had died but those blows were softened by a sense of inevitability. A few older people had faded from the margins of my life but their passing had not touched me deeply; it was almost as if they had left the country rather than the world. Until that June 6 I was, for one reason or another, almost unscathed emotionally.

At nine o'clock that night I knew something was wrong. Emotions have a life of their own and do not need logic to sustain them. Forgotten were those twenty-to-thirty- hour labors with successful outcomes. If nothing had gone wrong Richard would have called. Surely he would call now, at any minute, with terrible news. Any second the telephone would ring with word that I did not want to hear.

A kind of urgency shrilled along my nerves. I could not sit still. I could not talk to my wife. Although she is not Donna's mother, her alarm was almost equal to my own and mounting.

Fear feeds on itself. I thought about a life without Donna. I could not force that thought out of my mind. I remembered our first parting, when she left home to go to college. On the last evening, my heart ached with the knowledge that she would not live in our house again except as a transient. There is a terrible poignancy about endings. Never is a word that crushes hope. She would never again stand in the doorway of her bedroom to bid her mother and me good night. I would never hear the doorbell ring at the usual afternoon hour, and her voice, bubbling and alive, pervading the rooms with gaiety. We would never have long serious conversations about life and what the future held for her.

Never.

That had been a minor parting.

But now...?

Richard telephoned at nine-thirty.

Our worst fears, someone has pointed out, are those that never happen. Anxieties self-destruct if you give them time, and leave nothing behind but an ashy sense of anticlimax.

Richard said that after a long exhausting labor Donna had given birth to a healthy baby girl. The birth had occurred at seven forty-five that evening. He added he would have called earlier but in the excitement of being with Donna and the baby...

I told him I understood.

After so many hours of needless worry, the sudden release left me numb. Phantom fears, existing in my mind as if they had happened, left a residue even as they faded. I had discovered a new perspective about my feeling for my daughter. I loved her better than before; not just differently—a sophist's word: better.

But a change was imminent now that a granddaughter had arrived. First there had been Donna's husband Richard displacing me. Now there would be the baby, Emily. Would I be able to accept third place in the hierarchy of her affections? My head was brim-full of sharply focused questions to which I had only diffuse answers.

Images of our lives together, family photographs, old movies, still brought a familiar sweet nostalgic yearning. Could this be only a longing for my vanished youth, a recognition of shrinking time ahead? St. Augustine said that time rushes forward from the past which no longer exists into a present which has no duration and on into a future which does not yet exist. Time in its heedless path was about to shove my generation out of its way.

She seems always to have been a fact of my life. I cannot believe she has not always been with me, but she was born when I was just twelve days short of my thirtieth birthday. In retrospect, that childless man seems to have been awaiting her coming, moving toward a prefigured destiny. How could he not have known it?

For an important part of my life she did not exist. That is incredible to me now. She is here, she is real and all the might-have-beens are, in R. H. Tawney's phrase, "shadows attendant on the triumphant event." I carry a photograph of her in my wallet as a young girl of seven uncertainly astride a pony in Central Park. I look at that photo, which has seen a quarter century of wear, and bring back the moment, the click of the camera shutter, more vividly than I recall what happened yesterday. I hear her voice, walk with her again hand in hand away from that pony ring. She stops to point at a place in the ring where for a moment the pony took a wayward step toward the rail: "Right there," she is saying, "is where my horse *bolted!*"

I want her back. Not as the marvelous woman she is now, with all those connections to the world, but as that girl of seven. A small princess in a tower guarded by dragons, to whom I was Sir Lancelot or St. George. Now she has friends, a husband, a new daughter, a career as a professor in college. She lives in various disguises. When she was seven years old her principal connection was to me.

That little girl has grown up, but I accept that with a part of my mind and only with that. I have summoning powers. If I dared to exercise them, there would be unpredictable consequences. Sir Lancelot might ride off with her in time, never to be seen again.

A daughter is a father's link to immortality. She is what he has contributed to the world. In her bones and blood and genetic code a part of him is kept alive and is passed on to her children and her children's children. This is not the immortality most of us wish for, but it is something. We take what survival we can.

When I was young I was not sure I would ever want a child. The thought of being a husband, father, head of a family, a man with responsibilities, as the Spanish say un *hombre en serio*, was too intimidating.

They say every man has an instinctual need to reproduce his kind, but I doubt it. The desire to be a father is created by society, not generated in the psyche. "Human fatherhood is a social invention," Margaret Mead says, trying to distinguish it from the mother's biological bond to her infant. If fatherhood is an instinct, where did the instinct begin? It is rare in the animal world. Elaine Morgan says, "We tell our children tales about the cozy households of 'Father Bear, Mother Bear and Baby Bear' oblivious to the fact that Father Bear would certainly gobble up Baby Bear on sight if Mother Bear didn't give some rigorous training in shinnying up a tree before turning Baby loose."

After mating, most animal parents go their separate ways. There is no evidence that the father feels an aching void for his young, Why should he? He isn't aware that he is a father. Human beings say, "It is a wise father who knows his own child." How can animals understand the connection between a brief sexual romp and the amazing consequences that follow?

There are exceptions. The wolf, the fox, the African wild dog and the dwarf mongoose defy the rule of hogamous, higamous, animals are polygamous. The male parents of these species sign up for long-term associations with the female. The contract includes child support. As a father, the dwarf mongoose is practically Jewish. He participates in brood care, acts as babysitter when Mother leaves on an errand, totes the infants to and from the nest and even helps to groom them. If Mother should die, he and the older siblings will take over the feeding of the infant and Papa will do everything short of regurgitating his own food to feed them. The African wild-dog papa does regurgitate.

As you move up the evolutionary scale the paternal behavior is so unpredictable you can't blame an infant for getting nervous. Among primates the reaction varies from outright hostility (not too strong a word for a papa who eats his young) to the kind of care one would think only a mother could give.

Human fathers do not gobble up their infants. With that exception, they exhibit the same wide spectrum of reaction to a newborn. Some fathers don't stick around any longer than a purse snatcher. Those who do stay often react with hostility and indifference, quite similar to their fellow primates.

"The paternal instinct," Margaret Mead says, "is not an instinct at all. It is a learned response."

The paternal behavior among humans is at its most ambivalent during the period that precedes and follows birth.

The first time I totally accepted that there was going to be a baby was six weeks before Donna was born. We were house-hunting and a real-estate salesman brought us to a house. The woman who owned the house saw how pregnant my wife was and took us upstairs to show the nursery. A baby was lying there in a crib. All of a sudden, with a real shock, I realized I was going to have a baby that would sleep in my home and be my responsibility.

A month after Donna was born I was again struck by the incredible change that had happened. My wife and I were so busy we hadn't had time to think about it. When I did I wasn't sure I looked forward to my life as a father. I was tired of infant feeding and crying and diapering. It just didn't seem worthwhile; it wasn't turning out the way I thought. My wife and the baby were wrapped up in each other. The baby didn't seem to know who I was. We couldn't go out of the house without a flurry of arrangements—babysitter, bottles, burpings, bedtimes. Being a father meant being tied down. My daughter's demands would never end; all that had ended was my freedom. I was responsible for her being alive, and for the next twenty years I had to support her—feed her, clothe her, send her to college, pay her medical bills.

It was too much. I felt as if I'd committed some crime I had to pay for. I was suffering from a kind of postpartum paternal depression.

The social situation Donna was born into is swiftly becoming anachronistic. Twenty years from today the triad of mother-father-daughter will bear very little resemblance to what we know. But most adult women today grew up in a traditional household in which the father worked and the mother looked after home and baby. In that household a baby quickly learned that Mother was the one she could count on, the one who would comfort, feed, clean and soothe her, who would always love her no matter what. Father was a visitor who would come to give her a playful squeeze or tickle, but would not become involved with her daily care. In order to earn her father's love and attention she had to "be good."

An attractive, intelligent social worker with extraordinary recall of her childhood tells Donna, "Mom was a fact of life, like Rice Krispies for breakfast and a nap in the afternoon. Dad was a special treat, an occasion, a holiday. I used to love it when he'd play games with me. I clearly remember one game where he would sit on the floor and I'd toddle over to poke him with my finger and he'd pretend to fall over. How I loved that!"

It is not surprising that the father in a traditional home has little interest in babies. He is excluded from his wife's labor and delivery, and forbidden even to look at his child except through a glass partition in the hospital. When the baby comes home his first clumsy attempt to hold her is mocked by amused relatives who dismiss his incompetence as "just like a man." While his wife forms an instant emotional bond with the baby, he is excluded from the burgeoning love affair.

Furthermore, his needs are neglected by a wife preoccupied with her new role as mother. Housekeeping is abandoned, dirty dishes pile up, meals are slapdash, cleaning and marketing chores are neglected, sex is perfunctory and a night's sleep no longer knits up the raveled sleeve of care. Long quiet restful nights become short, noisy and active. Even a father who believes nothing in the world is worth waking up at two o'clock in the morning for has to wake up for a crying baby.

The traditional family has only one source of income—father, and money is his domain and worry. He is the man for whom the bills toll. Even if he is fully prepared to deal with the estimates he's read of what a new baby will cost, he soon discovers that whoever wrote those books and magazine articles would never hold a job as a cost estimator. By the ounce, a new baby costs more than Iranian caviar.

A child disrupts the routine of living and imposes other limitations. "I'd like to take a year off and write a book," says an editor at a major paperback house who is the father of three girls. "I've got a smashing idea and could get an advance to write it tomorrow. But the advance wouldn't be near what I'm making. And when the year was up I probably couldn't get my present job back. I decided I can't take the chance. I need that weekly paycheck to support my family. I'm in a plush rut and can't get free to do the kind of work that would give me real personal satisfaction."

A baby at home means that Father can't go out with Mother nearly as often as he'd like to. Even his best-laid plans go awry. One father planned a gala evening in Mannattan to celebrate his wife's twenty-fifth birthday—dinner at a fancy restaurant, tickets to *Chorus Line*, and dancing and champagne later at the Rainbow Room. When the gala evening arrived their three-year-old daughter was at home with chicken pox. They canceled their reservations and turned their precious tickets for *Chorus Line* back to a broker, who later reported he had been unable to sell them at such short notice. If the broker was telling the truth, there were two empty seats (sixty dollars with commissions) at an otherwise sold-out Broadway theater that night.

"My wife didn't mind so much," he told us. "She was too worried about our daughter. She didn't care about anything else." Not surprisingly, this father felt resentment.

The birth of a baby represents a crisis for most men, and not only for the reasons apparent to them. There are subconscious reasons also: a baby recalls infantile conflicts with their own parents, heightens their sense of dependency and inadequacy, intensifies their feeling of being separate.

"Some fathers are ill equipped to be effective parents," says a psychologist with the Russell Sage Foundation, "because they have a deep unconscious fear of assuming a real paternal identity. They consider child rearing to be an essentially feminine activity, and too much participation by them would be a threat to their masculinity. Their training has been toward aggressiveness and competition, qualities that are counterproductive for successful parenting. Such men find it difficult to reorient themselves to a giving attitude because their main function has always been to ensure the survival of themselves and their families. Baby care is peripheral to that chore."

Why then are so many babies still being born? Discounting the role of accident, what motivations impel a man toward fatherhood? After all, three million men a year become fathers. Why not take the advice of a twice-married friend of mine who says that all his life "I have managed to avoid having a baby in the summer. Also in the winter, spring and fall."

"I guess I wanted to find out if I could do it," explains a twenty-one-year-old millworker who lives in Lowell, Massachusetts. "Almost everybody I know has kids. I felt it was time I got started too."

"A child is a second chance," says a thirty-four-year-old accountant in Westwood, California. "When you get to my age it begins to dawn on you that you aren't going to set the world on fire. While you were growing up you were waiting around for something big to happen. You weren't going to be ordinary like everyone else. Gradually you realize it isn't going to be a happy ending. You look around and your friends aren't going anywhere. Nobody's that rich, nobody's that great, nobody's that happy. Before you go, you want another shot. You can make a human being who has a better chance to make it."

The most irresistible of human vanities is the urge to re-fashion a human being into a character of our design. Every father wants his children to avoid the mistakes he made, to seize the opportunities he missed. Through his child he can convert failure to success and come to the end of his life with a real sense of achievement. The philosophers tell us that the ultimate aim of conscious life is to extend itself, and a child helps him to achieve that purpose.

There are other motivations. If a man loves his wife, he wants to see a living product of their love. If his marital bliss is less than celestial, he may hope that having a child will revivify it. If the routine of living has become tedious, he may wish to fill up the vacant spaces with something more interesting and worthwhile.

Even before Daddy's Girl has been born, she has a lot of paternal expectations to live up to.

Robert's wife is a well-known trial lawyer, a domineering woman whom he says he married because she reminded him of his mother. Robert works as a fund raiser for a charitable organiza-tion. The job uses up his small store of aggressiveness, and at home he is meek. When his wife decided it was time for them to have a baby, she didn't let him know until she was three months pregnant.

They were blessed with a daughter, and very quickly Robert learned that he was unprepared to assume the duties of a father. His own childhood had been marked by dependency on a mother who was the Stronger One. His father was a cipher, never able to act on his own or assert himself.

Robert tried to do his best, but he had to be told exactly what to do. And he got contradictory advice from all sides: his wife, his mother and books that often disagreed with each other. He would have been quite willing to turn over the entire problem to the baby's mother, but she had resumed her career and made it quite plain that she had more important things to do than mother care. Robert was unable to rid himself of the responsibility for his daughter. When he came home from work at five-thirty he took over from a housekeeper who left for the day. He prepared dinner. Sometimes his wife came home in time to eat with him and their baby daughter, and sometimes not. It was Robert's job to feed her, put her to bed and get up with her at night.

At two o'clock one morning, he was wakened as usual by the baby crying. He prepared her bottle dutifully, but she pushed it away and kept crying. He began whispering to her angrily, "Why won't you take your bottle, damn it? I know why! You want your mother—you don't want me!"

The infant, with the unexpected sensory awareness that the very young possess, sensed Robert's fear and resentment and became even more unruly. To no avail he walked the floor with her, holding her and trying to soothe her. It was more than an hour before he could put her back in the crib and give her the bottle.

As she took it sleepily, a tiny aimlessly circling hand closed on his finger. For Robert it was a memorable moment.

"Not many people can tell you the instant in which their life began to change," Robert says, "but I can. It happened when I felt my daughter's little hand clutch my finger and hold on. Suddenly all my irritation was gone. I felt that we were linked together, that I had a commitment to guard and guide her through all the years ahead. We were both part of nature's plan to ensure the survival of the species."

Most fathers' experiences with their daughters are not as sharply demarcated, but we do know that somewhere in the first few months of a new daughter's life a relationship begins between father and daughter. It is not yet a profound attachment, but he ceases to think of her as a center of turmoil, robber of his tranquillity, despoiler of his home and usurper of his wife's affection, and begins to respond lovingly and patiently to her assertions of need.

The pattern is as various as the variety of personalities involved and is somewhat overshadowed by the intense rapport existing at this stage between mother and daughter, but in the very earliest months some interaction between father and daughter begins. The feeling of strangeness or hostility yields to the developing intimacy of two *persons* whom fate has linked together.

A continuous stream of minute events makes itself known in an event (the tiny clutching hand) that reflects but does not cause the change. From my experience there is no way of forecasting what sort of event will happen, and there is no way to prepare for it or avert it. I noted the physical changes taking place in my infant daughter and I recall how she behaved at six months, a year or two years old. But I cannot clearly recall what intervened to mark the emotional change in our relationship. That seems to me to have been part of the uninterruptable stream of life. I can only look back and wonder how in the world I got to love her as I do.

MOVING IN ON MOM

A father of a generation ago considered a baby girl to be more a mother's creation than his; she was like her mother because they belonged to the same sex, and ergo, a mother was more likely to understand her. A father and his infant daughter were divided by the great chasm of sexual difference. She would become initiate in the feminine mysteries: she would learn to wear slips and pantyhose and high-heeled shoes, sanitary pads and brassieres, and eventually give birth to another six-pound bundle that would make him a grandfather. In a glass darkly he dreaded the shape of things to come.

"My first child was a daughter, and the minute she was born I could feel the odds shift against me," a thirty-three-year-old father says. "I was shut out of the magic circle. It was like I was standing on one side of a wall and my wife and baby daughter were on the other side. If my first child had been a boy it would have been different. I know how to handle a boy just by reliving my own childhood. But with a girl I could picture myself in a few years locked in with females who didn't care anything at all about football, baseball or camping trips."

Many a new father does not adjust easily to the presence in his home of a small person of the opposite sex. His approach to her is wary and distrustful. Searching for a way to relate to this tiny female presence he looks toward an earlier prototype.

"The way I solved it," says the thirty-three-year-old father, "was to think about' how my mother would deal with her. I couldn't remember how my mother handled me as a baby, but I had a pretty clear memory of her as I was growing up. She was comfortable to be around and, well, reassuring.

"I could never be like her, but I could try to imitate the way she'd been. Maybe I couldn't compete with my wife at this stage of the game, but if I could get across to my little girl that I cared too, she'd find out eventually how much I did."

In the traditional household father cannot be as omnipresent and caring as mother. She wins diapers down on the question of who gives the most nurturant care. Psychologist Sol Gordon reports a study that revealed upper-middle-class fathers spent less than one minute per day on direct verbal interaction with their infants. A man spends more time than that brushing his teeth!

I quoted the Gordon report to a father who is raising five children, including four daughters.

He said, "I know I don't spend as much time with my kids as I—or they—would like. My job is too exhausting. I get up at six o'clock in the morning on weekdays to go to work and I don't get home until seven-thirty at night. By then my mind feels like a clogged sink. And the youngest children are usually in bed, with only time for a quick hello and a kiss.

"Their mother has to look after them so I can earn the income to support us. If I tried to take over a part of their mother's job, I'd be drained of the energy I need to do *my* job. Then no one would be happy."

But babies need affection and attention. In R. Spitz's *Psychoanalytic Study of the Child*, experiments are cited to show that an infant deprived of affectionate handling for an extended period of time suffers from a kind of sensory starvation which can result in mental disturbance or even have a fatal outcome.

The biological explanation appears to be that a lack of physical intimacy acts much like a lack of proper nutrition: the brainstem is not sufficiently stimulated and the nerve cells degenerate. The infant dies from a hunger for affection as severe as a hunger for food.

Since the traditional father at this point is spending more time with his toothbrush than with his baby, daughter must get the physical stimulation she needs from mother. Mother nurtures baby, guards her, teaches her; her presence is a daily, hourly influence; she provides all that is necessary for daughter's survival. Most of her physical and mental energy is devoted to the demanding chore of looking after baby.

One woman, after weeks of intensive baby care and little else, managed to get out for a short walk with her husband while a neighbor babysat. When a fire truck went shrieking down the street she turned to her husband and burbled: "See! See the pretty fire engine!"

Mother love, as Nancy Friday and others have argued, is not without its drawbacks. Precisely because it is so intense, so all-encompassing, it can keep a child dependent, clinging, unsure of herself when mother is not near.

I watched a mother's reaction when her two-year-old daughter was struck from behind by a swinging door she had just gone through. Before the two-year-old had a chance to realize what had happened she was swept up (from a now nonexistent danger) and mother began soothing her, "There, there, it's all right. Mommy's here with you."

Up to that moment the two-year-old's reaction to her mishap might have taken any form, but she was cued by her mother's concern. Suddenly the child clung to her mother and burst into tears. Mother pantomimed punishment for the door, striking it with the palm of her hand and warning it never again to hurt her little girl.

What was the child being taught? That the world is full of unexpected perils and mommy is her shield. Only mommy can subdue and render harmless the danger that surrounds her.

Only mommy.

Let us contrast a father's response to the same situation:

He sees the two-year-old struck by the door and hurries to her to assure himself that she is not hurt. Then he helps her up, brushes her off, tells her she is perfectly okay and sends her on her way. His message is also clear; risk and a certain amount of danger are unavoidable; mishaps are not traumatic events. Even if the two-year-old should begin to cry, he tries to distract her with a toy or move her to another room in order to interest her in some new topic.

An episode from Donna's childhood illustrates this point. Donna, her mother and I once vacationed briefly at a farm during the summer. A tiny fluffy yellow chick followed six-year-old Donna about the farmyard wherever she went. She became so attached to the chick that she wanted to bring it back to our city apartment.

Her mother offered no objection. If the child wanted it, why shouldn't she have it? I tried to caution Donna, pointing out that the chick would not be happy outside its natural environment. If she really loved it as she claimed, she would let it grow up as it was meant to do.

Donna was not impressed with my reasoning. She appealed to her mother and her mother appealed to me. We brought the chick home, kept it in an open box on the windowsill, and let it wander freely in our apartment. For the few short remaining days of the chick's life, Donna was happy.

Then the chick died. I'm sure this did not illustrate to Donna anything important about the nature of selfish love or how easily self-gratification can masquerade as love. But it provided an example of the difference between father and mother love.

Mother is assigned by tradition to the role of primary caretaker, and it has been presumed until quite recently that this was proof of a strong, affective relationship. Baby needs; mother feeds. But we now know that infants form strong attachments to fathers and to others who have little to do with gratifying their physical needs.

Dr. C. B. Pollard says, "A young child absorbs experience like a dry sponge soaking up water, drawing it in from all sides, from parents, siblings, friends, teachers. She uses this accumulation of impressions to fill in her outline of self. Most analysts now doubt that a child's character is formed at as early an age as was formerly believed. In assessing the importance of other than mother figures critical to character development of the child, we are turning more to the neglected figure of the father. His influence is strongest at precisely the age at which the foundations of her character and personality are being laid down."

Early researchers in the field mistakenly concluded that true intimacy between a father and daughter was rare simply because direct communication was demonstrably less than between mother and daughter. If intimacy could be measured by the amount of time spent with a child, that would be true. We have previously raised the question of interaction between a child and mother. Interaction can be stated another way, as the quality of time rather than the quantity. If quantity of time were the only measure of intimacy most children would be as "intimate" with their teachers, close friends, sisters and brothers as with their mother. And all of these put together would lose out to a television set.

The quantity of time spent with a child may be described as simple proximity, the quality of time as emotional proximity. Time and again women who declare they were much closer to their fathers as children have been dismissed by researchers who are wedded to the theory of simple proximity. To preserve a theory they ignore the evidence. A supposedly objective researcher even tells us, "Many women have the illusion of being closer to father than mother," and carries this to an odd conclusion: "The daughter may have got more of the pure unadulterated loving stuff with him (father) but there is no way she could have been closer to him." This confounds the already dubious.

The testimony of millions of women who say they are closer to their fathers cannot be ignored. Too many studies have clearly demonstrated that father's nurturing is as good as mother's, as affectionate, active and concerned, although occasion calls on him less frequently to prove it.

In a paper presented in 1977 to the Society for Research in Child Development, Alison Clarke-Stewart reported that in three-way play activity, with father *and* mother, children are more cooperative, involved, excited and interested in play with their fathers. This applies to male and female children alike. Over 70 percent of the children tested chose to play with father and preferred him as a playmate. By the age of twenty months children are as much attached to their fathers as to their mothers. And in the play area they are, at twenty months, significantly *more* responsive to play initiated by the father.

Accustomed to being the chief source of baby daughter's comfort and delight, mother does not view the growing attachment between dad and daughter with unalloyed pleasure. Donna writes: "I remember the first time Emily indicated a preference for her father rather than me. We had gone to a fast-food restaurant for dinner, and while Richard ordered the food Emily and I went to save a booth. As usual, I sat her next to me on my side of the booth and she snuggled up close. But when Richard came over with the tray and sat down Emily began to squirm and plead, 'Sit wif Daddy! Sit wif Daddy!' and wouldn't stop till we moved her over to Richard's side of the table. I laughed and passed it off lightly, telling myself that it was good for Emily to feel close to her father. But I missed her snuggling next to me and inside I couldn't help feeling hurt and rejected."

Nancy Friday writes in *My Mother/Myself*: "Beginning about 14–18 months and continuing to about the third year, the child begins to experiment with resistance to mother's demands on her. This try at self-assertion is marked by the almost constant use of the word No."

Mother's reaction is predictable.

"I couldn't believe it was happening when I came up against my daughter's negativism," says the mother of a girl now eight years old. "It began when she was around three or four. At first I thought it was simple stubbornness. When it kept on I began to be afraid there was something wrong with her character, some inherent flaw was showing through. I talked to my husband about it because I was worried she would grow up to be the wrong kind of person. He said it was just a stage in her development, that it wasn't going to be permanent.

"At last I had to face up to it. Her resistance was directed at me. She got along fine with her father. Better than ever. She was always hanging around him, wanting to talk to him. I couldn't understand why she didn't want me anymore. I always expected to be her favorite. I wasn't prepared for any tapering off."

This shift in the delicate system of emotional balances is not a wavelike motion but a tidal current. The pace of movement away from mother is slow, and she has no conscious awareness that anything important is occurring.

Mother's authority and influence do not, of course, disappear in this new stage of development. She retains the validity and importance that we grant, for example, to Newtonian physics. Newton's formulations are perfectly true as far as they go, but they are based on an incomplete perception of reality. Because mother cannot create the attributes necessary for further progress in social adjustment, her contribution is no longer as significant in an era in which we know that E equals MC squared.

The importance of her role continues to diminish as a daughter requires less than total care and her ability increases to deal with new situations. Daughter's struggle toward independence compels her to try to put her growing experience of life into a larger and larger frame.

Authorities agree that somewhere between the ages of three and five the partial rejection of mother is effected. This contradicts the general belief founded in sentiment and hallowed by tradition that mother continues to be exclusively important simply because she spends so many more hours in the company of her daughter. As we have seen, this does not necessarily constitute emotional proximity.

Indeed, precisely *because* mother is around daughter so much, she may tune out many of her childish questions and demands. It's hard to be "all there" for a small child all day long. But father, whose contact with daughter is limited, has not had his responses dulled by overfamiliarity.

A woman tells how, when she was a young girl, "Mom's attention was always being drawn off to some other problem in the house. The cooking, the marketing, a soap opera on TV, a telephone call, you name it. Even when she read a book to me I would get upset because she wasn't *listening*."

Her mother, interviewed later, said, "I always used to read to her before putting her in bed for the night. I was tired and I really wanted to be spending the time with my husband. So I wasn't listening—I wasn't sharing. She's right about that. My thoughts were elsewhere."

The daughter adds: "I always preferred to be with Daddy because that was playtime. He was never interrupted for other things. He belonged to me for whatever time we had together, and that was important. It made me feel loved—special."

Recently at dinner, Donna was absently supervising Emily's eating and at the same time trying to carry on a conversation with Richard. Little Emily tried to break in to get Donna's attention: "I don't know what I was talking about at the time, but it was interesting to me. I sort of waved Emily away, saying, 'Not now, dear. This is important.' Suddenly I heard her 'But Mommy, *I'm important too!*"

The sense of being shunted aside to make room for other people, other duties, diminishes the interaction between mother and daughter. The fact that the shunting aside usually takes place so that mother can spend more time with father sparks a primitive sexual rivalry: a competition for daddy's time and attention.

Mother's continual exercise of authority is another reason daughter rebels against her. She is the direct supervisor, the one whose writ runs to daily discipline and control. A daughter who needs to assert her developing sense of self must assert herself against mother. This, of course, risks alienation and a young child is in no position to alienate a parent on whom she depends.

Not unless she has someone else to turn to. And she has.

She has father.

As an infant, daughter is aware of her father's physical strength. At play, this is part of the fun of being with him. Who else can swing her so high and so far? Or ride her around on his shoulders so she can touch the ceiling? For a brief gleeful moment she actually shares his perspective on the world.

In her earliest formative years she becomes increasingly aware of his strength and, ironically, mother is the medium that conveys the message. If a jar lid can't be opened, mother calls for him. A repair job that requires physical power is always reserved for daddy. "When Daddy comes home he'll fix it," is a common phrase in many households.

Through mother, daughter begins to perceive father also as the provider and protector of the family and home, the bestower of blessings who insures that they will have food, clothing, gifts and a roof over their heads. The mechanism of transmitting this message is often fear. In the traditional home mother worries when father is late, frets over his health, caters to his whims, flatters and defers to him because he is the foundation of the family's security. Daughter observes that father is not only the earner, he is the taker-on-vacations, the awarder-of-money, the giver-of-gifts-and-allowances. Only he can take them to restaurants, encourage them to order what they like, instruct the waiter, pay the check with cash or a mere signature. In the three-to-five-year-old's world, father looms all-powerful, a household deity who controls her life from afar.

As Simone de Beauvoir observes in *The Second Sex*, "[the daughter] realizes that if the father's authority is not that which is most often felt in daily affairs, it is actually supreme....He supports the family, and he is the responsible head of the family. ...This is what the child feels physically in the powerful arms that lift her up...."

At whatever age the transfer to father as a role model occurs, the effect on mother is devastating. She has come to count on daughter's total dependency and exclusive love, and she makes an effort to restore the shifting balance and preserve the essence of their intimacy.

"I was the oldest daughter in my family," says a woman from a small town near Chicago. "Because I was the firstborn I was given almost the same privileges as an only son. My mother doted on me. I never had to do any of the picking up and putting away that a child is perfectly capable of. I dropped a toy wherever I felt like it and Mother picked up after me. I ate whenever I liked, and skipped a meal if I wanted to. I monopolized the conversation at dinner table, and answered the telephone so that all Mother's friends had to talk to me first.

"My father sometimes spoke up to suggest I ought to do more around the house— at least keep my own room tidy. Mother wouldn't concede that it was important. She saw no reason to force me to do anything. Even if my father gave a direct order, Mother would plea-bargain with him and get some sort of compromise.

"One time Mommy and Daddy began arguing about something he thought I should have done, I forget what. He said that when I grew up and had a home of my own I could live in it any way I wanted to, but while I was in his home I'd have to abide by some rules. Mother looked him right in the eye and said, 'It isn't your home. It's ours.'

"One Sunday in January we went sledding. It was cold and Daddy wanted to go back after an hour but Mother wouldn't hear of it because I was having such a good time. So I went over and told her I was feeling cold. We went home right away. It wasn't cold if Daddy was cold, but it was if I was.

"When Mother saw that I began taking Daddy's side sometimes she got terribly upset. She didn't want him to have any control. She began wooing me. The only important time to her was spent talking to me or playing a game or reading to me. But I wanted to be with Daddy. I looked forward to the time *we'd* spend together. There was so much I wanted to know that Mother couldn't tell me."

Freud describes this stage as moving from the oral and anal to the genital. Mother has guided daughter through her oral and anal stages and now father helps her to begin her genital stage. Striking as this explanation may be, it is not enlightening for ordinary purposes. It might be clearer to say that mother helps daughter to survive the stage of physical helplessness and now father must guide her through the stage of social helplessness.

Daughter turns instinctively to this strong parent for support in her new battle for independence. He is an armor she can wear that will protect her from harm. To win his favor is all-important.

Not unnaturally, mother reacts with jealousy and hostility. A woman friend of Donna's recalls that her father rarely if ever paid her mother a compliment but he was always extravagant with compliments to her. The daughter was aware of her mother's jealousy. When she won her third-grade spelling bee she waited until her father returned from work to tell him first: "I wanted him to know because he'd be proud of me. She wouldn't."

Whenever she was conversing with her father, they knew that as soon as Mother heard them she would summon her in to do chores. Daughter began to regard her mother as an antagonist; Father became more protective as he saw his daughter unjustly picked on; Mother complained still more to her husband about the shiftless ways of "his" daughter.

Mother's jealousy grew more intense as daughter grew older. On a trip to a remote village in Mexico, the mother insisted that her husband should converse with the natives in his scarcely remembered high school Spanish, although the daughter had won a citywide prize in Spanish. She explained, "Your father has a much better accent than you do." On another occasion the girl found her mother on her hands and knees going through her wastebasket. The father was away on a business trip, and her mother was looking for postcards her father might have secretly sent that the daughter had torn up.

Long after her parents were divorced the daughter was being blamed by her mother for "wrecking" her marriage, though by then the mother had remarried happily and called her first marriage a "prolonged, silly mistake!"

A 31-year-old professional woman recalls these incidents from her childhood: "My father and mother and I were having dinner with my mother's parents in a restaurant. I was six years old and I had just discovered that my father was the smartest man in the world. It was fascinating to hear him talk about real things—how restaurants prepared food, how it was all shipped from farms and ranches and ended up on our table.

"My mother interrupted and told him to stop talking to me and pay more attention to her parents. My father ignored her the first time and the second, but the third time she interrupted he answered her sharply. The next thing I knew she was screaming at him right there in public. He was so mad he got up and left the table.

"Whenever we went anywhere in the car Mother insisted she had to sit next to my father. She'd make a big point of it even if we were only going a few blocks. She didn't care if Father was annoyed. One winter night, returning from a movie, she crossed the street and walked on the other side all the way home. She wouldn't walk with us. Neither Father nor I knew what was wrong. Later I found out she was angry because in the theater she thought Dad spent more time talking to me than to her. I felt hurt, confused. It had never occurred to me that my mother might resent my relationship with my father. That was when I first began to think of my mother as a competitor, not a friend."

A 40-year-old psychologist told me, "When my daughter entered this phase, the first sign was that she no longer went to her mother with a problem. She only wanted me to handle it. She'd come running to me whenever she and her mother had any difference of opinion. That created a real dilemma. If I took her side, that might result in willfulness; if I told her she was wrong, that might undermine her self-confidence; if I tried to take over and direct her, that would weaken her mother's authority. On the other hand, if I let her go ahead and deal with a situation alone when she wasn't equipped to do it, that would be irresponsible. For the first time I was seeing how problems looked from the other side of my desk—and the solutions weren't so simple.

"Meanwhile, my wife was angry at my daughter's tendency to flout her authority. She called her 'stubborn, difficult, uncontrollable, unreasonable.' I tried to point out that there was no evidence of it in her relations with her friends, her grandparents or strangers, certainly not with me. That made my wife furious. She said I was taking my daughter's side against her and trying to win her away.

"There I was, knowing all about this shift of allegiance from mother to father, and still falling into the trap. It never occurred to me that my daughter was manipulating me. All I could see was her helplessness and dependency, her needing me.

"My wife knew she should be above anger with a child, but knowing it didn't help. She'd say things like, 'She's ungrateful. I take good care of her, the least she can do is obey me.' Or, 'She has to learn right from wrong. I only tell her things for her own good.'"

Rarely does an adult tell a child anything that is entirely for the child's own good. There are other elements present: a need to demonstrate the primacy of authority, to gratify one's ego, to instruct in patterns of behavior that the adult considers acceptable or to cloak anger in the guise of superior wisdom. The child resents the transparent lie of being counseled "for her own good," and therefore rejects the advice embodied within it.

At this young age, the child is experimenting with different kinds of behavior. She is trying to learn which behavior suits her best and will enable her to function successfully in the widest variety of situations. The process has been going on since infancy, with this important exception: as an infant she quickly abandons a type of behavior when it evokes strong negative reactions from mother. In the new phase of knowing that mother is neither all-wise nor all-powerful she is less likely to yield.

"I remember the first time it occurred to me that Mother might be wrong about anything," a 38-year-old mother told

Donna. "We had a dog named Fella, a lovely gentle cross between a Labrador and something hairy. My father found him shivering in a corner of our garage one night, fed him, and he stayed. Mother was afraid of him. She wouldn't let me go near him. She was always telling me how dirty he was, how undependable.

"One afternoon Mother had to visit a friend in the hospital and the babysitter didn't show up. Mother had to leave me alone but promised it would only be for an hour. She told me what TV program to watch, what toys and books I could play with and not to answer the phone if it rang. And, of course, I wasn't to touch Fella because there was no telling what the crazy dog would do. She warned me that on no account, not for any reason, was I to let Fella out of the house. He would run away and never come back. Not that she'd mind, but Daddy would be furious.

"Not long after Mother left I could see Fella had to go. I felt sorry for him but I was frightened of him too. Mother was late getting back. Fella began whining with pain. He was too well trained to do anything in the house. Finally I couldn't stand it anymore. I took him to the sliding glass door and let him out. I fully expected him to run away and get lost forever. But he didn't. After he did his business, he cantered around the back lawn until I called him. Then he came to me right away. He nuzzled me as if to say he was grateful, and I patted him. And I thought, 'Mother is wrong. He's a nice dog and we're going to be friends.'"

As her self-confidence grows, the accumulating impressions a young daughter receives undergo a sea change into opinions; opinions harden into convictions, and convictions become part of her developing character. Her experience must reach a certain point, a critical mass, before the change occurs that makes it part of her new outlook on the world.

"When I was ten years old I was interested in hearing from almost anyone, even negatively, that would help me to evaluate what kind of person I was," a young woman says. "One time, after an argument with my mother, I complained to my father that she was treating me like a little baby. He told me he couldn't go along with that, that other complaints might be true enough but my mother let me do pretty much as I liked compared to other mothers. I was fascinated by this glimpse from him of what my life was really like. It didn't matter if the comment was critical as long as it was true—a glimpse into a strange different mirror. Actually, by that age, I was pretty indifferent to what Mother thought, it no longer counted for much. What she said was just a reflection of how she was feeling at the moment. It was Dad I trusted."

Rivalry with mother for a daughter's affection fosters many different kinds of maneuvers by a father. For example, a daughter may be helping her mother clean up in the kitchen after dinner. She drops and breaks a valuable glass. Mother's instinct is to react angrily, but she doesn't wish to send her daughter running to her father for consolation so she restrains herself and merely cautions her daughter to be more careful. Then daughter breaks something else or puts something away unwashed or in the wrong place. Mother's poise cracks. She lashes out. Daughter cries, "It wasn't my fault!" and, predictably, Dad comes in to settle the quarrel and placate mother's unreasonable anger over a "simple accident." Like a crafty tactician, he chooses the proper place and conditions and by establishing himself in the role of the forgiving parent ("After all, she didn't do it deliberately") he also casts mother in the role of shrew and termagant.

As daughter grows older a father's maneuvers become more sophisticated. He needs procedures more suited to his purpose. A stratagem used with good effect on a daughter might be called "Love me because I'm smarter than your mother." The remark is the tip-off to how the game is played. A typical instance may help to demonstrate:

Daughter: Mom, I don't know what to do about Marian. She's asked me to go to her house and play.
Mother: What does your father say?
Daughter: He told me to ask you.
Mother: You like Marian, don't you? Why not go?
Daughter: I'm not really crazy about her. She's too silly and stupid.
Mother: Well, you don't have to go to her house if you don't want to.
Daughter: But nobody else has asked me. If I don't go to Marian's house, I won't have anyplace to go.
Mother: Why don't you wait awhile and see if someone you like better asks you?
Daughter: She would be awfully hurt if I did that.
Mother: Can't you ask her to come here and then invite someone else to join you?
Daughter: Oh, Mom, if I did that Marian would know I didn't

want to be alone with her. You just don't understand. I'll ask Dad.

The specifics may change but the basic pattern is the same. It is part of a daughter's growing up to reject suggestions from her parents. By having her go to her mother with the problem, father exhausts her patience with parental instruction. She says, in effect, "You just don't understand the situation." Then she returns to consult father again, who implies, "Love me because I'm smarter than your mother." This was the hidden purpose behind his sending her to mother with the problem in the first place.

Of course, father is unlikely to suggest a solution that mother hasn't put forward, but that doesn't matter. The point of the maneuver is not to solve her problem. Daughter probably knows already what she intends to do about Marian's invitation and doesn't need help. The real purpose of dad's maneuver is to get her to reject mother's advice and to renew her childhood contract with him. He will give her attention and affectionate concern in return for her acceptance of his Ultimate Authority.

I asked Donna if she could remember incidents connected with her transfer of allegiance from her mother. She writes: "It was all so gradual. There were times when I needed you more and times when I needed Mother more. I would still turn to Mother for comfort and reassurance; it was easier to cry with her and be babyish when I needed to. But increasingly I turned to you for advice and explanations of situations I didn't understand. Certainly I felt just as dependent, just as yielding to a powerful authority. At the age when daughters are supposed to begin their separation from mother they don't have a real sense of identity. Erik Erikson says we all have to develop an individual identity *before* we can begin to relate on an intimate level to another person. That includes parents. I hadn't developed a clear idea of who I was so I couldn't understand what was going on inside myself.

"My feeling is that it all happens in such minute stages it's hard to tell what's happening until the change is accomplished. It's as if you were adding a single degree of temperature at a time to a quantity of water. Suddenly the water turns into steam, and a difference in degree becomes a difference in kind. That's how the emotional change takes place."

What is a father's need? Toward what end does he use his newfound power to manipulate his daughter? He tries to make her conform to an ideal of femininity with which he is familiar because it is difficult for him to deal with any great variance from that.

A daughter finds father to be a different kind of animal from mother—and he is dealt with differently, by evading, placating, winning him over, not with the definite no-saying she uses with her mother. Wolfgang Lederer observes that a mother's love demands nothing more than her child's existence; father's love is conditional on performance. In Erik Erikson's phrase, a father loves "more dangerously."

"Whether a daughter is pretty or not," says Dr. Pollard, "has little to do with how a mother loves her. She can be colicky, petulant or obstreperous, but her mother's love can be taken for granted. As a result, such love is less important as a confirmation to daughter of her personal value."

"It didn't bother me so much when Mom was mad at me," Donna says. "She could rant and rave and, while I wasn't happy, I didn't feel seriously threatened. But a few quiet words of disapproval from you and I was devastated. I felt unworthy, unloved—and like a thoroughly 'bad girl.'

"One time I was on the phone to a friend, and you and Mom were out in the hall fighting. You were pretty mad. I asked you if Susie could come over, and you shouted, loud enough for her to hear, 'God damn Susie!'

"I hung up and waited a few minutes before I went out to the living room. Trying to be very grown up and reasonable, I said, 'I know you're upset but I don't think it was right of you to say that where my friend could hear.' You wouldn't listen. You were still involved in your fight with Mother. I knew you were wrong, though, and I resolved not to make friends until you apologized.

"We all went out to dinner in stony silence and then to a movie. I was miserable, even though I was sure you were the villain on this occasion. Finally Mom got up to go to the ladies' room—she always sat between us, of course—and I threw pride and principle to the winds. I leaned over and said, 'I'm sorry, Daddy,' although for what I didn't know. Then you said you were sorry too. We held hands for a minute until Mom came back. I felt as if a great weight had been lifted off me."

It's hard to believe that I was forty years old when this happened. But I have no reason to doubt it is true.

An interesting experiment by Dr. John T. Schowalter, professor of psychiatry at the Yale University Child Study Center, sheds light on a daughter's differing perceptions of her father and mother. Dr. Schowalter is interested in the role that dinosaurs play as a symbol in children's drawings. He writes: "Three-to five-year-olds who can't even pronounce the names of their classmates know the names, sizes, habits and number of bones in several dinosaurs." Dr. Schowalter believes this is an act of association: dinosaurs are seen by children as parent substitutes. To test his theory he asked children to draw vegetarian dinosaurs such as Brontosaurus. They were portrayed with aprons and feminine features. When he asked the children to draw the large-toothed carnivorous type, like Tyrannosaurus, the features became definitely fatherlike.

To get along with such a powerful and dangerous father, daughter must learn to conform to his image of femininity; she must transform herself into Daddy's Girl.

THREE

DADDY'S GIRL

A father wants his son to be stalwart, strong and self-reliant, "a real man," and his daughter to be his darling. "You're my pride, daughter, my shining pride," Loretta Lynn's father says to her in the movie *Coal Miner's Daughter*. That paternal attitude not only convinces a daughter she is wonderful but persuades her that no man fully appreciates her—except him. Where else can she find such all-enveloping approval?

A woman who speaks wistfully about how her father used to choose her clothes, oversee her makeup, teach her to fox-trot and carefully monitor boys who took her on dates admits that today when she confronts a problem she asks herself: "How would Daddy want me to deal with this?" Because he never allowed her to act independently, the only way she can solve a problem is by becoming him.

"The role of father as counselor, support and guide can be restricting to a young girl's development," observes Dr. Pollard. "As long as he is there, she is not completely free to grow into true independence. Like Moses, she may be granted a glimpse of the Promised Land but cannot enter into it. Even father's possessiveness, his attempts to manipulate her, are translated into a feeling that she is not ready for the risky venture of growing up. She does not have a sufficient store of experience to justify an individual perception of life. She is tempted not to fight too hard, to accept her limitations."

Listen to a young daughter as she admonishes her dolls, serves tea to them on her toy set and discusses the day's problems. She is the mistress of this household, and much can be learned from eavesdropping on what kind of mistress she fancies herself.

Her dollhouse husband is usually a figure of authority. When she arranges the furniture in her dollhouse she will consult her husband and promptly rearrange it on a signal that he does not approve. If his disapproval is unjustified, she will complain to a visiting friend but will not directly challenge him. Her complaints about him are always expressed to her friend or to one of her children. If she tells the dollhouse daughter that she must leave daddy alone because he is trying to read the paper, she is expressing her rivalry with mother. If daddy puts aside his paper to take daughter on his lap anyway, she displays her sense of the right outcome of that rivalry.

A father's manipulation is less visible because other emotions are being negotiated. The stresses and strains, tensions and rivalries, are balanced by emotional support, security, mediation and control. The intertwining is marked by hesitations, reversals, circular and sidewise movements that keep the basic direction of movement hidden from view, like a river running underground.

Donna writes: "I think something should be said about the advantages of being a daddy's girl when you're the right age for it. As a child I didn't have to be responsible for my own welfare, I always had you to advise and counsel me, and if real trouble came along there was you to lean on. I was having a pretty free ride. All I had to do was hang on to your affection and I had nothing to worry about. When I look back I think I was living in the Garden of Eden."

Does she deceive herself? Partly. She is not fully aware that while I wanted her to be someone, the someone was an extension of myself. I wanted her to grow up and see the world as I did, to love poetry and our beach house, the great men of history and her mother's lasagna, to wonder at the same wonders and delight in the same delights.*

A strong father may shape his daughter's character as a compensation for not having the kind of mother or wife he wanted. His daughter becomes his hope for the future, someone he can mold into a personality that will yield the kind of happiness that eluded him.

Rhett Butler, in the conclusion of *Gone with the Wind*, gives expression to this feeling when, in talking to Scarlett, he refers to the death of their daughter Bonnie: "As long as there was Bonnie there was a chance we might be happy. I liked to think that Bonnie was you, a little girl again...."

So much of a father's influence is conveyed indirectly that the extent of the influence has been underrated even by his daughter.

---

*Reading this, Donna commented: "And you succeeded very well! Indeed, there's a special quality to my feelings about certain things—a reflection, I think, of my unconscious understanding that our shared appreciation was part of what bonded us together."

Donna likens the situation to a chess game in which the queen is the most powerful piece on the board. The king appears, by contrast, nearly powerless—indifferent to the struggle taking place all around him. Nevertheless, powerful as the queen may seem, she can be lost and the game will go on. If the king is lost, the game is over.

A father can act as if he were Moses returning from the mountaintop with the Ten Commandments (except in these days there are likely to be Ten Thousand Commandments). He knows that it will be years before his daughter asks to check his handwriting against what the lightning wrote. Meanwhile, his lightest word, meant to have no more impact than a falling leaf, may drop like a falling safe.

"Nothing—absolutely nothing—was more important to me than to have your approval," Donna writes to me. "I wonder if you ever knew how much faith I placed in your judgment and opinions. When you gave advice your standard caution was, 'You don't have to listen to me if you don't want to.' How could I not listen? I couldn't form any idea of my own about the future or what was best for me to do. You were the one I relied on."

The following story was told to me by a close friend: "I recall driving into New York City with my wife and daughter, who was seven years old. It had been a long ride and I was tired. When my daughter asked me what was inside the great suspension cables on the George Washington Bridge I did not answer her seriously. I told her that one cable carried milk and the other chocolate syrup. When the cables met on the far side, I said, they merged to make chocolate malteds. I did not bother to underscore, as I usually did with gesture or tone, that my reply was meant in jest.

"Two days later she and a girlfriend came to our apartment after school. She asked me to tell her friend about the bridge cables because her friend didn't believe it. Shamefacedly, I had to admit having made up the story. That night my daughter was in tears. 'You told me a lie, Daddy! Why did you do that?'

"If I could have paid a thousand dollars to take back what I'd said, I'd have done it on the spot!"

Donna adds: "If you said something, there was no doubt in my mind that was the whole truth and the plain fact of the matter. Remember when we took a plane flight over mountains when I was small? The ride was bumpy and I looked to you, as always, for reassurance. You said, 'These small bumps are nothing! Why if a plane like this were ever really to go down, it would fall like an apartment house!' That's when my terror of flying began. Even after I learned that planes don't ever drop straight down, it was years before I could stop imagining myself inside a plunging apartment house."

Fathers, of course, find such complete trust and acceptance irresistible. One father tells me, his eyes suspiciously shiny, how when he was laid up in bed with a bad back he overheard his twelve-year-old daughter tell a friend over the telephone: "I can't make it tonight. I have a date with my best friend—my Dad." Visiting him later, she gave him a hug and a kiss. He apologized for not having shaved and she cut him off with "It's fine. You've got the kind of bristles I love!"

I still remember an occasion when I was suffering from a bout of hay fever and eight-year-old Donna told me: "Daddy, you have such a nice voice—even when you're sneezing!" And I treasure the memory of an evening when I intervened on Donna's behalf after her mother told her she couldn't wear lipstick to a party. I won the debate. Later I found that the framed snapshot of me she kept in her room bore the telltale imprint of—lipstick.

There is enormous gratification in playing the role of the all-knowing, all-wise counselor. As I have written elsewhere,* "Part of the joy of being a father is dandling a daughter on your knee while instructing her in some mystery of the universe. For a while you have a worshipful audience, entirely willing to believe anything you tell her."

In *The American Father*, William Reynolds observes that no one, neither "wife, son, mother, father, lover [nor] mistress can give Dad what his daughter can: approval and admiration for the doing of absolutely nothing. Father's girl can invest him with the robes of the true hero, and the sole quid pro quo is that he merely show up. Everywhere else father goes he has to earn his way for love, respect, money or whatever. Only his daughter gives her rewards to him for free."

In turn, father provides a vehicle through which a daughter arrives at an idea of her true worth. His approval and applause—his oedipal salute—demonstrate that she is worthy of his love. This circular reaction is familiar to students of human motivation.

---

*The introduction to *Word Abuse: How the Words We Use Use Us* by Donna Woolfolk Cross.

Daughter is reluctant to acknowledge the manipulative interplay with her father. Barbara, a high school senior, told us about a time she had wanted to sign up for a swimming class at the YWCA. She had never learned to swim because her father wouldn't let her go near the water. Many years ago, when her father was a young boy, his younger brother, two years old, had fallen into the family swimming pool and drowned.

"He told me about the terrible grief his brother's death caused his parents, how they emptied the pool and made it into a garden, planting a laurel bush directly above the site where the infant had drowned. I understood his feeling, but after a while I decided it wasn't fair I should miss out on fun because of something that had happened to him such a long time ago. Mother was on my side, and finally we persuaded him to talk to the YWCA swimming instructor. The instructor convinced him that I'd be well supervised, and he let me sign up.

"You won't believe this, but I gave up the swimming class after the very first lesson. I had a real terror of getting into water over my head. Isn't that funny? Dad turned out to be right. He was keeping me from doing something I was scared to death to do anyway."

Barbara believes her morbid fear of the water was always present, not passed on to her by her father. This is her way of resolving a conflict with him in a way that confirms the status quo and allows her to return to the role of obedient child.

The symbiotic attachment makes it hard for a daughter to resist as her father molds her into the desired image. One of our earliest interviews was with a high school principal whose nine-year-old daughter, after a traumatic episode with a mentally disturbed teacher, refused to return to school. Rather than compel her, her father undertook to tutor her at home. Every evening, and for a long session on Saturdays, he would go over with her subjects she would have been studying at school.

When she reached the junior high school level a serious dispute arose with the child's mother, who wanted her to resume her education away from home. The father opposed this, saying that comparative tests showed she was doing well with his tutoring. They consulted a psychologist, who advised them to send their daughter back to school where she could be with other youngsters of her age. But the girl did not do well in school. Her grades were so poor that she was in danger of being left back, and she only passed her final examinations with special help from her father. The psychologist was sure this was an emotional block, that she was making too little effort to keep up with her classmates.

Eventually her father withdrew her from school and resumed full tutoring at home. Instantly she began to make better progress, and on comparison tests with students at school she registered above normal grades. Her father was convinced his tutoring led to the improvement.

The psychologist disagrees: "With application there's no reason she would not have done well at school. She didn't want to—because her father didn't want her to. They actually had reached un unspoken agreement. On his part the agreement was: 'I'll help you--provided you continue to need my help.' On her part: 'I won't do well in school and that will prove I can't get by on my own.'

"As long as father and daughter live up to that agreement, they are able to sustain the old arrangement which both of them want. She will remain a totally dependent child."

A father can preserve his role of being above criticism and incapable of error only if his daughter is willing to remain or pretend to remain his admiring little girl. As Dr. Pollard sees it, "On the simplest level, we may draw a parallel with a man and his dog. The dog is devoted to him, will obey him, is programmed and implanted to love him. The dog welcomes him whenever he appears, waits on his moods, depends on him for everything. Above all, the dog never grows up; it merely grows old. Yet dogs make captives of their owners, for the owner comes to rely on this sort of devotion as much as the dog relies on the owner. In the far more complex human relationship, this mutual dependency is still observable."

One sunny afternoon on a Cape Cod beach I watched a father Indian-wrestle with his older son of about sixteen while a young daughter watched. Indian wrestling is a contest in which two opponents plant their right feet firmly against each other, using their left feet to maintain balance as they grasp each other's right hand and try to force the other off his stance.

The father was having a difficult struggle with his young son. Suddenly he was pulled off balance, losing the contest. His daughter became upset and sharply told her brother to "stop being crazy!"

The father, a macho type, insisted on trying again. Again he lost, and the daughter began to scream at her brother to stop. When her father tried a third time and lost, she ran off crying down the beach.

Neither father nor brother seemed to understand what was the matter. The explanation appeared simple to me. Watching her "all-powerful" father beaten upset the order of a universe in which, while he ruled, she was safe and protected.

I recall an evening at home reading a story to Donna at bedtime. Suddenly she looked up to say, "Daddy, you're so good to me all the time; I wish there was something I could do back for you."

Taken off guard, I answered, "You don't have to do anything. All you have to be is yourself."

I should have added, "and love me," for that is the fundamental bargain struck between dad and daughter.

THE TRIALS OF ADOLESCENCE

Reports a seventeen-year-old, "All I could learn from Mom is how to do the kinds of things she does—keep house, market, look after children. And of course look after Dad, which is her main job. Years ago I learned that if I asked her about anything important, she'd just say, 'Well, I have no objection if your father doesn't. Go ask him.'"

Only a generation ago—the world is changing that rapidly—a young daughter was usually prepared only for a career as a wife and mother, with possibly a brief preliminary period as part of the working force. Today more than half of young American women expect to work most of their adult lives. The importance and value of the work that women are doing steadily increases and, inevitably, so does the period of training needed to compete in the specialized job market.

Father is the parent most involved with long-range goals of the kind that concern daughter as she steps across the threshold of home and sees the world expanding beyond the horizon. The tests with which the new world confronts her loom more formidable than her skills, and she needs a yardstick to measure herself against the unfolding opportunities.

Donna says of this period in her life: "I wanted my freedom and at the same time I was afraid of the choices freedom would bring, the difficulties of survival in a harshly competitive world. I was also aware of the sacrifices that had to be made to send me to college—and on to graduate school if I held to my resolve of becoming a teacher—and I was worried I wouldn't prove worthy of the investment being made in me. I could see myself making the wrong choices, letting my life go out of control, ending up as a failure. The future was unpredictable—and unpredictability is terrifying. A young girl I know said recently, 'I ain't what I'm going to be, but I'm not what I was.' That about sums up what it feels like at that age."

This attitude is not confined to adolescence, but its existence at this stage assures the prolongation of adolescence. A daughter's feelings toward a protective and confining father become more sharply combative. Prompted by her contradictory requirements, she is alternately hostile and impulsively affectionate. Physically and mentally mature, ready for independence, more than ready, she still needs his guidance. But he appears to demand too much, to appreciate too little. She scorns his values, preferring those of her own generation, but simultaneously she longs for him to impose his authority. Vulnerable and willful, she yearns to be free but fears to be. She succumbs to feelings of unworthiness and lack of self-respect, while proclaiming: "I've got to be me." She is tempted by sexual freedom but alarmed that she may slip into promiscuity; she is tempted by drinking and fears alcoholism, by drugs and fears addiction.

"If my dad knew half the things I've been doing, he'd probably lock me up," a fifteen-year-old told Donna, then complained: "At home they treat me as a kid. I can't even go riding on my boyfriend's motorcycle. They won't let me decide anything for myself."

"What am I supposed to do?" her father asked me in the middle of our interview. "I can't possibly turn her loose and let her live as she pleases. I'd rather have her think I'm too strict than have her get into some of the scrapes I know I've saved her from. If I don't look after her, what kind of father am I?"

Naturally, father is reluctant to let go of his control when he knows his daughter has not completed her own system of internal controls. Inevitably, however, his direct control weakens. If he tries to reassert his authority, he merely proves how much changing circumstances have diminished it. His ukases and proscriptions do not have their former potency. An adolescent daughter's "stubborness and willfulness" is actually a part of maturing. It is not a bad streak in her character nor a sign of emotional disturbance. But father's solution is still more "discipline," which is a code word for punishment. The notion of punishment as a form of teaching is prevalent in our society. When dad sends daughter up to her room or forbids her to watch television or subjects her to the "silent treatment," he is employing a mild form of society's punishments: imprisonment, revocation of "privileges" and solitary confinement.

In areas where dad's will is not directly challenged, he is better able to accept that these activities should be corrected by teaching rather than punishment. A father would not punish a daughter who suffered an injury resulting from carelessness. He would soothe and comfort and caution her against repeating the mistake. Nor would punitive measures be required to improve a daughters table manners or teach her to dress herself or put away her toys. That kind of behavior can be modified by instruction, patience and sympathy. It is only when father's will is thwarted that he reacts in a punitive manner.

Father may claim he is acting out of love, but his actions are really an attempt to maintain control. They come into conflict with daughter's need to separate, and the result is predictable. As one young lady put it, "I don't understand what's happened in the last year. All of a sudden Dad is trying to push me around. I won't stand for that!"

This attempt to win a battle that time has declared lost—this last charge of the Old Guard (the Old Guard dies but never surrenders!)—is fated to end in a personal Waterloo for father. Daughter becomes alienated, no longer trusting him, no longer willing to believe that he understands her problems.

Some fathers try to restore the status quo by reverting to an indirect method. They revive the parental flirtatiousness that was so effective when daughter was younger and that helped her to form a more confident self-image: "They just don't turn them out any prettier than you," or "I take pity on the poor boys who are going to have to deal with someone who looks like you do," or "Why worry about a career? Your looks are a career all by themselves," may sound flattering, reassuring and familiar. But something more is now being said: "You're an object to delight men's eyes, even your old dad's, so don't be too serious about life or too anxious to grow up too fast."

To reject this appeal means rejecting admiration and love from the man whose admiration and love daughter has craved all her life. If she does not reject it, however, she will be diverted from the urgent serious task ahead of growing into a woman.

"If you're young and pretty, that's all you need," is father's message. All she needs for what? Not for a career, unless she is destined for television or movies or modeling. Not for a modern marriage in which a working wife is the norm. It is all she needs for the kind of relationship with men in which her chief function is to be decorative and to please. It is all she needs if her role in life is to give pleasure merely by *being* until the right man comes along to admire and love and support her. Just like dear old dad.

"I looked at my mother in the same way that a pieceworker in a factory looks at the supervisor who watches over her and criticizes or tries to hurry her up or makes sure her recreation period doesn't last too long." A woman of thirty is describing her attitude during her adolescence. "It wasn't until I'd begun living a life of my own that I realized my anger would have been better directed at my father. He was like the plant manager who laid down the rules. His rules guided both Mother and me, but he was always a kind of impersonal figure, so my resentment was directed at Mother, who was in direct charge and easier to get at.

"Up to a few years ago, I had a tendency to feel that Dad was more understanding than Mom. If you asked me, I'd probably have said, 'Mom tried her best, but we never really got along,' or 'Mom was always after me for something or other.' When I thought about some things she did I'd get mad. Then I finally got it through my head that she was only carrying out Dad's orders; she was between me and him. He was the general, she was only the drill sergeant."

Mother herself is partly responsible for this adolescent confusion. When her authority with daughter starts to slip, she invokes the Ultimate Authority: "If you don't do as I say, I will tell your father." She does not spell out what will happen then because a punishment unspecified is more to be feared than a punishment known. In similar fashion, a teacher threatens an unruly student, "One more word and I'll send you to the principal's office." No one knows what awful authority the principal may wield, but no one wants to find out.

With the active cooperation of mother, therefore, dad becomes the dominant figure in the household, a position confirmed with advancing years. Father is expected to administer the discipline beyond ordinary discipline and to inspire the kind of respect and fear that will keep his daughter in line—and keep her a child.

He is not the sole influence responsible for shaping daughter's adolescence. Her need for separation is directed at him because she perceives him, along with her mother, as an enduring figure. Her siblings are involved with their own problems of separation and growing up. Teachers are transient figures who come and go with each semester, and friends vary in importance with each new phase of growth. After the early-childhood separation from her mother, father remains the chief target of opportunity. He is there when the time comes for her to assert her identity and to meet the challenge of incipient adulthood.

Will he help her or will he delay her emergence from the family cocoon?

As she grows into adolescence, a daughter learns that she should not enter into open competition with her father. That role is reserved for her brother, who tests his strength against the many-antlered older buck in head-to-head competition almost from the time he feels his own strength rising. Sports is one way in which this competitiveness is expressed. Father and son compete in arm wrestling, in table tennis, in games of every kind. Both are aware that sooner or later this socially approved form of combat will end in victory for the young man. Father accepts this, though not always with the best of grace, because he knows that his son is growing into a man and will have to win other battles on similarly competitive battlefields.

His attitude toward his daughter is different. Charm, beauty and likableness are the attributes he prizes in her. Her need to emerge into adulthood is fully as great as her brother's, but because she cannot openly challenge her father her rebellion must take place in a different way.

"I began secretly smoking cigarettes when I was twelve," a young woman says. "At home I smoked in the bathroom, opening the window and turning on the exhaust fan to clear away the smoke and flushing the butt down the toilet. I took care not to spill ashes. I'd wrap them in tinfoil and put them in a drawer until I could sneak them outside."

A psychologist might say that unconsciously she wanted to be caught, or that her smoking was an incidental pleasure compared to the risk taking and her cleverness in avoiding inevitable exposure. When discovery came she did not defend her smoking or challenge her father's authority. At the end of a tearful argument with her father she promised she would not continue her "bad habit," "because I don't want to do anything that would cause you heartache."

This aspect is often overlooked: the reward for rebelliousness is not independence but forgiveness. This daughter's "offense" led to a triple payoff: she had her fling with the forbidden, she obtained absolution of guilt *and* she received the forgiveness which was for her a confirmation of love.

Dr. C. B. Pollard says: "The desire to offend, be punished and be forgiven is deep rooted in Christian morality. It is inherent in the Catholic's rite of confession and in the biblical account of Jesus, who offended the Romans, was cruelly punished, and 'forgiven' by One who had not forsaken Him.

"Self-reproach is a form of self-indulgence. The reward of repentance is not that the sinner will go forth and sin no more, but that he or she may go forth and sin again, knowing the route is never closed by which forgiveness may be attained. The sequence by which the guilt of transgression is discharged after the fruits of transgression have been enjoyed provides an open sesame to sinners. But the procedure does not move the transgressor in the direction of adulthood, which presupposes an acceptance of responsibility for one's actions."

A daughter's guilt is free-floating, seeking what absolution it can find. A fifteen-year-old girl felt she was no longer getting her fair share of paternal attention because she could not compete with her extraordinarily attractive sister. She began paying less attention to her appearance, dressing sloppily, not bothering with hair or makeup, gaining weight. This led to scoldings from her mother and stern lectures from her father—but also to an important reward.

After her father had lectured her, he would embrace her and tell her that no matter what, she was still his girl and he loved her. His admonitions to be less slovenly and to try harder to control her weight had no force equal to the reassurance thus given her. She was encouraged to seek more punishment—and more forgiveness.

In the course of a year she gained almost fifty pounds while her image changed from slovenly to gross. Her mother turned the problem over to the father, whose remonstrances were ineffective. Her standard reply to his lectures was, "Everyone else can eat and nobody blames them." This might be translated in psychological terms to read: "Do I have to do without your love just because I'm fat and unattractive?"

Eventually her father sent her to see a psychiatrist. She joined in group therapy with other young overweight people her age. For a while the therapy worked: she went on a diet and lost some weight. During one group session she asked the psychiatrist what he *really* thought of her. He told her she was making good progress. Unsatisfied, she demanded to know what the others in the group *really* thought of her. They concurred in the psychiatrist's opinion, and one girl even congratulated her on the fact that she was losing weight.

"You're not being honest!" the young woman replied angrily. "I have no self-discipline. Why can't you just say the truth? The truth never hurt anybody!"

She left the group and never returned. She could not continue an association with people who refused to play her game of criticizing and condemning, thereby enabling her to expiate her guilt and win their forgiveness.

I asked her psychiatrist how long this pattern of behavior could go on. "The only long-term cure is to induce her to recognize and confront the reason for her self-destructive behavior. With professional help, she might begin to treat the cause rather than the symptoms and stop designing her behavior to win the reward of absolution."

Rebellion against dad also springs from a daughter's secret desire *not* to grow up. She has been "programmed" to be dependent. A chief reward of dependence is not having to accept responsibility for one's actions.

A father leaves his sixteen-year-old daughter to "stay home and look after the house" while he and her mother go out for the evening. Looking after the house also entails taking the dog out for his evening constitutional. Engrossed in a television show, daughter neglects to do this. When her parents return they find that the dog has urinated all over an expensive rug.

Father: I told you to take the dog out. Why didn't you?

Daughter: It's not my fault. I didn't ask to stay home tonight. I'd rather have been out with my friends.

A dependent daughter finds a perfect scapegoat in an authoritarian dad. It is *his* fault for having restricted her natural inclination to have fun with her friends. He took charge of her activity for the evening, so nothing that went wrong can possibly be her fault.

Similarly, if father approves of that nice young man his daughter has begun dating, he tacitly accepts the risks involved in her continuing to see him. If at an early hour of the morning he goes downstairs to discover them in a passionate embrace, he may angrily order the young man out of the house. But when he tries to rebuke his daughter:

Father: I didn't raise you to be that kind of girl.

Daughter: You're the one who told me to go out with him. You thought he was nice.

What is omitted from her "explanation" is any reckoning of her own choice, whether she liked the young man enough or enjoyed his lovemaking enough to cooperate. What is important to her is that she does not have to accept grown up responsibility. She has abdicated it to her father.

Having such a useful scapegoat is a principal attraction of a daughter's surrender to paternal authority. There are parallels in other institutions than the family, in the Army for instance, where an order from a superior is never to be disobeyed. This is a given fundamental. *That is an order, Corporal.* Click of heels, salute, and *Yes sir!* This programmed dependence in the military is what led to the ghastly massacre at My Lai in which unarmed, defenseless women and small children were slaughtered because an American lieutenant had said, "Wipe them!" His order was obeyed. Neither humanity nor common sense availed because "he gave an order."

A daughter wins her freedom from responsibility in the same way, by surrendering her right to think for herself. Father and daughter take up assigned positions within the family hierarchy. There may be an occasional display of belligerence (dad) and petulance (daughter), but neither is allowed to have a serious result because a disagreement cannot be pushed to a point at which the character of their relationship would have to be changed.

What identifies this as childish behavior on the daughter's part is that she is not acting from her own appraisal of risks and rewards. Her values are thoroughly repressed. She operates not at the adult level of satisfaction but at the child's level of game playing. The consequence of such "pretending" is that what she pretends becomes real. She ventures toward selfhood and withdraws, both desiring and fearing; she becomes unable to function as a free woman seeking individual fulfillment and, worse, she cannot identify the cause of her maladjustment.

Conflicting desires are ever present in a growing daughter: the need to attach herself, the need to break away. Reconciling these irreconcilables is the task of growth. In cases where no reconciliation takes place, one conflicting desire simply vanquishes the other.

A twenty-one-year-old woman vividly recalls an afternoon eight years earlier in which, riding in a car with her father, she sang a "naughty" ditty she had learned in school. She has forgotten the words but assures me that "it wasn't very titillating—more silly than obscene."

Her father did not respond, so she sang it again. "I was trying to get some response from him, an acknowledgment of my cleverness, my wickedness—anything! But he didn't react. He must have told Mother because later that night she came into my bedroom to tell me I shouldn't sing 'that kind of song in front of your father.' He'd been very embarrassed and hadn't known what to do about it.

"I was so ashamed that I couldn't face him or talk to him for days. I'd done a bad thing. I wanted to make it up to him somehow, to prove I was still his good little girl."

A fifteen-year-old girl returned with her newly divorced mother to her grandfather's house in Rochester, New York. Having lived most of her life according to her father's rules, the mother was perfectly comfortable in his home. The teenage daughter was not. Even at fifteen, this independent young lady realized that there was something wrong with her mother's continuing dependency. She resisted her mother's attempts to make her conform to grandfather's rules.

One of these rules was a strict ten-o'clock curfew. No member of the house was supposed to be out after that semiwitching hour. There was also no television or radio after ten o'clock, and no telephone calls after eight o'clock, when dinner ended and grandfather retired to his bedroom to read.

Tension quickly began building when daughter refused to abide by these strictures. She was practically supporting herself, delivering Sunday newspapers, babysitting, mowing lawns. She had to pass up several babysitting jobs because of the ten-o'clock curfew. And because she was very popular at school, she got telephone calls after eight o'clock in the evening. She pointed out that there was no reason for her grandfather to forbid phone calls because it was easy to turn down the telephone and talk softly so that he wouldn't be disturbed.

Her mother, however, had been raised to be totally submissive. She was unable to give her daughter any support in the running dispute that developed with grandfather. From the mother's point of view, she was caught in the middle between a daughter insisting on her own rights and a father used to having his way without challenge. In her daughter's words, "She was so beaten down she wasn't sure she could act in any way. She was too busy trying to prove she was a good daughter to be a good mother to me." In fact, both the fifteen-year-old daughter and the mother were in need of better parenting.

The turning point in this generational conflict came when the daughter turned sixteen and began dating a young man in her high school. Often she stayed out beyond the ten-o'clock curfew. Grandfather began making sharp comments about the girl's nocturnal habits, and the mother became increasingly nervous.

One evening the parents of the girl's boyfriend invited her and her mother to dinner. The mother agreed to go reluctantly, but to her surprise had a very pleasant time. It was her first social outing in many months, and time ticked by swiftly. At ten o'clock, suddenly aware of the hour, she announced they had to be getting home.

Her daughter spoke up. "Mother, I want to stay—and so do you."

"You know how upset Grandfather gets when we come in late."

"We'll just explain that we were enjoying ourselves."

"Oh, I *couldn't* do that!"

The daughter replied smilingly, "Now, Mom, when we go home tonight I would like you to stand up to Grandpa and say, 'Look, I'm forty-four years old and I have a sixteen-year-old daughter, and I have a *right* to stay out past ten o'clock at night if I want to!'"

That got a laugh, even from her mother. But within a few minutes her mother found an excuse to end the visit and hurry home, where she apologized for being a little late. Clearly, this adult woman can no longer behave as an adult.

Adolescents today are much freer, much less trammeled by parental discipline. They have the freedom to make money, spend it, organize their lives, even discover sexuality. Yet, in a deeper sense, they do not move away from a father's control any more than did the teenagers of earlier generations. Too often a daughter is separate without being free, independent but still a child.

Most father-daughter relationships share a common feature: father becomes a refuge. For the self-proclaimed independent teenager the idea of home is no longer a specific location in space, whether house or apartment, houseboat or motor trailer. She needs an emotional center in her life which she can invest with the security she had as a child. In that sense, father *is* home.

New channels open to a young woman on the verge of adulthood: college, a job, her own place to live in, new friends. These may seem adequate replacements for a time. Inevitably, though, new anxieties arise and old emotional needs surge back with multiplied force. Her attachment to father as the focal point of her security can become so great that she is actually reluctant (reluctance as a signal of fear) to accept her new situation. She dwells within her fears like a spider in the center of a web, and continually scuttles back to remembered security.

"When a young woman calls home," Donna writes, "and talks to her mother, it's about the superficial details of life: what clothes she has bought, what people she's seen, what restaurants she ate at, and what favorite recipes she'd like to get because she's planning her first dinner party. When she talks to her father it's about more serious problems that have been troubling her. On her new job there's jealousy from an older woman who resents that she got a raise while the older woman didn't. How should she handle that? The boss asked her to do overtime work and then forgot to pay her. Should she ask for it or just pretend she was glad to cooperate? There's this salesman who came to the office and asked her to dinner but she doesn't know if he's married: how can she tell? There's a mean landlord who doesn't send up enough heat and won't make repairs because he's trying to force her to move so he can charge a higher rent: how should she deal with that? Et cetera. This is actually her way back into a pattern of dependency."

In later years, when a daughter begins to undertake the responsibilities of her own home and family, the psychological dependency on father recurs.

A successful magazine writer I know is also a renowned party giver and hostess. She was invited to a banquet at which she was to deliver a speech and be awarded a prize for a series of articles she had written. When the night arrived she could not set foot outside the door of her apartment. She simply could not. Finally, in desperation, her husband called her father. After a long talk with her father she agreed to go on to the award banquet and deliver her speech.

Clearly, the roots of this woman's problem lie deeper than mere dependence but her experience illustrates the prevalence of the syndrome.

Another woman, married to a close friend of mine, was brought up in a sheltered home environment. At twenty-one, she married and settled happily in her husband's tiny bachelor apartment. After a few months they had to move from their tiny "love nest" to a larger apartment. She was confronted with a new kind of challenge: to decorate and furnish, to cook and entertain, to be a wife and (probably) a mother.

She became increasingly nervous and anxious. Returning from a dinner party one evening, she had to walk close to the buildings because she was afraid something would fall from a window and hit her. When she got home she stayed there, absolutely unable to leave. This continued, except for trips to her analyst, for three years. In effect, she maintained the security of "home base" without having to accept the grown-up responsibility for living in it and looking after her husband.

Her analyst described her problem as an extreme case of "learned dependence" complicated by a severe personality neurosis dating back to the death of her father when she was a young child. Having got to the root of her problem, she then was able to get out of the "home" and function again.

Today she looks back on the experience and thinks she might have been spared the worst of her travail if she had been taught as a child to cope for herself.

A self-aware woman, she has never had a child. She says, "There will never be room for two children in my home!"

Some daughters run away from a safe well-ordered home where the father earns a good living and gives her a good allowance and the mother carefully attends to all her immediate needs. Time and again the daughters of middle-class parents end up living in miserable garrets with hardly enough money for food, yet they do not signal for help to their worried parents.

"She must be out of her mind," everyone says of the runaway daughter who abandons a comfortable home and loving parents to live in insecure isolation. But her need must be legitimate if she is willing to sacrifice so much for it. In many model American homes there is emotional hunger in the midst of plenty. Security is not love, and paternal love can induce emotional dependence.

Lois, a twenty-four-year-old woman reveals that, at eighteen, she took money her father gave her for her tuition and living expenses during a first year of college, and instead went to Europe. "I traveled around for a while and learned more than I would have in college."

Her father, embittered by what she did, virtually disowned her.

"I couldn't go back home, and I didn't really want to. I stayed in Europe and finally landed a job with Lufthansa, then got a better offer from my present company and moved back to New York. A man I used to know at Lufthansa also moved here. We have a lovely coop apartment in Manhattan. We're not going to get married until we work things out a little better between us. I expect to pay my own way in a marriage by keeping my job, but he expects me to be a full-time wife."

Later in the interview Lois remarked wistfully, "I want to marry someone who will be with me in a caring relationship, someone who won't make demands but who will look out for my needs, someone who will 'be there' for me."

Lois wants to keep the independence she has won but also wants the protective father figure she lost. Of such contradictory stuff are emotions composed. In shedding her role of dependent daughter and making the act of separation (an act that to her father appeared a betrayal of trust), she has still not moved far from her beginnings. She is still not sure how separate she wishes to be.

Many a young woman fails to understand what is implicit in letting daddy take care of her: she will not be treated as an equal. In asking him to protect and guide her, she must pay the toll-keeper at the gate. If she intends to become, in effect, his burden, she cannot reject his demand, "Love me, obey me, and I will see to it that you come to no harm."

If she accepts it, Daddy's Girl will continue to live in the grown woman.

Donna was present at a recent seminar in Syracuse on intrafamily problems. About thirty-five people were present, mostly women, and the discussion centered on mothers and children. A great deal of emotionalism was worked up during the course of the evening and everyone seemed to have some urgent message to impart. Donna listened with growing surprise because no one seemed to care about the father's role.

When her turn came she spoke on the role of the father in the family, especially as related to daughters. To omit a father from his proper role, she argued, was either a denial or a suppression of his importance in every woman's life.

Her argument turned the evening around, and the rest of the seminar was entirely devoted to a discussion of fathers. The women present began competing with each other to express their feelings. A surprising number confessed to having changed their minds about authoritarian fathers they had rebelled against when they were young. One woman broke down as she related how her father brought his family over from the "old country." "He was fifty years old, and in the old country children had to respect a father more than they do here. I was brought up to be afraid of my father. He had the right to punish us. Nobody else had that right. He demanded respect. Until I was twenty-two years old he would wait up until I came home at night. He would not go to bed until after I came home. That was all right in the old country, but not here in America. You're not supposed to have a guardian after you're grown up.

"But I miss having him to worry about me. It was kind of nice. I haven't felt safe anywhere since, not in my marriage, not with my children. I can't help it; it's the truth. It's how I feel."

The patriarchal ideal has yielded to the changing mores of a new society in which women are more independent, more responsible, more equal—but less secure. "I've had two divorces," one woman said during the seminar, "and I've got a current arrangement that I don't think will last much longer. I don't understand what we're supposed to do for each other, exactly what he owes to me and I owe to him. That was never true in my family. My father was Italian, and in Italy they define relationships better than we do. A father, the right kind of father, can give a whole family stability. A young woman is closely chaperoned. I have four sisters, all older, and their marriages were arranged for them. Not one has ended in divorce. I'm less happy now than if I had been married in the old way.

"My father passed away a year ago. I didn't go to the funeral. I stayed here and talked to my family on the phone, and they understood that the trip was too expensive and there was nothing I could do anyway. I'm sure it was one of those old-fashioned funerals at which everyone wailed and sobbed for two days and nights. And felt better. I don't feel better. I'm still mourning in my way.

"My sisters are not liberated or independent. Father gave them the rules to live by. I don't know what I am, except that I know I'm not free."

Said an attractive young married woman at the seminar: "My father is a very religious man. He really *believes*. His church is fundamentalist: every word in the Bible is literally true. Jonah and the whale. Noah and the ark. Adam and Eve. The whole works. That's how he brought us up. Religion is something that brings you together or drives you apart. I couldn't buy it. There were too many good people who didn't believe the way we did. I couldn't get it through my head why they wouldn't go to heaven while real bastards would, just because they believed. Any God worth believing in ought to have more sense than that.

"When I started to speak up about my doubts, Dad would take a strap to me. I thought there should be a more logical argument than that. A young man I liked didn't belong to our church and Dad wouldn't let him set foot in the house. We met on the sly. One time he called for me at the house and Dad threw him down the front steps.

"I make fun of Dad and his religion to my new friends and they laugh a lot. They're mostly agnostics. Bright, literate people— my husband's in the business side of publishing and we meet a lot of people like that. They're always on the lookout for something new. Psychoanalysis, acupuncture, drugs, the latest psychedelic experience. They're into sex and far-out music and radical chic. It's interesting in a way, but it doesn't seem to be going anywhere.

"The other night on television I happened to tune in a minister—a Bible shouter if ever there was one. I sat there smiling at how emotional he was getting, and all of a sudden there were tears in my eyes. I got to wishing I was back with Dad, the way it used to be. His life is impossible for me; I'd go crazy. But I was listening to that preacher, not with my own ears or brain but with my father's. I was getting a message in some part of me that is still hidden.

"Some people you can outgrow, but a father isn't one of them."

Women who feel that way are held in check by father's double harness of love and control. They cannot move forward and take their rightful place in a society of adults.

FIVE

PIGGYBACKING

She was thirty-four years old, had been married for twelve years, had a ten-year-old child, and still felt herself incapable of making a decision on her own.

"When I was a child my father controlled everything I did," she said in a subdued voice. "If it was possible, I think he'd have followed me to school and sat in the back of my class. As it was, I had to tell him every little detail of what went on from the time he left me in the morning to the time he came home. He didn't like me to have *any* experience he didn't know about.

"At the playground, if I was playing with friends, he'd be somewhere around, supervising what I was doing. Later, he'd ask me about how I got along with my friends, etc. If he didn't approve of somebody, the campaign would begin. 'Why spend time with her? She hasn't got very good manners.'"

You would think this woman was citing the problems she had with a troublesome, overprotective father. But: "My daddy really loved me. He's gone now but I still miss him terribly. It isn't the same with my husband. There'll never be anyone like Daddy."

Less than a year after our interview this woman was divorced by her husband. Shortly after that she nearly succeeded in a suicide attempt. She was still trying to find some way back to her daddy.

In *Passages: Predictable Crises of Adult Life,* Gail Sheehy writes that women feel "we are really kids who cannot take care of ourselves ... who must piggyback our development by attaching to a Stronger One."

The power of this symbiotic connection between dad and daughter lasts a lifetime and influences decisions a daughter makes throughout her adulthood. Most married women, whether they know it or not, have been secretly influenced in their choice of a husband by the "other man"—father.

Time and again in talking to grown-up women, some in their late forties, the phrase comes up: "I don't think my father had much to do with influencing my taste in men. My husband and my father are entirely different." These declarations of independence are usually made with an air of satisfaction, as if by rejecting the father as model a personal victory were scored. But the differences are usually in peripherals—physical appearance, sports and hobbies, type of occupation, even the amount of education. More basic attitudes, the kind of symbolic figure represented, are amazingly similar.

"My father is a psychically disoriented nitpicker," says the daughter of a wealthy Delaware family, a witty, sarcastic twenty-seven-year-old. "My whole adolescence was a minor series of adjustments to panic. There was always some way I was displeasing him. I became an emotional shambles. Other people envied me because I had such a brilliant father, so successful, strong, but they didn't know what I was going through."

What she was going through was a nervous breakdown that resulted in months of hospital care. "I used to go around putting vaseline on doorknobs," she says. "Nobody liked me. Just this one doctor, and I developed a kind of canine affection for him." She laughed an extremely brittle laugh. "He's the one who told me I was a product of the merciless warfare between the generations. He said I'd have to establish some sort of identity for myself.

"What I did was I married him. I knew from the start it wouldn't work. I think I married him because he didn't remind me of my father. His big attraction was that he liked me enough to want to marry me. That was about it. It was a quick failure because I wasn't able to give him what you might call normal displays of affection. Whenever he started picking on me he reminded me of my father.

"I didn't want to live with a man like my father—driven, emotionally uninvolved, overly success-oriented. I don't share those values. My father ruled like an absolute monarch. He made me feel like a buffoon, a nice, well-meaning, meaningless meddler who happened to be his daughter. On the other hand, I need someone strong. I'm incapable of managing my own affairs."

A father who lets his daughter see a circumscribed world in which women enact only predestined roles of wife, housekeeper, mother, is certain to have a limiting effect on his daughter's personality. There is nothing wrong with her playing these roles if she chooses them freely; the danger lies in being made to think of herself as incapable of handling a broader range of life situations.

The seal of approval only a generation ago was given more readily to the daughter who got married, raised children, kept a good home, entertained her husband's business friends and did volunteer work in the community. That ideal of womanhood was not created out of whole cloth by a magazine's editorial staff. The cloth was there waiting to be cut—to the exact specifications of what men wanted their women to be.

Because marriage was the highest possible goal, a woman had to behave in a way that would persuade a man to marry her. "I always felt that I came third in the pecking order," a woman confided to us. "My husband and the children came first and second. That kind of 'me-last' attitude has been with me all my life—and though I often resent the idea, I just can't seem to shake free of it."

Dr. C. B. Pollard says, "Women today who wish to know how they got to be the way they are must get rid of the blinkers of their previous conditioning and look at the paternal influence that molded their lives."

A self-educated businessman I know was skeptical of his daughter's academic achievement. When she brought home a report card with high grades he dismissed it as unimportant. "You're not going to be writing English compositions or doing algebra when you're married and have children. What they ought to teach you in school is how to be a homemaker. *That* would make sense!"

The girl's teacher told him his daughter had a genuine gift for writing. He replied, "How about her spelling and punctuation? That's what she ought to be studying. Her writing won't help her get a secretarial job. She has to know how to take shorthand and type!"

On graduation from high school, she was told by her father that he would not pay for her to "waste her time in college. If you want to go to business school, that's a different matter."

She did not go to college. In business school she became an excellent typist. She won fourth place in a statewide typing competition. Her father's reaction: "Fourth place! If you want to get anywhere, you've got to be *first!*"

Some men feel truly masculine only when the women in their lives are inferior. Whatever tentative foray a daughter makes toward escaping from sexist typing is accompanied by the instilled fear that she cannot achieve anything of consequence because she is a woman. She needs important allies—her mother, friends, lover or husband, an occupation or an ideology—to shake off the influence of a father who considers femininity to be an inferior status.

I should confess to having accepted this male chauvinist concept of femininity when Donna was a young girl. She tells me we were once engaged in a discussion of that fascinating subject: her future life. She wanted to know what I thought she would grow up to be. Incautiously, I referred to the statistical probability that she would "become a suburban housewife and doubtless be happy at it."

Confound her memory!

Since women entered the marketplace in increasing numbers, a pattern in their progress as executives has been noted. Women are underrepresented in the top echelons of management. Until recently this could be blamed on the policy of most companies not to elevate women employees to positions of high responsibility. But it is becoming apparent that many women executives themselves fear too much success, too much achievement. They are reluctant to try to reach their full potential because the effort might cost them popularity with men. They do their jobs well, but don't compete too strenuously.

Donna says, "Even very strong and successful women feel they are somehow incomplete without a man to lean on and look up to. No matter how prestigious or financially rewarding their careers, most still regard them as secondary in importance to the male's. One vice-president of a major corporation—who every day makes decisions involving millions of dollars—told me her husband, an executive in another corporation, refers to her job as 'Susan's hobby.' She added, 'And, in truth, I think of it that way. My job is something I like to do, something I think I'm good at. I enjoy getting out of the house. But Peter is still the breadwinner, the head of the household, the one responsible for our family's financial welfare.'"

These women are keeping the bargain they made with dad so many years ago—to be smart, popular, successful "good girls," but never smarter, more successful than dad. Having traveled that route in childhood, women find it harder to compete with men as equals. Far too many adult, intelligent women still allow their male colleagues to treat them not as peers but as precocious children

One administrative assistant whom Donna interviewed provided striking proof of this. "When I first spoke to her alone over lunch, she came across as an articulate, confident, self-reliant woman," Donna writes. "But when I accompanied her back to her office she underwent a startling change. She giggled—yes, giggled!—when male colleagues made comments on her dress and appearance, and acted flirtatious and charmingly bubble-headed. Later, when I asked her about the transformation, she admitted she deliberately 'played up to the guys.' She added, 'Once I wore a charm bracelet to which I had attached my Phi Beta Kappa key. One of the vice-presidents saw it and seemed a bit taken aback. "Hey, what's this? What've we got here—some kind of big brain?" I laughed and made a joke about getting it on the black market. Later I felt angry at myself for doing that. But the truth is I *want* my male colleagues to like me, and they won't if they feel threatened.'"

A forty-one-year-old woman admits that no matter how well she does in her job as research director in an advertising agency, "there is a part of me that wants to chuck it all."

She feels that she has succeeded merely to show she can do it, and does not consider herself successful because "I'm afraid that I scare men away." She is not trying to fulfill herself in her career but to impress a man—a pattern established when she was a young girl and never felt she had done well until her father told her so. "Whatever I did was to earn his respect and approval. I wanted above all for Dad to tell me he was proud of me." Today, she still wants men to indulge her, applaud her, admire her. Men will not share power with her for the simple reason that they don't have to. She can be bought cheaper.

Another woman in the same advertising agency had risen to be head copywriter. She credited her rise partly to the fact that "my father was such a big shot here." Her father was a famous radio and television producer at the agency during and after World War II. He is now retired, and his chief pleasure is in telling her about the top executives in the advertising field who once "emptied my wastebaskets" when he was at the agency. This woman did not tell her father that she held a position with responsibilities equal to those he had in his heyday because "I don't want to be in competition with him." She feared he would not love her as well if she ceased to be in awe of him.

Recently, this woman's husband was offered a chance to move, at a small salary increase, to another town. She turned down a big raise in salary at her agency in order to go with him. Her priorities continue to be the men in her life, her father and husband.

A thirty-eight-year-old woman was executive secretary to the vice-president in a firm of business consultants. She was the brains behind her boss's success, but she did everything she could to make it appear otherwise. She handled all his correspondence; he never had to do anything but affix his signature. She conducted interviews and made recommendations—but always pretended to be acting under her boss's direct supervision. She even wrote unsigned memos for him to take into business conferences, and later took pride in how many of "his" ideas were accepted.

While she worked late hours, he took off in the afternoon for cocktails or even for an occasional golf date. When he traveled out of town she waited by her telephone at home to consult with him if he needed her. One might suspect this was a familiar case of a secretary in love with her boss, but it wasn't. Her boss was a handsome dignified man in his sixties who had gone through several unhappy marriages but was now quite happy in his latest marriage. She herself was a happily married mother of two.

What he represented to her was a haven of security. Her father, an unsuccessful journalist, never had been able to provide properly for his family. She often advanced money to him that he could claim to have earned. This pattern of behavior was carried forward into her relationship with her boss.

When her boss retired recently he recommended her for a similar secretarial position with a young executive. He never once considered her for a higher position, although she had in effect been doing his job for years. Unwilling to settle any longer for less money, less prestige and more work, she resigned and took a position with a rival firm.

This story has a happy ending. She is now a vice-president on her own.

Psychologists have just begun to realize how much a father determines his daughter's attitude toward achievement. Marshall Hamilton, in *Father's Influence on Children*, observes that "a number of psychological problems and disorders, initially viewed as a result of inadequacies in the mother's behavior, appear to be influenced as much by father's behavior."

Happiness in Aristotle's definition is not an emotional glow but the fulfillment of our faculties. If we do not fulfill our faculties, we become disorganized and disheartened. A daughter who cannot achieve her adult potential will become passive and dependent.

Donna's interview with Eleanor was arranged with the approval of her therapist, who thought that talking about her problem might prove helpful. Her problem was emotional immaturity. She had gone to the therapist in the first place because although "I had everything I want," she felt restless and dissatisfied, with no goals or ambitions and "nothing to live for."

In a voice barely audible on the tape recorder, she tells Donna how her father said, "The important thing is to get along with people. A woman's job is to entertain and please, and her interests should center in the family." He told her the secret of getting along with people was to practice the four C's? Be courteous, complimentary, charming and cooperative.

At an early age Eleanor learned how to "play up to Daddy" in order to tease him out of irritable moods. She even kept her "little-girl" voice because her father was so pleased with it. Today she appears apathetic and listless. She admits that even the simplest tasks overwhelm her and cause her to run to Daddy to be told her failure does not really matter. His protectiveness is a continual summons back to her childhood.

"Mother used to scold me if I did something wrong. Daddy would just smile and call me a fumblefingers or a forget-head. He wouldn't even let me correct a mistake because 'you'll only make it worse.' But he never got angry with me. He always called me 'Norakins,' or 'little one,' or 'pushki'—affectionate names. I still don't like to be called Eleanor. It sounds as if someone is being cross with me.

"When I was small I was frightened of many things. This will sound silly, but when I was three years old Mother was making dinner at the beach house we rented for the summer. There was going to be a party. She was talking to Father about ice trays, and my father decided to keep the larger one out for drinks and 'put the little one into the refrigerator.' I burst into tears and ran from the kitchen. My father came after me to find out what the trouble was. After some coaxing I blurted, 'I don't want to be put into the refrigerator!'"

That amusing glimpse into the mind of a little child was related by her father to their friends that night, and for a long time afterward. Too long afterward.

When Eleanor was six years old television sets were beginning to appear in homes. Her father bought one of the earliest, a
fine Dumont set. Whenever he would turn the set off Eleanor
began to cry. Only after a while did her father discover that she
thought every time he turned off the set he was making the
persons appearing on the screen actually disappear.

That story about her was also told often. At age twelve,
Eleanor got up courage to ask her father not to tell it anymore. By
then she was not finding stories about her ineptness very funny
either. "I don't say he was wrong—I really wasn't very good at
things—but I wished he wouldn't keep bringing it up."

"What things?" Donna asked.

"Well, I never watched where I was going. Once I stepped on
an expensive watch that was lying on the floor. It was careless, but
I didn't appreciate the way Daddy made it the butt of a joke from
then on. 'Look out, everybody, here comes Miss Elephant!'"

"What was the watch doing on the floor?"

"I don't know. Daddy must have left it there. It was his
watch."

"Wasn't that careless of him?"

"I still shouldn't have stepped on it."

Eleanor either deliberately misunderstood what the question
meant, or would not accept its implications. She preferred to
blame herself.

"I just can't stand up to people," she complains. She has
begun to suspect that the origin of this problem may be her father.
"He was strong-minded and had definite ideas."

She went to a therapist because she had to "pull myself
together." Her husband, like her father, had been captivated by her
childlike ways, but she was impatient with herself because she
was unable to act as a mature woman. She had never held a job.
She had never had a checking account. The only money she
handled was a small weekly allowance. She had no idea how
much money her husband earned, how much money they had in
the bank, how much the mortgage payment of the house was, or
how much her clothes cost. Her husband picked her clothes and
brought them home for her to try on for size.

Clearly, a child-woman.

A daughter trying to establish an independent identity is
confronted by a father who under the guise of being her guardian

and protector tries to keep her love exclusively for him. He prevents, or at least postpones, her becoming a fully functioning adult.

Confronted with such a father, a daughter often reverts to childhood patterns, takes the safe course, and accepts further manipulation by other males in later years, especially by her husband. Her independence is compromised because she is "programmed" to let another dominate and direct her actions.

The parallel with hypnosis is close. A person who has often been hypnotized is ready to "go under" again at the snap of a hypnotist's finger. The crucial difference is that the hypnotic state is transitory, but childlikeness may endure throughout adult life. If she keeps internalizing the promptings from male authority figures, her own capacity for analyzing and dealing with a situation is reduced. At whatever stage of adulthood, she will be ready to offer compliance to anyone who will go through the ritualized steps.

"One of my friends," Donna says, "still feels obliged to attach to any department store bill a short note explaining to her husband why she made the purchase. She keeps the sales slips so she can return the purchase if her husband does not approve. This is a ritual act of exorcism—relieving herself in advance of the fear of criticism."

A woman programmed to act in this way is incapable of making an important decision. She becomes totally dependent on the dominant male and anything she does is tentative, subject to his revision or veto. This is not the status of an adult; it is the status of a child.

"My father made me feel that I couldn't do anything because I was a girl," says a young editor on a feminist magazine, "I began to think of myself as some vague fluttery helpless creature rustling about in a musty room. A lot of women still have to fight that image because of the way their fathers brought them up. They are taught to believe that a really feminine woman would never do this or that because 'that's what men do.' They lose confidence in themselves and their sex.

"I remember the first day I had to go to junior high. Dad took me for a trial run on the bus, showing me where to get on, where to get off. At twelve years old, it made me feel a little like an idiot. On the morning that school began he even wanted to ride with me on the bus. At least I talked him out of that. All my friends would have thought it pretty odd to see me with Dad taking me in tow!

"His excuse was that I was a girl—a condition apparently synonymous with incapacity. I pointed out that boys are not necessarily better equipped by nature to take the bus and a lot of other girls my age would be taking it. He finally let me go alone. A minor episode, but it sticks in my mind. In a small way I was allowed to prove my competence—not in terms of whether I was female or male, but as an individual. It would have been one more brick added to that burden women have to carry—of being unable to do things."

SIX

OBEDIENCE AND REBELLION

Leslie, at eleven years old, gave her father every reason to be proud of her. She was attractive, had an excellent disposition, lots of friends, and was a straight A student at school. Her father never failed to let her know how exceptional she was.

Although socially aware in other ways, he could be perfectly tedious on the subject of his daughter. Friends and business acquaintances endured interminable lunches and commuter rides with him in which he would bring out color photographs to show what a beauty Leslie was, and relate anecdotes *ad somnambulis* about how helpful and cooperative she was at home, about her cuteness and niceness, smartness and whateverness—as if her personal qualities somehow brought honor to him.

He suffered two rebuffs that I know of. A woman with a well-deserved reputation for bluntness asked directly, "You don't really think *anyone* is interested in that, do you?" when he was in the midst of a long recital about his incomparable daughter. And one evening, as he was busily setting up a projector to show a home movie featuring his daughter's violin playing, a friend with a reputation for dry wit remarked, "I hope you'll bear in mind that I'm the fellow who fell asleep during the chariot race in *Ben Hur.*" Neither rebuff deterred him.

As Leslie grew older she worked hard to maintain her standards of performance and deserve his praise even more. She took on extracurricular activities at school, and also became an accomplished musician. She spent several hours a week on her violin lessons. Her music teacher was so pleased with her progress that she arranged for a concert at a neighborhood music school. Midway in the concert, Leslie could not force her fingers to hold down the strings of the violin. She broke into tears and ran off the stage.

When Leslie could not resume her violin lessons her father sent her to a therapist, who discovered that this Perfect Daughter had been living all the while in a private hell. In order to keep getting father's praise, which she interpreted as proof of his

64

affection—she had set ever higher and higher standards of excellence for herself. In psychological terms, she felt she was being paid for accepting and surmounting new challenges.

The therapist advised Leslie's father to stop putting pressure on his daughter through praise. What she needed was simple reassurance that he would love her even if she were not exceptional. If she had that, she could develop her own goals and standards and decide for herself what badges of success she wanted to wear. "As a 'perfect' child her goal was only to fulfill his wishes, and she would have grown into an adult harried by feelings of worthlessness and inadequacy," the therapist explained. "Such women are unable to love others because they find it impossible to love themselves. They are victims of their own childhood."

A father is wrong to treat his daughter as if she existed only for his aggrandizement. No matter how exceptional she is, she can never demonstrate what a wonderful human being *he* is. She is an individual with an identity, problems, a history and a future wholly separate from his. Her sovereign and self-governing mind and nervous system lead to a differing outlook on the world.

Most fathers find this fact hard to accept. An example is a former well-known athlete whom I will call Thomas. I have changed the sport in which he made his reputation to further conceal his identity.

Thomas was a tennis champion in his youth, with every prospect of making it to the national championship. Then, in an elevator accident, he lost two fingers of his right hand. His career was over. He taught himself to play with his left hand but never became more than a moderately good player.

Thomas would have liked to train a son to win the championship his accident denied him. But, as fate would have it, he had three daughters, and only one showed any ability to play tennis. Thomas zeroed in on her. He spent hours every day teaching her everything he knew about the sport. Under his tutelage she won several minor trophies.

His daughter told us, "Somehow what I did wasn't enough. I kept trying to live up to what he wanted, but he was never satisfied. Many times I'd lock myself into my room and have a good cry."

At twenty-four, she fell in love and abandoned her tennis career in favor of being a wife and mother. Thomas felt betrayed.

To this day he remains bitterly disappointed because his daughter did not devote her life to making up for his failure to win a championship.

His daughter suffers mixed feelings about her decision. "There were a lot of good times, but I never felt I was doing it for myself. It was to please him—and I do feel like I let him down. And I resent him for making me feel that way. I wasn't cut out for Wimbledon. All I wanted him to do was love me and be proud of me for trying. He could never bring himself to do that."

Father's power over a daughter's development is a dominating force that she must defeat or come to terms with. Too often the way she comes to terms is summed up in the familiar phrase, "If you can't lick him, join him." If she "joins him," she denies her own need to separate and grow.

A forty-four-year-old father worked the late shift and didn't get home until one o'clock in the morning. But he always got up at six-thirty to make his daughter's breakfast and see her off to school while her mother slept. When she returned home he reviewed her homework assignment before leaving for work, then called her during his dinner break to discuss any problems. At that time he also planned her activity for the evening, what television shows she could watch, when she could complete her homework, what hour she should go to bed.

As she grew older, he kept trying to control her life. His daughter sensed that he was doing it to satisfy his own compulsion, although she couldn't find words to express it. "Sometimes I felt funny because Dad wouldn't let me do anything on my own. He thought he had my problems all worked out. But they weren't as simple as he thought."

She was particularly upset recently because her father did not approve of her boyfriend. The young man, seventeen, was badly crippled and used crutches. The first time her father saw the boy he advised his daughter "not to get closely involved. It's all right to feel sorry for someone like that but don't let pity get the best of you." She felt that was unfair and heartless, and continued seeing the young man.

As soon as her father heard of this he warned the boy to stop coming to the house. So his daughter began visiting the young man at his home. "I didn't feel pity for him at all," she explained. "All Dad could see was the fact he's crippled. He was the most brilliant person I'd ever met. All his teachers said he wrote beautiful poetry. He had deep feelings, and was much older than his age."

The father soon became alarmed that his attractive young daughter was romantically involved. "I always want you to solve your problems in your own way," he told her. "But you don't know the difference between sympathy and love—you're softhearted and innocent." The dispute led the girl to shut herself off from her father, and her attitude slowly changed from resistance to hostility.

The father wanted her to "broaden herself" by traveling and by getting away to a good college. She told him she had no intention of going anywhere without her boyfriend. Then suddenly the next summer she agreed to go to Bilbao and her father paid for a round-trip passage for her.

"This is my declaration of independence," she wrote to her father when she arrived. "I'm not going to let you run my life anymore. You still think of me as your sweet little girl, but I'm going to live my life the way I think best."

Soon afterward her father learned that her boyfriend had joined her. They lived together for a while, but toward the end of the summer she wrote that her lover had turned moody and neglectful and she was afraid of him. "He's not like I thought he was at all." Her father wired her to come home at once.

The young man never communicated with her again. He drifted from Spain to Paris, where he continued trying to get started on a writing career. At last report, he was working on the staff of a magazine.

As for the young daughter, she now accepts that she made a terrible mistake by ignoring her father's counsel. She will not defy him again. She has slipped back into the safety and comfort of being Daddy's Girl.

"A major problem in treating women patients," says Dr. Pollard, "is their conviction that everything that went wrong in their childhood has to be their fault. They are eager to accept guilt. By blaming themselves they don't have to blame their father, who is often the real cause of their problem."

One of his patients, a woman of twenty-eight, began suffering from feelings of deep depression because her father had been injured in an automobile accident. He had suffered a broken hip and other injuries that would require weeks and possibly months of care. Although she had a husband and three children, she felt she should drop everything to care for him.

"I asked her why she felt that way, since her mother was still alive and vigorous and able to look after her father's needs," Dr.

Pollard continues, "She told me, 'I won't have him with me much longer. This is my last chance to make up for all the bad things I did. He gave me everything, and all I did was take and take with no sign of gratitude.'

"A few sessions convinced me she did not have much to reproach herself about. For example, she told me her father had bought her a lovely grand piano but she had sneaked out of practicing and never got much out of the lessons he paid for. I pointed out to her that the piano lessons were her father's idea, that she had never wanted them and, in fact, had little talent for music.

"Nothing I said seemed to matter. She still felt she had let her father down and was anxious to accuse herself of childish transgressions. She carried her guilt around like a ball and chain; it was a bond to her father, a connection. I couldn't persuade her that her present depression might be disguised anger at how she had been manipulated. She wouldn't hear a word against him."

A daughter who trades in her own goals for those imposed on her, even if she wins her father's loving support, must resign herself to living as a child despite the crucial and ultimately painful difference that she is a woman.

A friend of Donna's told her of a time when she came home to find her father watching a preacher on television. Feeling sure that her father, an agnostic, was taking a dim view of the proceeding, she felt safe in making a slighting remark. Her father became quite annoyed: "After all, he's perfectly sincere about what he believes."

His inconsistency baffled her, but she did not blame her father for being inconsistent. She blamed herself for not perceiving the logic behind what her father said! As a young girl, if she pointed out an occasional mistake to her father, he would reply stiffly: "I stand corrected." She came to understand that the enormity of correcting him could never be offset by her being right. Fresh from her first year in college, chockablock with new knowledge, she boldly undertook to tell her father about conservation and the environment. She thought he would be proud of how much she had learned. But his rejoinder crushed her: "I've always been in favor of higher education for women. That's why I sent you off to college. Now I'm not so sure it was a good idea."

This young woman's subsequent history may be of interest. At eighteen she became involved in an intense love affair at college. She could not bear to be away from her boyfriend for a moment; she adopted the same attitude toward him that she had to her father. When he assured her it was "safe" two weeks after she had her period, she let him make love to her—and got pregnant. "I don't understand how I could have been so dumb," she confided to Donna. "I could have told him he was wrong!"

Her early training of yielding to a Stronger One was responsible. She had assigned her boyfriend the role of her father—and given him the unquestioning response learned in her childhood.

Piaget explains the attitude this way: "Any act that shows obedience to a rule or even to an adult, regardless of what he may command, is good; any act that does not conform to rules is bad. A young daughter is unlikely to measure what she does by her motive for doing it, but as to whether it conforms to the rules that have been laid down for her to obey."

A woman of thirty-eight was taught by her father as a young girl never to disagree openly with a man, never to speak her opinions too forcefully when in the company of men. "A silent woman draws men like honey draws flies," he would say. "A woman who talks too much ends up with the flies in her mouth!"

"Did you consider that good advice?" I asked her.

She smiled uneasily. "It was the rule in our home. My mother was actually much brighter than he was, but she sat around at dinner listening to Dad go on and on while not speaking a word. When Dad wasn't around she would keep us fascinated with stories about almost anything: she had a sense of humor about little domestic happenings that was like Erma Bombeck's. But she never spoke up with Dad present—not unless she was invited."

"How did you feel about that?"

"I accepted it as how things were, that's all. It didn't seem important at the time. I suppose it's one reason I'm the way I am. I can't express anger to a man. In my first job I was given a lot of unfair extra work without overtime pay. But I never spoke up. When I play tennis I never win from men I know I can beat. But I don't consciously *try* to lose. I remember how it was at home. Mother and Dad liked to play ping-pong. Mother always lost even though she could beat me much worse than Dad could. It didn't occur to me for quite a while that unconsciously she didn't *want* to win."

"And you think this has affected you?"

"I'm sure of it. I lived in Greenwich Village for a year and traveled uptown by subway to work. One morning I was going through an underpass and heard footsteps race up behind me. The next thing I knew a man grabbed me from behind with his hand over my mouth. He whispered, 'One scream and you'll get a knife.' I screamed anyway. He threw me down, felt me up, and then ran off. I never saw his face so I couldn't describe him to the police. The next day I was so shaken up that I signed up for a series of karate lessons. I wanted to be able to defend myself if anything like that ever happened to me again.

"After the first lesson I dropped out and forfeited the money I'd paid. I'd found out I just couldn't be aggressive toward a man, not even in karate class when he was simulating an attack. The only way I ever react to a man who treats me unfairly, even in an argument, is to cry. Tears are the way I express my anger. I guess my father helped to make me the way I am."

Denied an adult outlet for her anger, daughter is forced into childish tantrums and weeping. Her frustration is like a person trying to explain a complicated emotional problem while being restricted to words of one syllable. Too much must remain unsaid and unexpressed.

But repressed feelings don't go away. The feelings retreat wordlessly into the mind and fester there, often to surface later as physical symptoms. Many women who complain of being chronically deficient in energy, who suffer from migraine headaches or stomach ulcers or chest pains or asthma, are really suffering from the poisonous accumulation of repressed angers.

What is especially ironic is that these "female weaknesses" are cited by men as evidence that woman are "naturally" frail and need to be protected. One might ask: protected from whom? From men!

A woman who does not preside over her own life, who keeps trying to attain to standards set for her by someone else—all too often her father—feels a central lack of purpose. She is traumatized, a little caterpillar who was supposed to emerge as a butterfly and who has somehow not been allowed her natural evolution. She is imprinted with someone else's idea of who she should be, not with her own. She grows into an adult-sized child who cannot articulate her true self:

I could tell you
If I wanted to,
What makes me
What I am.
But I don't
Really want to,
And you don't
*Give a damn.**

---

*By Langston Hughes from "Impasse," *The Panther and the Lash* (New York: Alfred A Knopf). © 1967 by Arna Bontemps and George Houston Bass.

TWO
SEXUALITY

SEVEN

THE AWAKENING

Not long ago in a small apartment in Queens, New York, a young married couple was making love in the bedroom they were forced to share with their two-year-old daughter. Suddenly they heard her scream and saw her standing up in her crib and staring at them in the darkness.

Instantly, the couple parted. The mother went to the two-year-old and asked what had frightened her. The child pointed at her father. "He was hurting you!"

"Now you know Daddy wouldn't hurt Mommy. He loves Mommy, just the way he loves his little girl."

"I heard you! You were crying!"

"You're mistaken, dear. Now go back to sleep and I'll explain everything to you in the morning."

Later that night, discussing the problem quietly in the kitchen, they decided the best approach was to tell the truth, nothing but the truth—and no more truth than necessary.

In the morning, the child had forgotten all about it. Even when gently reminded that she had been wakeful during the night, she showed no interest, so their carefully prepared scenario was abandoned.

For the record, however, the young couple had decided to tell her that when people love each other and are married they like to play together in bed, and that was what Mommy and Daddy were doing. Just as two-year-olds like to play games, so adults like to play their games too.

It would probably have worked.

A similar incident occurred to the four-year-old daughter of a business associate of mine. She left her bed in the middle of the night and entered the unlocked door of her parents' bedroom as they were completing the act of intercourse.

"What are you doing?" she demanded.

Startled and understandably annoyed, the mother replied, "Why are you up at this hour? Go back to bed!"

The four-year-old ran out sobbing. Her parents dressed and went to her room to apologize for having spoken so sharply. Then the father inquired what had wakened her and brought her to their room.

"I was thirsty and wanted a glass of water and I knew you were awake."

"How did you know?"

"You were making noise. What were you doing?"

"We were doing our exercises, that's all."

After a few perfunctory questions, the four-year-old appeared to be satisfied. Her father brought her a glass of water and she went promptly to sleep.

But the episode apparently wakened her curiousity about her parents' noctural activity. She developed a habit of knocking on their bedroom door at almost any hour of the night. If she found it locked, she began to cry and beg them to let her in.

In a recent survey 10 percent of the women interviewed said they recalled having witnessed their parents making love. The question of what, if any, sexual stimulation this caused was not definitely answered. Half the women remembered having a significant emotional reaction, but even these said their reaction was of very short duration.

A very young daughter's sexuality is, at first, nearly indistinguishable from a feeling of affection. She gives her father hugs and kisses and sits in his lap. However, these signs of affection are also means by which sexual feeling is conveyed. They are, in Don Quixote's phrase, "the other side of the tapestry."

The behavior of dads and young sons is far more restrained in its physical expression. This may be an unconscious response on father's part to the suggestion of homosexual behavior. There is also the "macho, he-man" image to contend with. One authority has suggested, "A loving and gentle father is consciously or unconsciously looked upon as a psychological failure in the sense that he isn't really a he-man."

With a daughter, none of this applies. One father tried to explain to me why he felt so differently about his little daughter: "God knows I love my son, who is three years older. I realize he's going to carry the family name and all that. I'm proud of him, but I don't look at him and have my heart turn over. When I think about him I don't get a choke in the throat or an ache in the heart. A friend said to me about his daughter, 'She just wipes me out.' That's a good way of putting it."

Every father falls in love with his daughter. I cannot recall the steps, the now untraceable progress of emotion, which has carried me from the moment I first saw Donna behind a glass wall in the hospital. The nurse held her up for me to see. That red, squawling, slope-headed infant with the peculiar tuft of hair was flesh of my flesh. My first thought was: *She's ugly, even if she is my daughter.* At the time, I was quite capable of retaining my objectivity.

I am no longer objective. Now everyone tells me what a lovely woman Donna is, but the only time I am close to being capable of judging for myself is when I see her at a remove—as during her television appearances. That glamorous creature who appears from behind the curtains on cue as Johnny Carson introduces her is my daughter. But she is also an image on a screen and I see her briefly that way. Otherwise, she is a face so familiar she might have been looking back at me from my mirror every morning of my life.

The physical bond that unites a father and his preschool daughter is designed by nature to serve a purpose. The formation of a strong and secure attachment between a father and daughter allows her sexuality to grow within the emotional bond.

Alex Comfort observes, "Some degree of parental seduction at the unconscious level seems to be necessary for human females to establish full function. Sexual response in women is based on presexual learning ... Fathers are there to imprint girls for sexual adequacy."

The attraction between father and daughter is not expressed in overt sexual terms. In "roughhouse" play, a young daughter is lofted, cradled as if in a sling, swung as if being "flung away." Her squeals of delight are the measure of the real game being played. Roughhouse on the intimate level is a portrayal of their relationship—holding her tight while making a symbolic rejection of sexuality. Other roughhouse games, such as "pretend" wrestling with its close body contact, turning daughter upside down when she's wearing a dress so that her undergarments are revealed, crushing her with bear hugs, all have obvious elements of sexuality.

I was present when a young daughter and her father played a "rushing" game they had just invented. The daughter "rushed" at her father, and each time he intercepted and broke the force of her charge without hurting her. This rushing toward father's arms only to be turned away at the last moment was repeated again and again with childlike indefatigability, until at last father ceased his resistance and accepted her into her arms.

As he looked over at me, he was perspiring and red-faced. "Did you ever see a girl with so much energy and determination?"

he asked. "She could wear down a mountain." He was really saying: "What do you expect me to do under the circumstances? I'm only human!"

Recently I saw a young father, on his return home from a business trip, greeted by his young daughter as if he were a long lost lover. She ran into his arms, buried her face in his neck and clung to him. They lip-kissed for as much as fifteen seconds (if that doesn't sound long to you, get out your stopwatch) while his wife stood nearby waiting her turn to greet her husband. I detected a nervous strained quality in her smile—a conflict between the good-humored acceptance expected of her and what she was secretly thinking.

This father would be terminally offended if I told him there was sexuality implicit in the greeting, that this was more than the innocent exuberant welcome of a young girl and that he was a coconspirator. Sexual feelings between father and daughter are unthinkable, so the idea is dismissed in advance. Some fathers go so far as to prove their rejection of the unthinkable by contrary behavior. Says Dr. C. B. Pollard: "Many of my women patients— particularly those with psychosexual problems—tell me that when they were children their fathers were undemonstrative and unaffectionate. 'I know he loved me,' goes the litany, 'but he never showed it.' By their conduct, these fathers might have been trying to show that no incestuous thought could possibly exist in their minds."

By the age of five a young girl is undergoing her first real sexual surge. The reality of the "unresolved desire of a child for sexual gratification through the parent of the opposite sex" was known in Greek legend several millennia before Freud.

The polarities of human emotion are closer in nature than emotions of the middle range. Extremes that seem opposed are linked by an invisible bond. An undemonstrative father appears to be at the opposite pole from an overly affectionate father, but they are brothers under the id. In the sense of being unaware, neither type is innocent.

A young daughter practices her sexual wiles on father because he represents danger and excitement, safety and shelter. Encouraged, she will test her powers further. A very young girl will dance for her father and end up whirling into his arms; she will parade naked from her bath in front of him, try out seductive gestures and mannerisms that she has learned from watching actresses on television or mother at home. Her intent is not to get daddy into bed or to steal his affections from mommy, but simply to win acknowledgment of her developing charms. Daddy's reaction may vary from mere approving laughter to a responsive sexuality.

If approval is denied, a young girl will try even harder until she approaches the limit of physical intimacy permissible in such situations. One mother intervened when her four-year-old daughter got into the habit of "riding horsey" naked on her father's foot. Another father drew the line when he entered his daughter's bedroom at night and she pulled down her pajamas, turned on her stomach, and asked him to give her a goodnight kiss on her bare behind.

Seductive games are often played between daddy and young daughter at bathtime, a practice that probably began when baby was only a few weeks old. Daddy's soft caressing touch in the bath and the all-over body powdering that follows are a time of squealing delight in many households. Nor is daughter likely to object when having her genitals soaped and rinsed and softly toweled dry.

The overture and response are as clearly marked as in any other kind of sexual fondling. But it is not perceived that way by the father. To be more accurate, he does not choose to perceive it that way. However, the sensuous handling of the genital area is known to be a source of pleasure even to extremely young infants. Most fathers will admit to a "sensual" pleasure in bathing their infant daughters. They balk at the word "sexuality" because that has unwelcome connotations. They refute the suggestion that there is any kind of sexual approach involved.

I quote verbatim this passage from one interview:

"Isn't it at least possible that by directing an infant's attention to the genital area as a source of pleasure the risk increases of her continuing to use it in that way? I mean, of course, by masturbation?"

"A baby that age doesn't know what it's doing."

"How about an increased tendency toward masturbation in later years?"

"You can't say one thing causes another. Anyway, nothing like that has happened with Eloise (an older daughter, now nine years old). She grew up normal."

"Normal?"

"She's never had any interest in that."

Men raised in an earlier tradition of sexual repressiveness have trouble accepting female masturbation as a normal part of

growing up. Many still subscribe to old myths about masturbation's harmful effects. Two generations ago the usual parental
warning was that masturbation will either make you blind or drive
you insane. The warning was apparently devised on the theory
that the more extreme the consequence, the more effective the
deterrent. Some doctors in that era prescribed incredible treat-
ments for young girls, such as removal of the ovary, cutting the
genital nerves and even removal of the clitoris to "solve" the
problem. The practice still survives in some Arab countries.

Modern authorities, in an attempt to reconcile old myths and
prejudices with new trends and discoveries, have settled on the
theory that masturbation is a serious problem only if practiced to
excess. But a father will fight like a tarpon against associating
what he considers this morally dubious activity with his pristine
clean daughter. At the first sign that a young boy is suffering from
Portnoy's Complaint father will begin searching for evidence to
confirm his suspicions, but he will disregard evidence that his
daughter has discovered the delights of self-loving. A young boy
who retreats into the bathroom with a copy of *Playboy* is presumed to be guilty, while a young girl who goes there with a
romantic novel is exempt from suspicion of any offense worse
than excessive reading.

A recent survey found that most fathers are disturbed by the
idea of daughters masturbating. Working-class fathers have the
strongest negative reaction. Some believe the practice has to be
stopped, even to the extent of punishing a daughter who engages
in it. Others agree that masturbation ought to be discouraged but
are not sure about the best way to do it.

Among our interviews on this subject is one with a father
who was rather proud of the method he used to "scare" his small
daughter out of masturbating. He enlisted her pediatrician, who
during her next physical examination advised her "not to handle
her genitals too much" because she was developing an enlarged
clitoris, "almost the size of a full-grown woman." The pediatrician
did not mention that many young girls have similarly large
clitorises.

One father told me he became "concerned" about his daughter when she was four years old because "she was always touching
herself, sometimes right in public where anyone could see. I
caught her beneath the dining room table, straddling one of the
curving support legs and riding up and down on it. I talked to our
family doctor, who told me it was a phase most kids go through

and she would stop it in time. That wasn't good enough. I laid down the law to her and now everything is fine. She's not touching herself anymore."

More likely his young daughter simply learned to carry on her masturbatory activity where no one will notice. As one woman told Donna, "I learned very early that touching myself there was 'not nice.' I remember one time when I was quite small, I was in my room listening to some story records and massaging my clitoris. I didn't know what it was then, of course, I just knew that it felt good to touch. I was happy and relaxed. Then my father came in to ask me something. I don't think I'll ever forget the look on his face when he saw what I was doing. 'Stop that!' he yelled. 'That's disgusting!' I was horrified. I didn't know what I'd done wrong. For a time I stopped touching myself, but then I started again. Only this time I knew I was being naughty, and I listened carefully for any footsteps approaching my room."

Masturbation is the particular aspect of daughter's developing sexuality that a father finds most distasteful. Unconsciously, he wishes to keep his young daughter from taking the first bite of the forbidden apple because that marks the beginning of her growing up—and away from him. A father whose attitude toward his young daughter is basically seductive ("Thou shalt have no other love before me") is threatened by any form of activity that may displace him as her principal love object. As long as she remains entirely innocent, she can be entirely his.

Despite his best efforts, however, he cannot prevail. The process of sexualization is irresistible and irreversible, and begins earlier than most fathers think. Rarely is daughter as innocent as dad would like to believe she is. One father told of watching his four-year-old daughter get ready for bed. A button stuck on her pajama top and she couldn't pull it down over her head. She uttered a subdued "Oh, *damn!*" from under the flannel.

Her father grinned and helped her to pull the pajama top down over her head. "Did I hear my girl say a bad word?"

"No, Daddy."

"I'm sure I heard you say 'Oh, damn.'"

"That isn't a bad word."

Delighted with this proof of her innocence, he explored further. "What would you consider a *bad* word?"

"Fuck," she replied.

We interviewed a man married to a woman who had to supplement their income by working as a cocktail waitress. From the time she left home at eight o'clock in the evening he was in charge of their children, a five-year-old girl and a nine-year-old boy.

The boy was self-sufficient, but the girl missed her mother. To comfort her, the father allowed her to sleep in his bed. At eleven o'clock he would go to bed himself. One midnight, he woke to discover his young daughter pressing her body lightly against him. Not knowing what to do, he pretended to still be asleep. She began to rub her vulva against his thigh with a regular rhythmic stroking.

At the first opportunity he rolled over to his other side. In the morning he told her she could not sleep in his bed anymore.

One woman recalls "wonderful Sunday mornings" in bed with her parents when she was only eight or nine years old. "The Sunday paper had a large comics section which I read while Dad and Mother divided up the rest of the newspaper. Best of all was when Mother got up to make breakfast. Then I had Daddy to myself. Sometimes we'd have pillow fights or wrestling matches. I'd try to pull off his pajamas and he wouldn't let me. By the time Mother called us we'd show up very respectable for breakfast, but I'd be brimming over with laughter inside. If I caught Daddy's eyes, I'd bust up for sure."

For her, the roughhouse games apparently still had no sexual implications.

Sigmund Freud believed in a period of sexual "latency" in children from the age of six to puberty. The first five years were marked by masturbatory and oral orientation, which receded in favor of activity in other spheres, an exploratory time in which the child discovered the world. True sexual interest and development did not recur, in Freud's view, until puberty.

Freud's view is not widely accepted today. When girls go to school they segregate themselves socially from boys, and this persists until early adolescence, which covers the time period of Freud's hypothesis. But the segregation by sex does not mean girls have lost interest in boys, or vice versa. Among themselves they talk freely of falling in love and getting married. They have crushes on boys their own age and also on older males: brothers, teachers, male friends of the family, and of course television and movie and rock-and-roll stars. This is hardly symptomatic of sexual latency.

A father trying to deal with a daughter's developing sexuality is handicapped by his lack of training, education and experience, plus the taboo involving any form of sexual intimacy between father and daughter. To paraphrase George Bernard Shaw's famous remark about parents and children: "There may be some doubt as to who are the best people to deal with daughters' sexuality, but there is no doubt that fathers are the worst."

A father would like to be more open in discussing sex, but the topic makes him uncomfortable. "One of the hardest problems is to get them to use certain words freely in talking to their daughters, words that they have always been taught were 'dirty,'" says the director of a YMCA Parenting Center who conducts a class for men who wish to develop their parenting skills. "Many of these men could not refer to parts of the male or female body without flushing or stammering. Yet in another setting they probably tell raw jokes about sex. That seems a contradiction but isn't. They can't discuss sex in an objective, straightforward, impersonal way, but the telling of so-called dirty jokes is their emotional release, a blowing off of steam. Having a forum to discuss sexual problems within the family in a serious adult way is the best thing that could happen to them—and to their families."

The typical father is confronted with a dilemma: he is the object of his daughter's first sexual feeling and he also takes on the role of guardian of her innocence. The way he resolves the dilemma is to keep her unaware of the fact that there is anything to learn about sex. "As a little girl," Agnes De Mille says, "I was taught that the part of the female anatomy between the knee and the shoulder was not to be revealed. It simply didn't exist."

Yet almost as soon as a daughter understands that she is a girl, she understands that her father is a man. His feeling of unease about the difference in their sexes communicates itself. The crucial role he should play in her sexual development—establishing a standard by which she can conduct herself as a female and judging the progress she is making toward adulthood—is hindered by his reticence.

"When I was a little girl Dad thought it was cute when I showed up naked in front of him. He told me I had a pretty body. Now you should see the fit he throws if I wear a bikini to the beach!"

This fourteen-year-old's complaint finds echoes in other similar comments from teenaged girls: "I used to bother my dad with all kinds of questions about sex. Right after Mother explained about menstruation, a couple of silly questions I asked Dad became famous in our house. I wanted to know, 'Is it true that men don't get a period because they've got that thing down there blocking it off?' and 'After I get my first period, how long do I have to wait before you can help me to make a baby?' That was okay then, but I couldn't talk like that anymore. *Anything* about sex is strictly off limits."

In interviews with daughters of various ages, we did not encounter a single instance in which a daughter was not aware of her father's feelings on the subject of sex, although he never communicated them to her directly.

A father of two girls, sixteen and eleven years old, prides himself on the fact that "I never in any way have made my daughters feel that there is anything dirty or sinister or wrong about sex. That's Freud's hangup; not mine. I would never want them to feel guilty about anything they do."

His sixteen-year-old daughter agrees that her father never had led her to believe sex was dirty or wrong. "He's not a prude or anything like that. But he's not too keen on me knowing much about it either." She relates an occasion in which she slept over at a girlfriend's house. Her friend has two older brothers, eighteen and twenty-one. "When Dad heard that her brothers were in our room after midnight—even though we were just playing Pit (a popular card game) I could almost see steam coming out of his ears. I told him it was all perfectly innocent, and he sort of nodded and let it pass. But whenever I've asked to stay overnight at my girlfriend's house again he always finds some excuse. Because of that night."

To a father, his adolescent daughter seems in more danger than a preschooler. "Hold me real tight, Daddy," a six-year-old daughter says, and her father is charmed. When she is sixteen, he regards the same request much differently.

Her need for affection has not changed. What has changed is that she has passed the age for "nonsexual" affection and entered into the vulnerable age in which physical expressions of affection are associated with lovemaking. Now dad sees his role chiefly as her protector, whose task it is to save her from the dangers of sexual knowledge.

A recent news item provides an ironic illustration of a young daughter's awareness of her father's attitude. The daughter of a politician was arrested with half a dozen teenagers in a raid on a house where they had been having a heroin party. As the father was leaving the station house with his daughter after posting bail, she was overheard to say, "What's to worry, Dad? None of us were having sex. Hard stuff really kills that."

EIGHT

THE DEVELOPMENT

Someone has said that a sexual thought passes through a man's mind approximately every thirty seconds. The frequency diminishes with age and satiety, but no doubt this is true for the concupiscent young male.

For a father to send his innocent young lamb into the midst of that wolf pack is unthinkable. His attitude has the blessing of society. The concept of the young male as victimizer and the young female as victim is built into our laws and social customs. A young man who takes a young woman's virginity without benefit of clergy or even intention of marriage is a vile seducer. Somehow the young woman has lost whatever the young man has gained and so the act is akin to theft.

A young woman who spent a summer waitressing at a Catskills hotel told Donna, "When Dad found out I was living with George he flew to the hotel and gave me all kinds of hell. He wanted me to come home with him and promise not to see George again. I told him he was being silly, that when young people really like each other sex helps them connect in a closer, deeper way. What was wrong with that? His answer was the old 'Why buy the cow when you can get the milk free?' I couldn't make him understand that my relationship with George wasn't a *business* transaction. No one was buying—or selling—anything!"

Father can easily inhibit a daughter's progress toward full sexuality. As instructor, model and target of opportunity, he may discourage the early signs of sexuality or unwittingly encourage traits that can cause difficulty later in his daughter's sexual adjustment. A feeling that boys are "dirty, hairy, uncouth creatures" is often fueled by a father's desire to be "protective." The message *Beware the Wicked Them, Trust the Good Me* is part and parcel of a father's attempt to keep her from "growing up and away."

"When I was old enough to be interested in boys, he was always warning me not to let them take advantage of me," says a woman about her father. "Boys were not to be trusted. They were always up to something wicked. I began to look at them as spiders weaving some giant web to catch poor helpless me."

A daughter's developing maturity increases her father's desire to keep her under his control. He tries to make the larger world appear full of unsuspected dangers. *Trust Daddy, I have charted the perils and will steer you safely by. You will be safe as long as I am with you.*

"I used to rely completely on my father's advice," a twenty-eight-year-old woman says, "especially where men were concerned. I felt he understood men. He told me how to talk to them, how to keep them from getting fresh. He told me how to dress when going out on a date, never to wear anything that would call attention to my figure. It was years before I discovered his advice was based on a fear of my getting involved with a man. My ideas about men got all mixed up with worries about venereal disease, injury to my genitals, the danger of getting pregnant. Talking about sex with my father was supposedly very open, very advanced, but most of our discussions got around to the dangers of having sex.

"If I liked a young man, Father would be very critical of him: 'That's got to be one of the homeliest boys I've ever seen!' He would find a way to knock him down, usually something that had to do with his family or educational background: 'I know his family—all shiftless no-goods. He'll grow up the same way. The apple doesn't fall far from the tree.'

"One day I brought a special boyfriend home to dinner. My father knew he was special, and he really got on his back. He corrected his table manners, even showed him which fork to use. When my boyfriend spilled some of his wine on the rug my father was furious. He told him how much the rug cost, what it would probably cost to clean it and how it would never be the same. I wanted to dive under the table and not show my face. My boyfriend was humiliated; he didn't even know how to apologize. Finally he made some lame excuse and left. I cried in my mother's arms for an hour. I hated my father for what he'd done.

"Late that night, from my bedroom, I called my boyfriend to tell him how sorry I was. One thing led to another, and the next thing I knew I sneaked out and met him at four-thirty in the morning. We drove to a motel. We fooled around but we were both too scared to do anything.

"In the morning I began to worry about my parents. I called, and my father said he would call the police because I was underage—only seventeen. He said if the young man had 'put so much as a hand' on me, he'd have him sent to prison. When I told him nothing had happened his attitude went like this: 'Come home to your daddy. You're my little girl and I love you and I only want what's best for you. If I did a wrong thing and hurt your feelings, I'm sorry. Please come home so we can all sit down and discuss this like grown-ups.'

"I did go home, and I never saw the young man again. Because of what happened, his family sent him to a college two thousand miles away. Dad and I still fight about the men I date. I'm twenty-eight years old and still living at home. I'm still a virgin. To tell the truth, I feel desexed. I've got this feeling that things have passed me by and I missed my chance."

As Gail Sheehy observes in *Passages,* "There is no good reason to give up the love of her father except that it tends to keep her a little girl for life."

Says a well-known newspaperwoman, "I recall Dad telling me, 'I really like you so much better when you look your best.' But when I was a few years older and began having my hair done and using nail polish and lipstick, everything changed. Suddenly he began making fun and ridiculing. I never could figure that out." In another part of the interview she refers to a comment her father made when she wore her first bra: "I never heard of a girl wearing a bra on little pimples." Clearly, he was disturbed at the developing sexuality that wearing a bra connoted.

The onset of a daughter's adolescence inspires a father's fear of impending separation. It happens too fast for his peace of mind. "As far as I can see, my daughter thinks boys are from Mars, strange creatures she doesn't need anything to do with," a father tells me with pride. "She's got a lot of interests that have nothing to do with sex!"

His daughter is thirteen. I would be interested in hearing his reaction in two or three years. Like most fathers, he will probably connect her growing up with a growing away from him.

A father lies awake at night, contemplating further losses to come. "As Time takes from you, I engraft you new," says Shakespeare, but as time adds to a daughter's sexual attractiveness it subtracts from her father's. He can contrast his graying hairs and increasing corpulence with her glowing complexion and slim young waist, his slowing gait with her exuberant stride, his creaking muscles with her supple agility. Love and envy are not strangers.

"I became worried about my fourteen-year-old girl," a father confessed. "In a little more than a year she'd stopped wearing braces and being too plump. Suddenly she had a figure worth showing off in tight jeans and sweaters. She was always on the telephone with her girlfriends. All they ever talked about was boys, boys, boys.

"She kept a diary which had a lock and a little key she wore on a chain around her neck day and night. She was so secretive about it that I began to think she was having a love affair. I cut open the strap on her diary with a pair of scissors so I could read it. God, I wish I hadn't! It was nothing but a lot of purple passionate prose. It was clear she thought she was in love, but it was all platonic. It was also embarrassing to read. Sincere gush with most of the words misspelled—no wonder she got such terrible marks in English composition! I put the diary back in her desk.

"But I had to tell her what I had done. It was one of the worst moments of my life. A look of betrayal came over her face. Then she said, 'I hate you for that,' and went back to her room. I'd never been so depressed. For an hour I sat, trying to think of some way to apologize. I made up a little speech telling her how wrong I'd been, that I had no right to share in experiences which were hers alone.

"Then I looked up and she was standing in the doorway. She came over and put her arms around me. She said, 'Daddy, I'm sorry for what I said. But I was so *angry!*' I tell you, my heart damn near split. I realized she had a much finer nature than mine. I made my little speech and promised nothing like that would ever happen again."

This problem was essentially one of maturing—for father.

A man whose story appears in another part of this book wrote me the following letter about his lovely fifteen-year-old daughter: "We went to her brother's wedding a week ago, and I guess that started us both thinking about her future and what kind of a man she would marry. It was my first insight into how the young are thinking these days. And I don't understand what's going on.

"I've raised her to be a nice girl in the best sense of that term. She's interested in sports, she's a good conversationalist and a cheerful person to have around. She's also quite attractive. But her telephone never rings. We sat together at her brother's wedding and had a long serious discussion about what boys expect from a girl.

"It hurts to have your fifteen-year-old daughter tell you she's a 'social dud.' She gets to meet boys, so that's not the problem. Her high school has more boys than girls. A lot of other girls have dates. My daughter hasn't resigned herself to not having any, but she's tired of being ignored, of coming home and spending all her time studying or watching television.

"I'm afraid she may blame me because I've steered her in a certain way. I don't know how to convince her that while it may be hard right now, it'll make her happier in the end.

"At the same time she's scared of what she sees happening to her friends who are making out with boys. Once they've slept with a boy, any other boy they date expects as much. It's like they've put on an "I'm available" arm band. She told me about one girl who always has sex with a boy after a first date because it's not worth fighting about. She claims it's easier to say no the second time because then the boy doesn't blame you, he worries that it's his fault because he wasn't a good lover!

"Meanwhile, although my daughter hasn't given up, she's starting to wonder. There's one boy who's showing some interest, although he has pretty wild ways. The girls are all crazy about him and the feeling seems to be mutual. But I don't like the idea of her becoming one of his girls.

"I raised my daughter to be romantic about love, but that doesn't seem to fit in with how girls her age behave. I still hope there's someone out there who will appreciate a really nice, sincere, old-fashioned girl. If there isn't, the next generation of wives and mothers isn't going to have much respect for marriage vows or set a very good example for their children."

Peel back the surface of this father's argument and you find unanswered questions. His definition of a "nice" girl is one who does not have sex or even engage in heavy petting. That criterion was not obeyed even in his era. Today's wives and mothers, if they are honest, would admit to not having been strictly "nice" in their youth. The sexual hungers of adolescence are too hard to contain.

Nor does his argument allow for the changing sexual mores. He wants the standards of his day to be inviolable by the new generation. But old standards are under review everywhere we look, in movies, television, newspapers and magazines, in advertisements, in dress, in language, in schools. If society's standards are changing, then behavioral norms must change within society.

What a father really wants is to keep his daughter from growing up like her peers, because that implies rejection of his values. To peel back still another layer, it means acceptance of a rival to himself.

A young lady, having been away at college for a year, wrote her parents that she would be home for the Christmas holiday and was bringing a friend. The friend turned out to be a young man.

"It couldn't have been more of a shock to her mother and me," the father says. "I pointed out to her that we only had one extra bedroom and he'd have to sleep on the living room couch. She just laughed. 'It's O.K., Dad, we're *pinned*.' As if that solved everything.

"Her mother and I debated whether we should allow our daughter to sleep with him in our home. My wife contended we'd be giving implicit approval to the arrangement.On the other hand, I pointed out, there was no use pretending that we would be protecting her virtue. We finally decided not to interfere.

"In addition to everything else, I didn't like the young man. He went around all the time in a cowboy hat and jeans. Never made any effort to help around the house. We had some heavy snow and he did mention that he liked to ride the snowblower. So I let him, and he drove the machine into a buried tree stump. I had a repair bill of a hundred and fifty dollars. When he left he said he'd probably be back again at Easter. My wife and I both thought, Oh, no you won't, buster. Fortunately, our daughter's affair ended before Easter and we never saw him again.

"But I still wonder: Did I dislike him because he was unlikable—or because he was sleeping with my daughter? Probably the latter. It may be the new morality but that doesn't mean I have to like it!"

One father's confrontation with the "new morality" came when he discovered a diaphragm case in his daughter's bureau drawer. He asked where she got it, and she told him she'd gone to their family doctor to be fitted.

"I called up our doctor and gave him what for. He pointed out that the fact my daughter had come to be fitted for a diaphragm didn't mean she was promiscuous. 'A diaphragm doesn't cause anybody to have sex,' he said. 'But it can save her a lot of grief if she ever decides she's ready for it. That decision is often pretty spur-of-the-moment and then it's too late for the protection that a diaphragm would give her.'

"But somehow I couldn't stand the thought. I didn't want to become a snooper who every time she went out on a date tried to find out if her diaphragm was missing. I sat down to talk to her and I was too embarrassed to speak out. It was obvious that she wasn't a virgin anymore but I finally managed to say I hoped she wasn't bedding down with every boy she went out with. She answered, 'Why should I? I don't *want* to bed down with every boy I go out with!'

"I tried to explain honestly and clearly how I felt about it, but she got more and more impatient. We got into a real deadlock when I tried to get her to explain her reasons. Why did she want to have sex with boys she wasn't terribly serious with or engaged to? 'Because it's fun,' she answered. 'Is that so different from you? Isn't it fun for you?' I said it was different because her mother and I are married. At that point she burst out, 'Oh, Dad, things aren't like they were back in the Dark Ages!'

"I wish I could have gone deeper into her motivation. I don't believe it's right just because it's fun. Sex has gotten cheap. All that counts is doing it, not whether two people care about each other or have a relationship. It's sick!"

Despite what this man thinks, premarital sex is not an invention of the last quarter of the twentieth century. In my day, there was something a little ridiculous about a young woman pretending that she had no idea what a young man had in mind when they drove onto a little-used road dubbed "lovers' lane." Her duty was to keep up a stream of mindless chatter on any topic in order to disguise the fact of her awareness.

These are the lubricant hypocrisies that keep the wheels of romance turning. My generation subscribed to a theory of sexual morality that did not jibe with what we practiced. The new generation is more honest and less guilty. Young people today do not share the sexual hang-ups of their parents. To them, the idea that a woman might be loved for her virginity is irrational, for that kind of love is doomed not to survive a normal wedding night.

In discussing the difference between a father's attitude toward premarital sex in society and his feelings on the subject when his daughter is involved, we should bear in mind that each generation adopts the vocabulary of the oncoming generation while stubbornly holding fast to basic lessons it learned from the generation now receding into the past.

A striking example of this occurred recently during a conversation Donna had with a woman friend whose father, a teacher in a progressive school, espoused liberal attitudes on the subject of young people living together before marriage. The young woman had called her father to say she was moving in with a young man. "It made sense. Roger and I were seeing each other every night anyway, and I was staying over at his place. It became a pest to have to go back to my room every few days to pick up the mail.

"My father really flipped when I told him. He warned that I'd be making the biggest mistake of my life and I'd live to regret it. I couldn't have been more surprised, but in the end I decided to go ahead and do it.

"Whenever my father telephoned after that he was very cool to Roger. Just said hello and then asked to speak to me. He was always saying how 'very strange' it was to call a man's apartment in order to talk to me and how he 'didn't feel right' about it. After about six months, during dinner at our favorite Italian restaurant, Roger proposed. My father flew out for the wedding. Since then he's back telling everybody that young people ought to live together before marriage, that it's the only sensible way to get to know each other!"

As the attitude of society toward sex evolves, so does the attitude of fathers toward their daughters. However, this happens at a slower rate, for tenets are harder to dislodge from an individual father than from the volatile society in which he lives. He clings to the idea that he has a kind of proprietary interest in his daughter's body. She may inhabit her body but she cannot own it, cannot make the decisions about her sexual activity without the approval of the absentee owner.

It is only a step from this attitude to the kind of obsession described by Eric Berne in his book *Games People Play*. He tells of a father who always waited up for his teenaged daughter to return from a date so that he could examine her and her clothing to make sure she had not had sexual intercourse. The "slightest suspicious circumstance" would cause a violent argument.

A less extreme form of the same obsession is the father who closely interrogates his daughter after a date. Beneath his oblique questions: Did you have a good time? Where did you go afterward?

Is he a nice boy? is the weight of the unspoken: Did he get fresh? Did anything happen? If she appears seriously interested in a young man, father's questions will sharpen. The questions stop only when he becomes sure of the worst because, at that point, he doesn't want to know.

Eric Berne also observes that the quarrels set off by paternal prying usually end with daughter going to her bedroom and slamming the door, and father going to his bedroom and slamming the door. Their hidden motivations are being acted out and the slamming of bedroom doors serves a symbolic purpose beyond the display of mutual anger. It emphasizes that father and daughter have separate bedrooms.

NINE

RIVALS

A fifteen-year-old girl was having her first mad crush on a young man who was a member of the high school football team. Instead of going out on dates, she had to accommodate to his rigid training schedule.

"He has to be in bed asleep every night by nine o'clock," she complained to Donna. "And weekends are all shot because he's working out or catching up on his studies. I'm not too happy about any of it, but what can I do? My father says I ought to give him a dose of his own medicine."

"What does he mean?" Donna asked.

"That I ought to get more occupied with my own problems and stop waiting around for him. Then he'll miss me and have to figure out a way to be with me."

The girl took her father's advice. Not long after, the young man acquired a new female admirer who usurped what time and attention she had been getting. She became furious at her father. "Why did I ever listen to him? He's ruined everything!"

Her father, in turn, was clearly hurt by his daughter's attitude. "She came to me for advice and I gave it to her. What did I do wrong?"

He might be surprised to know that her anger was proportionate to his offense. At least that is what Dr. C. B. Pollard replied when we posed the question to him. "She was angry at being manipulated and deceived by her father. Intuitively she sensed a deception had occurred—even if he was not consciously aware of his own underlying motives. What he advised her to do led to the elimination of a rival for her affections, and was meant to do it.

"She may also have had her own secret motive. After all, she sought out and accepted advice that she did not really believe would work. Child-daughter was saying, in effect, 'This is my problem and I'm putting it all in your hands.' Parent-father was replying, 'I understand your problem and will tell you what to do.'

"She also had the satisfaction of being able to tell her father, 'See! You're not as smart as you think!' This relieved her of responsibility for losing in a situation which she probably had begun to suspect was unwinnable."

Wheels within wheels. For our purpose, it is enough to point out how subtly a father can manipulate his daughter to eliminate a potential rival.

When a teenaged girl begins dating, a father becomes upset at the sight of a boy's arm casually flung about her shoulder. Every gesture of affection signifies danger. One rueful man, confessing to his anxieties, put it: "You don't have to be the father of an adolescent girl to suffer—but it helps!" Believing his only motive to be the protection of his "little girl" from the evil designs of Other Men, father measures each young rival who appears on the scene with suspicion: is he the one who will victimize his daughter? One woman says that when she was a girl her father lectured every young man who dated her: "I'm putting my little girl into your hands and I expect you to take good care of her."

How did she feel about that?

"I was pleased that Daddy cared about me. Some boys were put off by him. But they always acted like perfect gentlemen because of what Daddy told them."

Too many liberated fathers, whose relationships with their daughters were formed in an earlier era, find a variance between what they say they believe and what they believe. The experience of a friend of mine illustrates the wide gulf between logic and emotion and between expressed and felt beliefs.

At fifteen, my friend's daughter informed him she was no longer a virgin. "I acted in the civilized way that I expected of myself and as I knew she expected that I would. However, some time later something happened that revealed to me how much I was suppressing.

"Late at night we heard a terrible hammering on the front door of our house. A young man's voice began to call loudly for my daughter. She ran into our bedroom in tears. She told us this was the young man she had been going out with and that she'd broken off with him because he drank too much.

"I got up and went in my pajamas to the door. The young man was still banging on the door and yelling for my daughter to come out. Suddenly I felt a terrible surge of rage. I flung the door open and waded into him without a word of warning. He was drunk and unable to defend himself. I gave him a terrible beating. The next morning there was still a small pool of his blood, like a ceramic, on our front doorstep.

"As you see, I behaved in a very civilized way."

Since prehistory, human beings have been dominated and controlled by powerful unconscious processes. In Darwin's concept of the primal hords (which Freud adapted), there is a violent and jealous father who drives all his sons away as soon as they are grown because he wishes to keep all the females for himself.

In Freud's version, the brothers who are exiled by the powerful father eventually come together, kill and devour the father, and put an end to the patriarchy. In the fundamental sense this scene is repeated in modern times by the suitors who eventually appear to claim and carry off his daughters. In this inevitable "conquest" by other men, father sees himself as abandoned, in effect killed, and helplessly devoured by his own consuming jealousy.

Fear that his daughter may be prematurely encouraged to experiment with sex inspires father to be wary of malign influences. These include magazines, books, films and television shows which help to create the "wrong" attitudes toward sex.

A student in a class that Donna teaches told her she would not be allowed to read an assigned novel because her father would disapprove. Her father censored all her reading as well as her movie and television watching. Donna learned that the father had gone to a high school principal a few years earlier to protest the teaching of biology. "Apparently he believed that the knowledge she would inevitably pick up in the street and hallways, locker rooms and washrooms was somehow better for her than what can be found in a textbook."

One young woman's experience with her father is worth quoting at some length: "He never wanted me to look grown up. I had to wear clothes that were too young for me. My hair was always done up in braids and I wore socks and low-heeled shoes or sneakers. I'd complain to my mother, but she was afraid of him and she'd say go talk to your father if you've got a problem. I had a lot of friends who'd tell me straight out, 'You look awful—like a little kid,' but my father wouldn't let me wear anything that would make me look older. I thought he hated me, that he was out to ruin my life. I began to think of myself as unattractive. I didn't believe I could get a guy to look at me even if I did dress up.

"Finally, there was this boy who seemed to like me. We had a geometry class together and whenever I'd turn around I'd see him three rows back, just staring at me. One afternoon as we were leaving school he caught up with me and offered me a cigarette. That was a big deal—smoking! It made me feel more grown up. Then he asked if I'd go out with him and I said 'Okay,' as though it wasn't going to be my first date.

"We went to see a movie. I remember everything about it, what the seats were like, how he bought popcorn, how he finally sneaked his arm around the back of my seat and onto my shoulder. Nothing else happened, but I was as conscious of his arm there as if it had been a red-hot brand lying there.

"By the fourth date we were kissing and I let him touch my breast. There was a lot of guilt and I felt as if I had done something really wicked. I told him the truth, that I'd never let anybody do that before, and he asked if I wanted him to stop. So I said I didn't really mind his doing it.

"I told Mother that I'd been 'making love' with this boy I liked, and was surprised at the way she reacted. Then I realized what she was thinking and explained it wasn't like that. I told her about the kissing and touching. She said I should be careful and not lose control of myself. I don't think she knew how she scared me. Don't lose control of yourself. The words kept drumming into me.

"Mainly I worried about my father finding out. I imagined all sorts of punishments, from being locked up in a closet, to bread and water, to being thrown out of the house. My father believed in punishment. In the end it wasn't my mother who told him; it was my best girlfriend, the one person I trusted most. She did it because she was jealous."

The young girl's fears were realized. When her father discovered she had been seeing a boy, he said she was "too young for such foolishness," and forbade her going out with her boyfriend. She had to report home directly from school. If she was even a few minutes late, she was "disciplined." This included corporal punishment.

As I showed this interview to Dr. Pollard to solicit his opinion, I remarked, "It's hard to believe there are fathers like this left in the world."

"Not hard to believe at all," Dr. Pollard assured me after reading it. He went on to explain: "The Puritan tradition teaches that fornication is basically evil and the only reason for it to exist is to keep the human race going. The idea that sex might be fun is alien to that whole tradition—and our forefathers managed to write the concept of 'sex as sin' into the laws. Only in the present day is the power of the Puritan idea beginning to weaken, but obviously this father believes that sexual temptation is to be avoided at any cost."

The use of corporal punishment as discipline is part of the syndrome. Paternal violence toward the young still meets with approval in many quarters. The proverbial advice to fathers is still quoted: "A child ought to be whipped at least once a day. If you don't know what it's for, he does." The pronoun is interchangeable; it just sounds better to call the victim of corporal punishment "he" because sexual implications are not so apparent. "Strict discipline" are code words for physical punishment. When physical punishment is inflicted by a father on a daughter, the line between punishment and the covertly sexual becomes tenuous.

Unrealistic expectations about the sexual experience prolong a daughter's emotional tie to her father. Since she was a child she has been thinking about sexual relations, which she is encouraged to believe are the highest possible refinement of feeling, a transfiguring event. This concept becomes so ingrained that long after she experiences the earthbound reality she may go on dreaming an impossible dream. Her endless quest for the indescribable transcendant joys of Ultimate Orgasm ends in a sense of letdown so sharp that she may decide, as one twenty-five-year-old woman told us she had, that "Sex is simply not worth all the sweating."

Sexual discontent makes a young woman nostalgic for the perfect love she has known in her relationship with her father. Why can't she reduce other men to a similar role of unsexual companion and provider? The sexual drive of young men is basically selfish, interested almost solely in gratification, ready at all times to move on to new sources of gratification. It does not provide the reassurance, support, caring, that conveys paternal affection. A teenaged girl who is treated as a play partner or a sex object finds her "romance" a tension-ridden intense overture that leads to nothing, and she emerges from such shallow and painful experiences to seek shelter again in the love of her father.

Donna recalls discussion with me on the subject of virginity. She was fourteen and in no imminent danger of losing it, but she wanted to know how important it was to be a virgin when she married. I had on occasion, and to persons of both sexes, quoted with implicit approval Anatole France's remark, "Of all the forms of sexual aberration, chastity is the strangest."

Needless to say, this was not the reply I gave to my daughter. She remembers my telling her that the question of whether sexual relations occurred before or after marriage is largely irrelevant, but that the first time is an important emotional event and I did not think a woman should share it with someone she was not really sure she liked.

That answer apparently pleased her enough to keep my reputation as a sage intact. But I also told her the story of a young woman who decided, at nineteen, that she had waited too long for her sexual initiation. Because she wanted to "get it over with," she picked up a man in a restaurant and took him back to her apartment. The episode was unsatisfying and cast a pall over her subsequent experiences. This very attractive woman had many sexual adventures after that. "If a man really wants to, why not?" she said. "What's the difference?" She never married and was very unhappy.

Ah, Machiavelli. At her age, my daughter's convictions were shaky and subject to the influence of a father standing on the relatively firm ground of experience. My real motives were beyond her suspicion.

One woman recalls overhearing as a young girl her father boast that her mother had "never known any other man." She determined that she, too, would "save herself" for her future husband. She refused to see a young man again if "he tried to get fresh." Despite this attitude she managed to have "good, friendly" relationships with some men. Then, at twenty-four, she met the man of her dreams. He respected her desire to save herself for marriage, but he was soon to be drafted for service in Vietnam. He wanted her to "commit herself" to him, and suggested that they spend his last weekend together in a motel.

She agreed, then began to regret it. Finally she told him she could not go through with it. He assured her that he understood and it would not change his feeling for her. He asked her to consider herself engaged to him, and on the day he left for Vietnam he bought her a diamond engagement ring.

They exchanged letters for a while, then his letters came less frequently. At last he wrote that he had "spoiled it" with another woman and considered their engagement broken. She returned the ring.

At thirty-three she is still "saving" herself. Her daddy passed away last year, but she appears to have condemned herself to a loveless, sexless life—in order to please him. I doubt he would be pleased.

TEN

HOW DO I LOVE THEE?

I have never kissed my daughter on the lips. We kiss on the cheek or place our cheeks in contact as we hug or embrace.

I do not consider lip kissing to be an especially carnal act nor do I look askance at fathers and daughters who greet in this fashion.

Why, then?

The only answer that comes to mind is that I would not feel comfortable doing it. Obviously this is due to my sociocultural conditioning. In my youth there was a definite prescribed order to dating intimacy. At the end of a first date a girl might let you kiss her good night. Or this reward might be put off to a second date in order to show how "nice" she was. A girl who kissed with an open mouth was offering real encouragement. The big forward step was to touch her breast. Touching the breast was, in fact, such a crucial turning point that the event was subdivided in order to emphasize its importance into whether you touched the clothed or naked breast. If you touched a girl's naked breast, you breached her inner defenses. Her virginity, even technical virginity, might provide a temporary rallying point against the inevitable, but for every practical purpose the battle was over.

This brief description of the state of the art of seduction in my youth may explain why I consider lip kissing an act of some significance.

When Donna was in her early teens she became self-conscious about going out with me alone, claiming that I looked younger than my years and therefore we might be mistaken for a couple on a date. Not boy and girl to be sure, but man and nymphet.

This was flattering but struck me as on the far side of preposterous. So I made light of it. Walking past strangers, I made overhearable remarks about motels and asked Donna what time her parents expected her home in the morning. Donna defended herself with a loud emphasis on "Father" and "Daddy" in her replies while laughing immoderately to make clear to eavesdroppers that I was joking.

Then one evening as we were strolling down the street a boozy panhandler weaved over. I gave him a quarter; he glanced at us knowingly, smiled and said, "Ahh, young love!" before staggering away.

That was another occasion on which Donna learned that I was not infallible.

Neither the avoidance of lip kissing nor the joking about being each other's date is what anyone would label incestuous behavior. But they are ways of sublimating, or dealing with, latent desires.

Few human relationships contain as much ambiguity as incest. The confusion of the customary roles of father and daughter, the conflicting and even contradictory emotions, secret anxieties and motivations, all lead to a tangle as hard to unravel as the Gordian knot. All that is clear is that at some point the attraction between father and daughter enters the danger zone of physical sexuality.

During the difficult period in which my marriage to her mother was dissolving, Donna became the one person I trusted with the painful secrets of my private life. Only much later did I realize that her mother was also confiding in her. We shared a compulsion to seek her advice as if she were not only an adult but our closest friend.

After the divorce, we continued trying to keep our separate relationships with Donna on the previous level of intimacy. Neither her mother nor I felt we could afford to lose her sympathy and affection, not when so much else was being lost. Neither of us reckoned the emotional cost to her of being caught in the middle between two people she loved.

I have tried since to understand and, if possible, to forgive myself for such uncaring behavior. I cannot. The man I am now does not approve of the man I was. My behavior was exploitive and, in seeking an easier way for myself, I made my young daughter a part of my problem.

(The palms of my hands are wet as I write this. I am forcing myself to confront in words what an emotionally abusive father I was.)

The similarity of emotional abuse to sexual abuse of a daughter is greater than the difference. In both, a daughter is vulnerable because of her youth and the closeness of the relationship. The trauma she suffers is severe because a fundamental betrayal of trust is involved. She believes, at least in part, that she is responsible for her plight, and cannot be relieved of guilt because she cannot confide in anyone.

Against these similarities set the chief difference: emotional abuse is not directed at the daughter's genital and sexual regions. Most would add that emotional abuse of a daughter does not involve force or violence, but this is based on a misunderstanding of the nature of sexual abuse, which is rarely accompanied by physical assault. A 1969 study revealed that only one in two hundred instances of physical abuse involved sexual abuse. The underlying motivation of a father who beats a child is hostile and sadistic, more likely to derive from individual pathology than from sexuality. The sexually abusive father has no intention of doing physical harm to his child. The victim is usually compliant, and the offender relies on authority and persuasion to achieve his purpose.

Sexual abuse and physical abuse also differ in the age and sex of the victims. Sexual abuse is directed mostly at preadolescent females, while physical abuse covers the whole of childhood and spares neither sex. Infants are quite often the objects of severe physical abuse, while the peak years of a child's vulnerability to sexual abuse are between eight and twelve.

Incest occurs more frequently than all other forms of sexual abuse put together. The frequency with which it is reported in recent years has increased with repulsive rapidity. Only ten years ago the first center for counseling both the victims and offenders in incest cases was opened in San Jose, California. Today there are over fifty-one such centers.

Reports indicate that father-daughter incest, in particular, has reached epidemic proportions. One authority estimates that three quarters of a million American women aged eighteen or over have had such an experience, and that 15,000 to 20,000 new cases occur every year—a truly startling statistic.

There has been a proliferation of confessional books on the subject of father-daughter incest, several movies have dealt with it, and recently a young woman victim, Katherine Brady, appeared with her father on Phil Donahue's nationally syndicated television show. The victim's mother was also present for the occasion.

Mr. Donahue emphasized that the Brady family was a typical midwestern, middle-class, "Norman Rockwell" family. They went to church and paid their bills, and both mother and daughter sang in the church choir. Katherine Brady's father and mother were carefully shielded in darkness onstage while Mr. Donahue discussed with Katherine the incestuous relationship with her father that began when she was eight years old and continued throughout her adolescence.

> *Mr. Donahue:* I assume that this had to do with fondling and some sort of attention that you were getting that went beyond the normal hugging that we expect fathers to give their daughters.
>
> *Ms. Brady:* That is correct ... I remember feeling guilty about it from the moment my father told me not to tell anyone, especially not my mother. I felt that because of the tone of his voice, because he said that, I couldn't share it with her, that it was something awful, and that I was doing something bad. Thus, I was bad. Thus, I felt guilty.
>
> *Mr. Donahue:* And the encounters with your father became rather routine then, didn't they? ... Was it daily, three times a week?
>
> *Ms. Brady:* No, the routine as it developed, especially my adolescence, got to probably two to three times a week. Ultimately, as we developed this routine, as the years went on, it was a ten-year relationship.

When a member of the audience wanted to know why Katherine had told no one, she replied:

> *Ms. Brady:* I obviously couldn't tell a soul. There wasn't anyone I could trust. It occurred to me to talk to a person next door who I liked, whom I had babysat for. But I didn't want to lose her respect. I worked for a doctor during a high school summer. I thought, maybe if I tell him, but then, you know, what, what will happen to me? He won't like me.

As it happens, Katherine Brady did not tell anyone until she was over thirty years old. This interview is remarkable not alone for its candor, but for how clearly the identifying marks are set forth: Katherine's youth, the closeness of the relationship, trauma suffered because of a betrayal of trust, the fact that she believed herself at least in part to be responsible, and her inability to confide in anyone.

The point was also made that it is wrong to think of incest in terms of physical violence; that it is more properly defined as emotional violence. Most revelatory of all is Katherine Brady's insight into why fathers have incestuous relations with their daughters. After observing that she did not believe her father's motives were entirely sexual, she adds: "There was a long period during adolescence when he was the only person I saw, I was totally dependent on him. I couldn't run away. *I think incest creates terrible dependencies.*"

Many girls involved in such a relationship are seen by others as "good girls" because they are so rarely in conflict with their parents. The sexual bond enables father to retain his dominance over his daughter's life. Out of fear of discovery, he tries to prevent her from having outside contacts. Her sexual interests, which should have begun to move in an outward direction, remain within his control. The lack of outside contacts makes it more difficult for her to gain a perspective that will enable her to appraise what is occurring as unnatural.

The fifteen-year-old daughter of a thirty-eight-year-old insurance salesman in a Westchester, New York, suburb began to suffer badly from a colitis that would not respond to treatment. Her doctor finally advised her to seek psychiatric help. The analyst discovered that for some years she had been her father's lover as well as his daughter.

Her mother was a career woman who often came home late at night. "As soon as my mother calls from the office to say she won't be home for dinner that night, he starts in," the girl told her analyst. "It's part of my regular routine, like my keeping house and cooking dinner. He's nice to me whenever we do it. And I guess I feel in a way I'm keeping our family together."

After several years, however, hidden conflicts began to surface. Her attacks of colitis were her way of appealing for help. When confronted with his daughter's testimony this father tried to justify his conduct in several ways. He pointed out that he had never completed the act of intercourse with her and therefore she had "suffered no damage." Because she could not have become pregnant, he did not feel he had committed a wrong but was actually helping to "educate his daughter sexually." He added that he had only begun paying attention to her because his wife was not paying attention to him: "She was not satisfying my needs. A man needs relief, and I am not the kind of man who would ever go to a prostitute or anything like that. It's not the money. I could afford to pay, but I never would."

Most cases of incest reported to social workers come from poor families. Earlier researchers thought that the correlation between incest and poverty was significant, and attributed the causes to overcrowding, family disorganization, social incompetence and the frustrations and emotional maladjustment prevalent among lower strata of society. They overlooked a simpler explanation. More cases from lower-income brackets were reported because social workers were in a much better position to observe the poor. The upper middle-class and affluent were more likely to have the resources to hire professional help to keep the problem from becoming a scandal.

The latest studies, including one on child molestation which uses a scientifically selected and more unbiased sample, reveal that a large percentage of upper-middle-class girls are victims of incest. More and more evidence of sexual abuse among the affluent is now coming to light. Incest apparently knows no race, class, socioeconomic status or geography.

No definite personality pattern has emerged for the incestuous father. In Nabokov's famous novel *Lolita*, the protagonist Humbert Humbert's sexual preoccupation with children is conditioned by a pleasurable childhood stimulus. But a negative experience could as easily have caused the same effect by driving him to compulsively repeat the experience in an attempt to change the outcome. Sexual involvement with a daughter can begin for many different reasons, including some that seem to have no enduring roots in the personality—unexpected opportunity, a time of emotional stress, the denial of other sexual outlets, the age of the offender and the age of the child, even the sort of sexual activity engaged in plays a role.

There has been a subtle change in the public conception of an incestuous father. In the nineteenth century, Krafft-Ebing described such men as psychopaths and moral degenerates, if not actually feebleminded. We now know the stereotype to be false. Only a small proportion of the offenders is psychotic. A plethora of studies during the years 1954–72 revealed a more human portrait: The incestuous father almost invariably gains the daughter's cooperation or at least passive agreement.

Surprisingly, the majority of reported cases of incest do not result in intercourse. Far more frequently the "crime" consists of genital handling, exhibition or masturbation.

A daughter "loses herself" in an incestuous relationship with her father. She reaches a stage of dependency that amounts to immersion in his stronger character.

"I felt a very great attachment to my father as a person," one nineteen-year-old woman reports. "When he became my lover it was like I was being born all over again, learning about life. There were so many things I didn't know, and he was teaching me.

"I was never much of a feminine person. My figure was lean and hard, I had muscles but no breasts. Other girls seemed to act different from me. They would cry and I never did. A lot of people didn't even know I was a girl when they first met me. My hair was cut short and I wore my brother's outgrown clothes. I didn't feel I had a gender until my father made me feel like a girl. Then I wanted to be a girl for him.

"After a while I began worrying somebody would find out. I could hardly stop thinking about it. I did badly in school because I couldn't concentrate. I wasn't popular and I didn't try to be friendly because if anyone got close to me they might find out.

"When I was fifteen I met a nice boy. He was a year older than me, the studious type. He wore glasses. We began spending time together after school and he helped me with my homework. He was really nice and I wanted to talk to him about what I was doing with my father. But I was afraid of losing the one friend I had.

"My father found out about him and began asking questions, mostly about what we did when we were together. He said he was the only person I really loved and no one else should matter to me. He'd say, 'You don't do our things with him, do you?'

"I never told him much about what went on between me and my friend. For a long time nothing did. Then we sort of drifted into it.

"Meanwhile my father kept giving me a third degree. It got so bad that sometimes I would stand on a street corner and not know whether I wanted to go home. One evening I packed a bag and walked out on the street and got into the first car that offered me a ride. The driver was an older man, about thirty. He was a salesman going to another city. I hadn't given any thought to where I was going to sleep that night, so I ended up going with him. We went to this hotel room.

"I began doing it a lot and got known to the police. They notified my parents and my father came to see me. He treated me as if I was still a kid. He said he was responsible for what happened because he hadn't stopped me from running around with strange boys. I got hysterical. Imagine him pulling a line like that!"

Says Nancy Friday, "More than in any other area of our lives, we expect sex to grow us up." An incestuous liaison preserves daughter in her childhood state like a fly in amber.

Dr. Henry Biller, in his book *Father Power*, contends that there is an important difference between sensuality and sexuality in a father's relationship with his daughter. Dr. Biller argues that sensuality is the physical enjoyment of being close, touching and caressing, which is a natural part of fathering and is not the same as real sexuality. Fathering contains a more overtly "sexual sensuality" than is usually conceded, and fear of this "erotic component" is too often exaggerated, causing a father to reject his daughter simply because he is afraid of producing a "sensual pleasure" in himself.

"By accepting your own sexuality and recognizing the sensual component of fatherhood," Dr. Biller says, "you will make it easier for you and the child to remain close. Only in disturbed or immature people does such natural sensuality lead to overt sexuality. You must have confidence in your own ability to distinguish between the two."

Most theories cast the adult as the sole offender. In the Katherine Brady interview mentioned earlier, Phil Donahue made a tentative stab in another direction and was quickly rebuffed.

Mr. Donahue: At age eight there was no way for you to really know what was going on, was there?

Ms. Brady: No.

Mr. Donahue: On the other hand, as I read your book, you were a very insightful little girl.

Ms. Brady: Children don't seduce grown men. And I know that I did not seduce my father.

Overt seduction by children is comparatively rare. But what is known as "victim precipitation"—the kind of action we recognize in those people who leave their cars unlocked with the keys in the ignition or who carry unlatched handbags into subways—should not be ignored. Failure to give proper weight to victim precipitation is part of our general reluctance to recognize the "dark side" of a young daughter's psyche, or to put it more precisely, her unexpressed sexuality.

Nevertheless, the idea that young girls may be active contributors to an incestuous relationship has steadily gained currency. The popular conviction, founded in the pre-Freudian belief that children are by nature innocent, is seriously challenged for the first time. Authorities contend that a child is partner to some degree in her own seduction if she acts suggestively, fails to discourage the initial proposition, accedes to it, then allows the situation to continue by not reporting it to anyone in a position to stop it. Many sociologists who have interviewed victimized daughters report that the girls make some form of sexual overture during the course of the interview. To this evidence might be added the insight gained from psychoanalysis that a daughter in her fantasy life wishes for sex with her male parent but is too young and too lacking in experience to clearly distinguish fantasy desires from her real ones.

There is, undeniably, a heightened excitement for a young person in performing any act, particularly a sexual act, that breaks a social taboo. To the pleasure of the act is added the thrill of risk taking and the sense of power resulting from assertion of individual will against the customs and laws of society. Oedipal rivalry provides a still further source of excitement. A daughter may not only wish to win her father's love, but to defeat and diminish her mother. Anger generated in her by the long struggle for daddy's affection is resolved by a triumph over the maternal rival. The prize is more than her father. It is a way of expressing her sexuality, responding to the inner irresistible drive to create and live a sexual life. As one of the principals in the family triad, she cannot bear to be treated as an outsider.

Wardell Pomeroy reports the incident of an adolescent girl who became upset because her father was so physically affectionate with her mother. One evening, when her parents were embracing, the daughter suddenly burst into the room, naked and pleading, "Please make love to me tonight, Daddy. I'm better than she is. Try me and see!"

Granting that there may be a predisposing element on the part of the victim in some incest cases, those who emphasize it commit the error of oversimplication. They overlook its proper rank in the hierarchy of explanations.

No guilt on the part of the victim can equal the guilt of the offender. The unwary driver who leaves car keys in the ignition, the foolish woman who leaves her handbag clasp open on entering the subway, is not an accomplice in the crime. The crime is committed solely by the criminal.

The following case history may make the point clearer. A woman recalls her adolescence: "I was going with this boy and we got pretty physical, though we never went the whole way. The boy was an Egyptian, very handsome. My father caught us one night on the living room sofa and practically went crazy. Called the boy all sorts of names—a foreigner, a dirty little greaser. He threw him out of the house and refused to let me see him anymore. He said he'd beat him up if he ever came to our house again.

"At the same time he felt free to act as he pleased with my friends. One girl in particular who was very pretty. She had dark hair that went all down her back. One night my father started running his fingers through her hair and telling her how beautiful it was. I was terribly embarrassed, and later I asked him not to act that way with my friends.

"He just smiled and said I shouldn't be jealous—that I was still his favorite. That night he came into my bedroom and lay down on the bed beside me. He said he was going to show me how much he liked me. He kissed me and felt my breasts. He said if I had to learn about sex it might as well be from him. Then he began touching me down there. 'Do you like it?' he asked. I'd done it to myself but I wouldn't admit it. He took out his penis and made me hold it and stroke it until it got big. But I wouldn't let him do anything to me. The next morning I told him if he tried to do that anymore I'd have to tell Mother. He never did, but we were never easy with each other after that."

The young woman's previous sexual involvement with her boyfriend might have aroused her father's interest, and her compliance with her father's advances might possibly be defined as "victim precipitation," but the incestuous incident *would not have occurred without the father's initiative.* To blame the daughter as his accomplice is to say that a woman who leaves a window unlocked in her home is conspiring in the burglary that follows.

If someone were to ask the question, "Is incest abnormal?" the universal reaction would be a thunderous "Yes!" Outrage is the sensible response, the only attitude that would not label one as a wild-eyed extremist or, worse, a secret offender.

There is, nevertheless, an underground consensus that contradicts that overwhelming moralistic referendum. One part of the public mind stubbornly continues to believe that incest is not as terrible as generally portrayed. A multitude of jokes, limericks, anecdotes and folktales deal with incest in a different, unserious way, a countervailing message that indicates the "ultimate taboo" should not be all that ultimate.

V. Rudolph, in his book *Pissing in the Snow and Other Ozark Folktales*, quotes the following typical example: "Jack has been seduced by his sister Jill. 'Golly, Jack,' says Jill, 'you're much better than Paw.' 'Yeah,' Jack replies, 'that's what Maw always says.'"

In a similar vein is the story of the hillbilly who, when he discovers his prospective bride is a virgin, refuses to marry her. "If she ain't good enough for her own family, she ain't good enough for me!"

By smiling, we acknowledge at least a modicum of truth in this reappraisal. We never smile at the truly shocking.

Fiction, which reflects where our culture stands at a given period, also gives us a different, constantly changing view of incest. From the nearly incomprehensible hints of incestuous love in *The Well of Loneliness* by Radclyffe Hall, we have moved to the explicit detail of current fictional shockers. Popular novels chart the steady movement of the topic toward popular acceptance, and newsstands regularly display magazines featuring articles that confirm the theme's general interest. In the highly successful Academy Award-winning movie, *Chinatown*, released in 1975, Faye Dunaway has a sister who is also her daughter—born of a sexual union with her father. The erring father, John Huston, not only escapes punishment for his "crime" but gets permanent custody of his granddaughter-daughter!

Freud, by identifying the desire to possess the parent of the opposite sex as a nearly universal part of human nature, made it a discussable topic rather than a forbidden mystery. The term "abnormal" fails of an objective definition; any attempt at definition begins on close examination to crumble at the edges and turn soft at the center. The basic condition on which most judgments of "abnormal" behavior are based is what is necessary for the survival of the species. That is why heterosexuality is considered "normal" and homosexuality is not, why onanism is unacceptable and incest is condemned. But even the "survivability" definition is challengeable. One of the earliest and greatest of human civilizations, the Egyptian, did not consider incest either a crime or a sin. Indeed, incest was prescribed for some Egyptian rulers, since only female members of his immediate family were worthy of marriage with the pharoah sun-god!

A working definition might be that incest is a sexual relationship in which the desire and behavior is normal but the object of the relationship is abnormal. Any attempt to pin down the nature of incest by further definition is like trying to make a necklace of worms. The effort is not worthwhile. To discover if incest is a minor aberration or a true perversion, it is better not to rely on social authority but to go to life.

"My mother accepted part of the guilt when I told her," says an eighteen-year-old whose confession of incest with her father was made after his death. "She never forgave herself after I brought it out in the open. She said she chose to marry my father, so whatever he did became in part her responsibility. I can't convince her that what happened wasn't her fault. It was *his* fault. Until we both accept that, we can't go back to living normal lives."

An interview with the girl's mother proves revealing: "I have two daughters and I never let anybody bother them. Even if somebody just patted their shoulder or pinched them, it would upset me. I know what my youngest is going through. Her father was the vainest man who ever lived. He would spend an hour in front of a mirror primping, combing his hair, patting lotion on his face, powdering himself. He was a great hit with the ladies. A week after my daughter was born, legally, another woman was giving birth to his illegitimate child. How do you like that?

"He was a tyrant at home. Treated his daughters like his personal property. Wouldn't let them date, or play cards, or dance, or touch any kind of alcohol. They had their 'privilege time,' which, believe it or not, meant that they could come and kiss him.

"As he got older and began to lose his looks he became impossible. No one could tell him enough that he was still handsome, that he wasn't getting old. The week he died I found out about him and my beautiful daughter. She'd rejected him at first, but he took her love as his right.

"As far as I'm concerned what he did was rape. He had the physical power to make her submit even if he didn't actually use it. She was afraid of him. One time her sister disagreed with him about something at the dinner table. He picked up a fork and drove it right into her hand. Crazy! He should have been locked up.

"It helped his macho if he could bully a woman. I should have known what he was capable of. It was already set up in his mind. What happened to my poor girl is my fault."

No evidence supports the notion that certain men are predisposed toward incest. The overwhelming majority of male offenders do not have a previous history of any sexual hang-up. They are not Peeping Toms, adulterers, exhibitionists or child molesters; they are not even interested in having multiple sexual relationships. Unlike the father just cited, most offenders have good relationships with their daughters. It is the "good" relationship that makes seduction so much easier.

"I had a certain level of trust," says a young woman interviewed in the psychiatric ward of a New York City hospital. "I mean, who thinks a father is going to try anything? The first time it happened my father was reading a sex magazine. He called me into the bedroom. I was thirteen. He invited me to sit next to him on the bed and look at the pictures. I asked him why he liked looking at naked women, and he laughed and said it turned him on. Then he showed me his erection and said I could touch it. I did but it made me feel funny, so I stopped. Then he told me to take my clothes off and he would show me something that was very important for me to know about sex.

"I did what he told me. He began fondling me and then started to make love to me, you know, orally. I knew it was a bad thing to do, but I let him do it because it felt good. He told me not to tell anyone about what we'd done because they might not understand.

"Whenever we were alone in the house after that he made love to me in the same way. When he asked me to do it to him, I didn't want to, but I did. Then it got hard to refuse. I began trying to find ways out of being in the house alone with him. I didn't want to be a bad girl."

Donna spoke with many victims of father seduction. There is no space in this book to recount their stories at length, but I will briefly synopsize a few.

A ten-year-old girl whose father, a photographer, made her pose for pornographic pictures which he later sold to underground publications here and abroad.

Teenaged twin sisters who had run away from home to escape the sexual attentions of their father. They became part of a teenaged vice ring in order to support themselves.

A young married woman of nineteen who said her father had made her pregnant and then quickly arranged a marriage for her with a young man who still is not aware that the child is not his own.

A sixteen-year-old girl who, after being seduced by her father, turned to drugs—and was arrested for possession of heroin. Her father blamed her for "disgracing" him,

Most poignant was the story of a fourteen-year-old girl, daughter of a semiliterate unskilled laborer, who won a prize for an essay she wrote in her high school English composition class. For some reason her father decided this was a put-down of him, implying that he wasn't good enough to be her father. One night he came to her bedroom and said he would prove to her there was a lot she had to learn about life that she would never learn in books. Then he forced her to have oral sex with him.

"After that night he was very distant and cold to her," Donna reports. "It was many weeks before she got up courage to ask why he had done that to her. He denied it ever happened. The way he phrased his denial was interesting and revelatory. He warned her not to tell lies with her 'dirty mouth' or she'd be sorry."

Recently an unusual situation developed concerning the son of a friend I've known for twenty years. The son was planning to get married. Before long, though, a quarrel broke out between the two fathers over arrangements for the wedding. Whenever the two fathers met, a violent dispute started over the most trivial details. At the engagement party, for example, the young woman's father became very angry because she called my friend "Dad" and embraced him.

Matters went from difficult to impossible, and finally my friend suggested to his son that he and the prospective bride elope in order to avoid further controversy. Each set of parents would then contribute what the wedding would have cost, and the money could be used as down payment on a home for the newlyweds. The young couple thought that was a fine idea. When the young lady's father found out, however, he accused my friend of a double cross and told his daughter to break her engagement. His reaction was so extreme that no one took it seriously—except the young lady. She was so shaken by her father's demand that she asked to postpone the wedding. Her prospective husband informed her that they would either get married on the date planned, whether in a formal wedding or an elopement, or they would not marry. The decision was up to her. To everyone's surprise, she decided not to get married. Her official reason: "I don't think I'm mature enough. I'm not ready to take on the responsibility." Privately, she confided to the young man that this was not her wish but "Whenever my father tells me I'd better not do something I usually see it his way. That's how he brought me up."

Some weeks later the young woman wrote her former fiance a long confessional letter. She admitted that she had been having a long affair with her father that ended only "at the time of our engagement," and she had hoped by getting married she would break her father's hold on her. She realized now she had been unfair to "use" her former fiance in that way and hoped he would forgive her.

A 1979 study concluded that a father's seductive attitude toward his daughter has profound and unpredictable effects in her later life. One frequent result is sexual promiscuity. The psychological pattern goes like this: The seductive father attempts to impose restrictive rules, supposedly to guard against sexual misconduct, but actually to prevent her from transferring her affections to anyone else. Her rebellion against the restrictions takes the form of promiscuity.

Dr. Alexander Zaphiris, a leading authority in the treatment of incestuous families, says that the extreme psychological damage suffered by incest victims often ruins their lives: "Over half the prostitutes in one penal institution are incest victims. So are thirty percent of the felons and twenty-five percent of the women convicted of sexually molesting young girls."

Dr. Zaphiris, an associate dean of the Graduate School of Social Work at the University of Houston as well as an educator, social worker and lawyer, has dealt with over 1,500 cases of incest. From this extensive experience he drew a profile of a typical incestuous family:

- Incest usually occurs in a large family, though the family may be of any race or religion and from any income bracket.
- The offender is usually the father, and the victim is usually a daughter. Mother-son incest is rare.
- The father victimizes one child at a time, while preparing younger ones to assume the role as they grow older.
- When confronted with his offense, he usually denies it, or tries to blame it on overuse of alcohol or drugs. In some cases he claims he is teaching his victim "the facts of life," or even that she seduced him.
- The father's incestuous behavior usually begins in the daughter's infancy. "I have never seen an incest victim who

is not conditioned as an infant," says Dr. Zaphiris. "The conditioning process may be done unconsciously, and customarily involves some form of sexual stimulation in the guise of normal fatherly affection."

- The father is usually selfish, jealous, timid, overprotective. The mother is passive, hostile, jealous, and overly dependent on her husband.

Studies indicate that fathers of delinquent girls are much more restrictive with them than fathers of nondelinquent girls. What is puzzling is that after a time the delinquent girls do not resent their fathers but usually put the blame for their delinquency on their mothers. Two recent research projects agree that during a period of confinement for delinquency, the attitude of delinquent girls becomes more favorable toward the father. Mothers are described as "emotionally disturbed" and "selfish," while fathers are "worriers" and "jealous" but overall "he loves me better than my mother does." The father's motivation is seen in retrospect as "loving" and his behavior is viewed as a component of his love.

For an explanation we turn again to Dr. Pollard: "Women often have an unconscious need to reinvent the past by going back and making a 'bad' father into a 'good' one. This is a familiar reaction to psychologists. The transfer of blame from father becomes evident during analysis. A question I often ask, 'Do you consider your father to be one hundred percent guilty and responsible?' is met with an almost universal negative.

"This attitude represents a reversion to the daughter's childhood conception of mother as the chief rival for her father's affections. A daughter who is labeled a delinquent sees herself as being punished for loving her father, and therefore mother must somehow be responsible."

When we move from the daughter's viewpoint to the father's we find a striking difference in their stories. In the father's account, as Dr. Zaphiris indicates, there is usually a note of self-justification.

"From the first night, my wife didn't like sex," a forty-four-year-old construction superintendent told me. "She always said it hurt. I couldn't get her to go see a doctor. She said there was nothing wrong with her and she was willing to do whatever she had to. But it got so I had to have a couple of drinks before I could work up the nerve to ask her.

"We didn't have sex more than a couple of times a month, so I had to fill in with masturbating. It made me feel like I was a boy again instead of a grown man. After our kids came, there was nothing at all. She wasn't interested in me and I got into the habit of going out with other women. They were plenty glad to have me. The women where I was working did everything but whistle at me. Some were prettier than my wife, but I never promised marriage to any of them. I had three kids by then and divorce was out of the question.

"Our first kid, a daughter, was my favorite. She always had time to spend with me. We had good times together and I gave her extra spending money. Her brother and sister didn't know about that, nor her mother either. My wife was so busy with the house and kids that I took to bringing my daughter along when I went bowling or to a movie. When we got home my wife would be angry and slam around the house, complaining how she never got took anywhere. I told her any time she was ready, I was, but I knew she never would. That wasn't what was bothering her. She didn't like how my oldest daughter favored me, and vice versa.

"One night I wanted to go out bowling, but my daughter had homework to do, studying for a test. I sat around the house getting more and more depressed. I tried to get my wife to pay some attention to me but as usual she wasn't interested. She said she had a backache from all the housework and cleaning. The same old malarkey. When she went off to bed I had a few drinks. The next thing I knew I was knocking on my daughter's door.

"She'd been working late on her homework, and hadn't been in bed long. She wore a pretty nightgown and at her age she already had a figure. I sat on her bed and told her how rotten everything was, how her mother made me feel I wasn't much of a man and didn't really care about me. I just wanted somebody to talk to.

"Well, she tried to make me feel better. But I'd had too much to drink so I just sat there. And the next thing I knew I was petting her. Then it got out of control and I couldn't stop. Afterward I could have killed myself, I was so ashamed.

"I promised it would never happen again. We tried to keep away from it, but it happened again. Gradually I let her take the place of my wife. And she was a lot better wife to me than my wife was."

The note of defiance and self-justification is probably false. Psychologists tell us that the most damaging emotional consequences follow from actions which run counter to what we fundamentally believe. Both a daughter and her father who transgress the social and moral taboos against incest suffer some form of emotional disturbance created by their guilt. Everyone who flouts authority must pay that price, and it is higher than most reckon it to be. The guilt-ridden are surrounded by menacing shadows, unable to enjoy what they are doing or to stop.

THREE
SPECIAL PROBLEMS

We have described what might be called a psychosexual history of the developing relationship between father and daughter. In this imposingly tangled skein of human emotions we have discovered a thread of meaning, deceptively simple, yet omnipresent in the relationship.

Fundamentally, the necessity for a young daughter is to expand into and fulfill her adulthood. Father is able to exert a counterforce to that fulfillment. Often his daughter does not need a directive; she feels within her psyche the partly real, partly imagined power of paternal opposition. The message he communicates is: If you do this thing of which I do not approve, you are removing yourself from me. The father receives the ego boost of bending her to his commandment and thereby keeping her dependent.

A daughter trying to maintain a tenuous connection with her father finds it difficult or impossible to answer him as she should: "I am no longer willing to accept you as the one who has all the answers to all my questions, all the solutions to all my problems. I am going to rely on myself, my own intuitions, my own intelligence, my own view of the world." Such a reply might cut the last remaining link. She also fears a blow to her shaky self-confidence: "You may go off on your own if you want to, but you don't have what you need to survive without me. You will sink in the stormy seas through which I might have guided you."

Most fathers believe their daughters are obligated to follow their advice because, after all, it is so manifestly clear that fathers want the best for their children.

They do. But they also want them to remain children.

The question should now be asked: Do special circumstances alter the syndrome which we have described? In seeking an answer to this question, we will continue to follow the method prescribed by Harvard anthropologist Beatrice Whiting: "Don't bother with social science ... Stick to the lives of real people. You don't need scientific studies to show how various human lives can be."

120

ELEVEN

ABSENT FATHERS

Divorce is clearly becoming a part of American life. Each year at least one and a half million children are involved in a divorce, and the number of divorces granted every year keeps growing. It is estimated that by the nineteen-nineties fully forty percent of children will not be living with both their natural parents. The so-called traditional family, in which mother and dad and the children live together under the same roof, is in the process of becoming obsolete.

"All happy families are like one another," said Tolstoy in a famous quotation. "Each unhappy family is unhappy in its own way." Certainly each individual divorce is unhappy in its own way. Each family has to make a separate and difficult adjustment, and children are intimately involved in the whole painful experience.

In a divorce the daughter is an innocent bystander. She is part of a conflict over which she has no control, in which she cannot take sides, and in the outcome of which she has no hope of victory and every expectation of defeat.

In addition to trying to cope with emotional conflicts, she worries about practical problems. Will she have to move from her home, will she be poor, will she keep on seeing whichever parent moves out? She has had no previous experience with divorce—no child ever had a divorce—and the concept represents a threat to the stability and order of the only universe she knows. Why did mother goad and taunt her father, why did father bully and tyrannize her mother? Such actions are inexplicable. As an adult she might have tried to reconcile the antagonisms and in the process have learned something of their nature; as a child she is condemned to play a passive role.

A career woman, describing her childhood, told me she rarely saw her father after he divorced her mother and moved to another city. It was not a "loving, close relationship" and he was "hardly aware of my existence." She summed it up with: "He didn't care about me and God knows I didn't care about him."

Then she stopped, stared at me and her face crumpled. "Oh, he was such a bastard!" She began to cry. "And I loved him so. I tried so hard to make him love me back!"

The bond that unites father and daughter is buried deep and is based partly on hidden yearnings, fantasies, the need for a strong protector.

To his daughter, a father is a powerful metaphor for the opposite sex and a rebuff from him is transferred to future encounters with men. What this woman expected from men has become a self-fulfilling prophecy: betrayal, desertion and neglect. She compels each man she meets to reenact her father's abandonment of her. She clings childlike to each lover because of her inner unsatisfied need, and eventually her sheer emotional intensity drives him away. "What I'd like," she told me, "is to find a man who'll stick around for at least three weeks. Is that too much to ask?"

It is interesting that she only becomes involved with older men—old enough to *be* her father.

When father leaves home, a daughter feels betrayed. One young woman explains, "I felt *tricked*, as if he had never really loved Mother or me. He'd just been living with us while all the time keeping this terrible secret." Even though she had witnessed the arguments preceding the separation, the final parting was still a rejection of her.

One fifteen-year-old says, "I felt very lost, very down. When Dad came to see me a week later we were like strangers at first. I didn't know what to say. Then he said, 'You know, whatever happens, dear, I love you just as much as ever.' My heart went thump, and the next thing I knew I was sobbing in his arms."

It seems a paradox that while more and more marriages are breaking up, the importance of marriage is becoming magnified. But there is nothing paradoxical about it. Marriage represents security in a world where every wave seems about to wash the ground out from under our feet; we value it more even as we are losing it.

The other night I was at dinner with old friends, a married couple and their two daughters. Both young women are in their early twenties. Both vividly recall a time when they thought everyone's marriage was dissolving, because within our small social group there had been four divorces in a couple of years.

"All the people we knew who used to come to our house," Julie said, "were suddenly coming with different partners." Susan added her recollection of an evening in which their own parents began arguing. The sisters, then in their early teens, huddled in their room and came to the conclusion that there was going to be a divorce. Why should their parents be immune to the strange plague striking everyone?

Fortunately their parents remain happily married, and Julie and Susan are long past such childhood terrors. But their fear is understandable. We all believe Chicken Little when he tells us the sky is falling. It takes a great deal of experience to learn that the worst doesn't always happen. Not even if parents *do* get divorced.

A divorced man observes with humorous exasperation: "Some people seem to think that the only way a father can love his children is if he lives in the same house with them. I tried marriage and it didn't work for me. I've got two kids and I'm divorced. My wife is a buyer for a big department store in San Francisco. She has a nice apartment with a great view, lots of men friends, and a woman who helps her with the responsibility of looking after the kids. She's being the sort of person she always intended to be. Three cheers for her! I wish her luck, and I mean that.

"As for me, I see my kids at Christmas and Easter holidays. My daughter Deborah, who's just starting high school, spends most of her summer vacation with me. There's a woman with me, it's a living arrangement. Deborah's had to get used to that. I won't get married again, that's for sure. But I wouldn't mind having some more kids!"

We were unable to arrange an interview with Deborah because her mother didn't think she should expose her to any kind of interrogation. "I believe you mean well, but I'm just afraid something might go wrong."

It might be useful to examine two other reactions among the divorced fathers, thirty-eight in all, that Donna and I consulted in compiling the case histories for this chapter. The thirty-eight divorced men live in six different cities, and more than half have remarried. Seven have again become fathers.

Typical is a man who told us he thought the divorce had been best for everyone, including his children. "I didn't have confidence I could raise three kids alone, so I didn't ask for part custody. I have greater economic and social independence and a much fuller life. I just can't see it as a tragedy. It wasn't a good marriage and the kids were under stress. They're better off without all the grief of living in a home where the parents didn't like each other very much. I've decided that a lot of people are taken in by the so-called attractions of traditional marriage. They say marriage is for having kids, and I say all right. I've had kids and I'm paying to help bring them up. Now, who do I owe? A big change is taking place right under everybody's eyes. Men are finding out there are a lot of different ways of living your life and bringing up children. Alternative life-styles. That's the real story of what's going on in this country today!"

Another man complained that his former wife, in divorcing him, had left him with an unfair burden. "She was free as a breeze, but I was stuck. I've got a business I can't run alone, so I had to pay somebody to work at the store. And I also had to pay somebody to be with my kids while I was working. My oldest girl was thirteen and it would have been a while before she could have been any real help in either place.

"I married again, a nice woman with two grown kids of her own. I sent my kids back to their mother. I'm willing to pay for them but I can't take the responsibility of raising them, and it wouldn't be right to ask my present wife. She's got enough on her hands, looking after me and helping me to run the store. Her grown kids help too. When my own children are older I'll be glad to have them back. Meanwhile they're better off with their mother."

It has long been considered a disadvantage to be reared as a "fatherless child." The expression itself, "fatherless child," is so allied with misfortune that it can bring a tear to the eye. But the reality behind the stereotype can be very different. Children deprived of their fathers may be poorer but they are also more self-reliant, and in most instances grow up to be quite as successful as fathered children. They are likely to be smarter, more cynical and worldly, more career-oriented.

Adrienne is a good example. After her father, with whom she felt she had a strong, deep-seated relationship, abandoned his wife and family, Adrienne took over as the responsible adult. "In effect," she says, "I forfeited my childhood. I was a grown-up at an age when I should have been getting started in high school. The family had to go on welfare and it was a really hard life. Then my mother got leukemia. Toward the end she didn't recognize the other children. She wanted only me to look after her and I did until the day she died."

Adrienne put herself through college, and on graduation got a job with an import-export firm. (Significantly, her father had been in that business.) Now, at thirty-six, Adrienne is a successful businesswoman who appears to have made a remarkable adjustment to the disappointments and difficulties of her childhood and the loss of her father.

A woman Donna spoke to, a model who works for a well-known cosmetics firm, was afraid she would lose her job if they found out she was a mother with two children. She left her twin daughters in the custody of her ex-husband. When he took a job overseas in Hamburg, Germany, she decided she would rather have her children live with her. Her ex-husband agreed. "I suppose it would be nice if we could all get back together and be a real family," he wrote her, "but I know in my heart that will never happen. And young children need their mother."

"They need a father too," the woman added, "but I hope to supply their needs. They have a deep affection for their father and can always go to visit him whenever he wants them to. But he's not their boss anymore and I think they're better off for it. They could never stand up to him or be as fresh as they can with me. In our house there's not only a women's liberation movement, there's a teenage liberation movement. My former husband is like most men: he has no real confidence in a woman. That attitude, I believe, was leading to a lack of self-confidence in his daughters. That's all cured now. He's not their protector, they're not his protected. That doesn't mean they're not going to be great friends."

Jane Fonda suffered a tragic rupture in the symbiotic tie to her famous father. Before her twelfth birthday Henry Fonda left his wife and family for what was announced at the time as a trial separation. Jane's mother became so disturbed that she suffered a nervous breakdown and had to be treated in an institution. She died there, and for a time the truth of how she died was kept from Jane, who only discovered what happened when she read that her mother had committed suicide.

This was sufficient trauma for any twelve-year-old. But Jane went on to make her own career and eventually to reach a new rapprochement with her father as an adult. The fear and anger she had felt at her own helplessness, her sense of betrayal, were directed into speaking out boldly against injustice afflicting others.

The Chinese symbol for crisis is a combination of two words: danger and opportunity. What distinguished Jane Fonda was her ability to turn crisis into opportunity. Rather than bewail her misfortune or search frantically for another authority figure, she pushed forward toward adulthood and responsibility. Her growth was accelerated rather than brought to a halt.

The maturity and independence that often characterizes daughters of father-absent homes is achieved with no small amount of pain.

Dr. Pollard says, "Teenage daughters involved in a divorce situation feel sad and confused. They blame themselves, at least in part, for what happened. Initially, their fathers are romanticized as they wish to remember them rather than as they were. As the daughter grows older, her still-present visible mother also changes. She doesn't grow in intelligence or stature or authority— not in the daughter's opinion. She gets older, more nervous, more interfering and bothersome. Only father remains beyond change— the daddy of memory."

The problem is made worse when mother tries to convince her daughter that "daddy is the bad one." A thirty-year-old woman recalls, "Mother played the martyr, telling me that the divorce was all Dad's fault. He was a good-for-nothing who never earned enough money, who went to bars with his friends instead of coming home to dinner. He spent afternoons in front of the TV watching sports instead of taking us out. He never bought me pretty clothes like the other girls had. She was always so negative about him. But the more she tried to make me not care about him, the more I resented her. I wasn't going to let her take my daddy away from me."

Another young woman tells how she felt when left in her mother's custody after a divorce. "I didn't understand about laws and courts. I thought Daddy let me go to Mother because he didn't love me. I was hurt and resentful. Until I was in college I'd have told anyone who asked that I was my mother's child. But I always yearned to go to that other house where Daddy lived. When Mother took me there to spend one of my prized weekends with Dad, what a sudden rush of happiness I felt! When I had to leave, it was like the end of the world. I memorized every street sign and the location of certain stores so that I could find my way back if I had to. Whenever I'd get really angry at my mother I'd go into my room and have an imaginary talk with Father—and my anger went away. I realized I didn't resent him—I missed him."

A young teacher says, "I always felt it was important to stay close to my father. He was an outgoing, cheerful man. I never could understand what he saw in my mother. When they separated I was nine years old. I had absolutely no doubt that she was at fault. If I could have, I would have chosen to live with my father. But he traveled so much—he was regional sales manager for a liquor company—that I couldn't live with him even if Mother had been willing to let me.

"Mother tried to turn me and my younger sister against him. I never let her get away with that. He sent money to support us and that meant he loved us. When Mother spoke against him I wouldn't listen. I would tell my sister how Mother lied.

"When Father came and took us away for a day or maybe for a weekend I felt it was Christmas. I dreamed of growing older and being able to look after him. I would keep house for him and cook and never make the mistakes Mother made that drove him away."

Often it takes years for daughter to come to a realistic assessment of her absent father.

Lorraine is the daughter of a successful portrait artist, whom she idealized as a very young girl. "When I was fifteen my parents were divorced after a rather messy scandal involving my father and another married woman. What Mother called his 'infidelity' only made him more glamorous in my eyes. How could he help being madly attractive to other women? If they set out deliberately to have an affair with him, why should he resist? Anyone who didn't understand that was naïve and unsophisticated.

"Mother was awarded custody of me, and my father went abroad to live in London. I still felt very close to him. I looked forward to his letters, and read them over and over. The summer I went to visit him in London was the high point of my life.

"He was living with a woman, but not the one my mother divorced him over. I wasn't prepared to find this woman was exploiting him, taking him for all she could get. I couldn't understand why my brilliant father didn't see through her. She got whatever she wanted. Underneath she was laughing at him. She was only interested in his money and what it could buy for her.

"I tried to tell my father that, but he shrugged it off and told me she had a good critical mind and had been very helpful to him in his work. Helpful! He'd painted several portraits of her and was taken in by her 'Oh, my, you're so wonderful.' Was it for somebody like this he had divorced my practical, down-to-earth, sincere mother?

"I returned from that summer in London in a different frame of mind. That fall, as a senior in high school, I took a course in art appreciation. I thought that knowing more about art might bring me closer to my father. In class I was exposed to the work of really fine artists, some I'd never heard of before. I realized that my father's financial success was due to his ability to please a mass audience. His work was shallow, sentimental, flattering—second-rate.

"A few months later, the day before my eighteenth birthday, my father married the woman he'd been living with in London. That completed my reevaluation of him, and I stopped thinking of him as being exceptional. Maybe he sensed that I didn't have my old attitude toward him because there was some sort of estrangement on his part too. Or maybe his wife gave him all the admiration he needed, so I wasn't as important to him anymore.

"Now I live at home with Mother—we get along fine. But I still get teary when I see her in the morning sleeping on the right side of that queen-size bed; the left side is empty. And when I pass the building where my father had his studio I feel a little sick with sadness. I carry a picture of him in my mind: he's never more than forty and I'm still his little girl in hair ribbons."

The little girl grew up. Her reappraisal of her father did not end their relationship; it merely put her father into more realistic perspective.

After a divorce, a young daughter is left with a residue of guilt. This was apparent on a television program in which Fred Rogers (the "Mister Rogers" of children's television programs) interviewed children aged eight to ten on their feelings about their parents' divorce. One child said, "Maybe half of my school is divorced ... maybe half of my class, a lot of people. Divorced."

Fred Rogers interviewed several children to obtain their reactions to their parents' divorce.

"You always knew all the time that both your mom and your dad loved you. Didn't you know that?"

"Not at first."

"What did you think then?"

"That it was all my fault for doing it, so that they'd get divorced. Till I learned."

"How did you learn?"

"My dad talked to me and my mom talked to me."

And another girl: "Sometimes I have a talk with my daddy about why he got the divorce."

"You sometimes ask him about that? What does he tell you?"

"He just says it was a fight. He doesn't tell me the rest of it."

"And what do you think might be the rest of it? ... Some children think it may be their fault."

"Yeah. They gets real scared."

Another girl gave her perception of what divorce meant: "I remember that every morning my mommy and my dad and me would sit at the table. And one morning he wasn't there ... It is *so-o* hard. A divorce."

In the halting, difficult speech one hears more than the literal bare meaning of words. "Hard" spells out an incommunicable feeling: "I can't see my father anymore because he lives in Philadelphia, and he doesn't call me anymore and I haven't wrote to him yet and I don't know his number. So—it's hard."

Where do children get the idea that they are somehow at fault? "Probably their childhood omnipotence," says Fred Rogers, "in which they feel that everything they do influences the whole world."

Where guilt is involved, we are all children. When we are good we are rewarded; when we are bad we are punished. If one is good enough the reward must follow, and if something bad happens it must be that one was bad. Some children think if they are very, very good maybe their parents will get back together again.

I spoke to a psychologist who was recently divorced. "My daughter says to me, 'If you were going to get a divorce, why did you ever get married?' Her real question is 'How do you stop loving someone?' and behind this is an unspoken fear: If you stopped loving Mommy, maybe you will stop loving me. I tell her that grown-ups don't stop loving children; they stop loving grown-ups. But I'm not sure she's convinced."

It does not make sense to a child that grown-ups who once loved each other can stop loving each other. If they can, then parents are not parents forever. In that lies the root of children's fear about divorce.

"My father was a famous man, a movie director," says a young woman who has married three times, but has never "felt close" to any of her husbands. "Everyone remarked on his insights into people. But his ability as an artist was a lot greater than his ability as a father. If I charted a path from my childhood to where we are now, I'd have to say that he's been trying harder and harder in a rather bewildered way. He's very nice to me now, and I'm sure he's proud of me. But he'll never be the kind of father I hoped for."

What did she hope for?

"I try to think back to the warm, good times, to what I liked about him. But all I remember is my mother telling me how he resented her for getting pregnant, and how he tried to make her have an abortion because he was afraid a baby would interfere with his life-style. They separated not long after I was born. He was always attracted to other women and she wouldn't stand for that.

"I wanted to love him. When he came to visit I spent the whole day in a kind of 'Daddy's coming!' excitement. We'd go out together but his mind was full of work and there was no room for me. He told me I was closer to him than anyone else on earth. 'Who do you love best—your mother or me?' he'd ask. I didn't know what to say. I was his child, but there has to be a certain minimum amount of contact to maintain a relationship."

Says Dr. Pollard, "A daughter cannot expect her absent father to be her dream lover and to fill her days with adventure and romance. She wants to make unlimited calls on his strength and intelligence, but men have other problems that originate at work, in their remarriages, and in their sex lives. Children are only a part of the equation, but it's hard for a child to realize that."

The situation can be as difficult for fathers as for their daughters. Martin, a thirty-six-year-old accountant, moved out of an apartment on the West Side of Manhattan that he had shared with his wife for fourteen years. Their two children, a daughter, eleven, and a son, nine, continued to live with their mother. Martin had always been close to his children, particularly to his daughter, and he wanted to rent an apartment close by. His wife became very upset, saying that if he lived in the same neighborhood he would make it impossible for her and the children.

Martin reluctantly yielded, partly because his wife was in such a highly emotional state. He found an apartment some distance away on the fringes of the Soho district.

After he moved to his new apartment his daughter visited him. He asked her advice on furnishings, draperies, bedspreads, and carefully took notes on her suggestions. They had lunch and strolled about the neighborhood, noting places and restaurants they might want to visit on subsequent occasions. As he was about to put her into a taxi to go home, she suddenly turned and grabbed him fiercely about the waist: "Oh, Daddy, I don't want to lose you. Not ever!"

Martin says, "That night I woke up with a terrible feeling. My daughter was crying for me and I couldn't make her hear or let her know I was there. I couldn't breathe. I got up and paced the floor. What had I done? I had made a terrible mistake! I was as important to my kids as my wife was. I'd put as much love and care into bringing them up. It's not one of the Ten Commandments that a child can live only with its mother.

"I asked my wife for some kind of joint custody or even to let one of my kids live with me some of the time. She flew right off the handle and made some nasty insinuations. I went to a lawyer."

That was where Martin got a real shock. "He told me my chances were practically nil. He read to me from a guidebook on family law in which it said that a father was not qualified to look after his children. He told me about the case of a mother who was really cruel to her kids: the daughter was sometimes chained to the bed in her room and she had been in the hospital several times, once for a broken arm. A psychiatrist said the mother was unfit to be a parent, and investigators from Family and Children's Services found that the father's home would be a much better environment. Both the father and grandmother wanted to take care of her. There was testimony from social workers and from hospital personnel who had treated the child. Despite all that, the court ruled that the daughter should not be given to the father. She was put in a foster home. Talk about sexism! As far as the law is concerned, raising a child is as much a woman's job as giving birth in the first place. It doesn't matter what kind of mother she is, just as long as she's a mother. It doesn't matter how good a parent a father may be, he's still a father!"

We talked to several lawyers who assured us that the situation in courts is slowly changing to grant a father more rights as a parent. As for the present, however, this case history is not untypical. Many a divorced father still has to do his parenting from a distance.

No doubt that for most fathers this is a wounding experience. "Divorce is one of life's great traumas," a forty-five-year-old man told us, "a real postgraduate course in suffering. When I couldn't live with my wife and kids, I couldn't live with myself. I got obsessional. I'd take out the family album—one of the few things I took with me—and look at the photographs of my wife and me and the kids. I wondered at how happy we looked, how innocent it all seemed. The idea of a family is your life. How could I go on living without a life?

"I kept asking myself, 'How did I let it all get away from me?' I noticed in almost all the photographs my wife and kids were making real eye contact. But I was looking off past the camera, my attention fixed on something else. I wish I could project myself into the man in the photograph and think what he must have been thinking. He wasn't thinking about his family, that's for sure. He was tense, abstracted, worried by other problems.

"I feel sometimes that I'd like to redevelop or retouch the photographs and give the poor bastard some brains. I stare at him but he never stares back."

This man blames himself for his broken marriage and is self-flagellating in his descriptions of the "waste, the lies, the stupidity, the pain" that preceded the divorce. A drinking problem led to abuse of his wife and children and to a nearly fatal automobile accident in which he and his family escaped only by a miracle.

"Sometimes I just get numb and sick and I'd like to bury it all and forget it. I can't. It's a hollow right in the middle of my life. My kids came to stay with me for a week when their mother was in the hospital. When they left I stood in the empty bedroom and didn't know whether to remove all traces of their visit or to leave the damn bed and the rollaway cot unmade. I settled for keeping the half-empty cereal boxes. They're still on the kitchen shelf. And I've got the crayoned note my daughter wrote, *Thanx for evrything*, (sic) *Dad. We had a great time.*

A thirty-two-year-old mother, who has a low-paying job, struggles to support her two daughters. They live not far above a subsistence level. The common-law father of the children, from whom the mother is separated, makes minimum payments for child support.

"He's always complaining to me about our daughters. He says he'll stop paying if I don't get them to act better. He says our older daughter, who's fourteen, is running around in bad company. She don't study, she and her friends just smoke pot. He wants me to keep her from going out with them.

"I talk to my daughter about this and she says he just wants her to stay home without any company. I don't know who to believe. Anyway, she's planning to drop out of school and get a job out of town where her father won't bug her all the time. I tell her she's too young to get working papers, but she says there are ways around it.

"I don't want her father upset so he'll stop making payments. I work in a store and we have a hard enough time. It all looks scary when I look ahead. I tell my daughter if she can get around the working papers, she ought to get a part-time job and stay right here to help out. Her father wouldn't mind. But when I mention her father she gets mad. She says, 'He's got no rights here anymore. I won't do what he wants; I've got to do what's right for me.'

"Well, I know how she feels. I don't say she's wrong. I was like her when I was her age. My father tried to run my life. He was a strong man. He wouldn't let me be myself.

"Now the same thing's happening to my daughter. The other day she had a big fight with her father. She's going to leave school and get a job and live somewhere else. I don't know what will happen to her. If her father hadn't left us, he might have been able to change things. But I don't think so. I don't know if I'd have done much different than what my girl is doing. She's got a right to her own life."

A father who was in the Coast Guard abandoned his family when his daughter was only eight years old. The grown woman has not forgotten. "She has explained why he abandoned her in a dozen different ways," says Dr. Pollard, her analyst. "She's finally settled on the fact that he had to leave because it was the call of the sea. I expected her to quote John Masefield at any minute: 'I must go down to the sea again.' She kept a picture of him in his Coast Guardsman uniform next to her bed and wrote to him every week, though she never got more than one or two postcards a year.

"After he left the Coast Guard, her father became hard up for money because he'd become a heavy drinker. She was a young woman by then, with a good job. She'd meet him for lunch and slip money to him. She reported to me that during one lunch her father said she had been a 'pesky kid,' which was why he hadn't wanted to spend much time with her. And she agreed with him. In effect, she was entering into a collusion with him against her younger self—revising the past to explain why he had not been able to love her.

"For several weeks she did not come to my office. Then she called to tell me her father had died. When she did return I found how it had happened. She was at home when a taxicab driver came to the door. He said her father was downstairs in his taxi, very ill, and he had asked to be brought to her. But he was too sick to come up. 'I think he's dying,' the driver told her. She went down with him and found her father dead in the back seat.

"She still cannot get over the fact that her father told the taxi driver to take him to her house. She keeps bringing that up. To her, it constitutes proof that he must have loved her all the time!"

It is so necessary for some daughters to believe that their fathers loved them that their belief will persist in the face of any evidence to the contrary. They are even able to maintain a dependency that never really existed!

TWELVE

FATHER AS HOMEMAKER

A few years ago in public hearings before a Senate committee, a well-known sociologist, Jessie Bernard, testified about the changing aspects of family life. She referred to the increasing importance of the father in child rearing: "The trend of the times is in the direction of greater sharing of the child-rearing function." She cited a study in which one out of three young men responded positively to the idea of helping with the rearing of their children, and she called for a relaxation of the "restraints imposed by unrealistic stereotypes that currently make it difficult for men to participate fully in child rearing." What she proposed is already coming to pass.

At forty-one, David, an advertising sales representative, was earning much less than his wife Cathy, who was head of an interior design service. One day they figured out that if David stayed home, they would actually save money. He could look after their two children, a daughter eleven years old and a boy of eight, and replace their full-time live-in housekeeper with a part-time cleaning woman. This would free the housekeeper's room, giving them the extra space they needed and sparing the additional expense of a planned move from their comparatively cheap rental apartment to an expensive cooperative. Most important, their children would not be deprived of both parents at a critical time in their young lives.

"I wasn't sure how the arrangement would work out," David admits. "Cathy was afraid it wouldn't be good for my self-esteem if I kept house and raised the kids while she was supporting the family. I told her, 'Look, I'm not the best advertising sales rep in the world, but I can be the best father in the world—if I have the time to work at it! Being a full-time father will give me a lot more career satisfaction than I've ever had.'

"I've been doing it now for two years and can tell you that being a homemaker takes a lot more brains and diplomacy and plain hard work than being an advertising sales rep. I don't know where the U.S. Department of Labor gets its nerve saying that homemaking skills rate down at the bottom of the list along with jobs that pay a minimum wage."

What of the children? A prominent textbook widely used in American colleges states: "A child whose father performs the mothering functions, both tangibly and emotionally, while the mother is preoccupied with her career can easily gain a distorted image of masculinity and femininity." That textbook was written in 1968, an eon ago in the rapid evolution of the modern family.

What is actually occurring in the United States today does not support this evaluation. The massive infiltration of the labor market by women has changed everyone's conception of what is a "natural" feminine or masculine role. In a two-income family there is, obviously, no clear demarcation between homemaker and breadwinner.

David's daughter is now old enough to make a comparison: "I feel I'm pretty lucky because my dad is around for me to talk to when I need him. I don't have to fight to get his attention like other girls do with their fathers. I like having my dad around, and I admire him for what he did. He didn't care what people thought. That's beautiful."

Not many men are willing to accept David's solution. "If I couldn't earn a living for my family, I wouldn't feel like a man," is the common reason given for rejecting it. Doubtless there is social embarrassment. When one man meets another for the first time a warm-up question is sure to be: "What do you do?" If the answer is, "I keep house and look after my kids," the response is likely to be uncomfortable silence. Not having an occupation—doctor, lawyer, architect, businessman—robs a man of an important symbol of his identity.

Working wives have blurred the boundary lines between the types of duties each parent performs at home, but certain tasks are fixed and hallowed by tradition. A man who challenges the basic division of labor threatens the masculine conception of what is a man's proper role. He is still supposed to be the provider, not the homemaker.

Researchers and experts in the field almost without exception attribute to the mother unique capabilities as homemaker and care giver. But in concentrating their attention on the feminine and masculine duties within the family they neglect the important change taking place in the relationship of working parents with their children—especially the change in the father/daughter role.

Cathy is beginning to realize that her relationship with her children is deteriorating. "David is cooking for the family because he is a good chef, and the children are clearing dishes and putting them in the dishwasher. Housecleaning is done by a woman who comes three times a week, but David helps the children tidy up their rooms and make the beds. After school my daughter helps him do the marketing, although he still makes occasional trips for minor groceries when we are about to run out. For the rest, my husband tries to make sure everyone does what they do best. If anyone wants to switch around, they do. David doesn't feel that chores are something anyone should feel programmed to do. My daughter makes a terrific chili, and when it's chili night she cooks. My son waters the plants and looks after them, strictly on his own. David spends as much time as he can with the kids, and on Saturday morning he even gets up early to watch my son's favorite television programs while I sleep late.

"An ideal arrangement, except that one person isn't included. Me. The mother. I'm practically a stranger. The other day I was looking at snapshots of the four of us a few years ago—David, me, our two children. We were a family. I was loved and needed. That isn't true any longer. The children don't need anyone but David; they're a complete unit without me. 'One for all, and all for one,' and David is the one.

"I asked him what he will do when the children grow up. He'll have a real problem to resolve when he isn't the be-all and end-all for the kids. He just laughed and said, 'I'll start on a new career. I may even go to work for you!'"

Cathy is trying now to make time to be with her children. She insists on being alone with the children on Saturdays from noon to six. David is not to interfere. "I told him to find something to do that will amuse him—take up golf, or join the Y, or go to the museum and to any movies that aren't G-rated, which is the only kind he's been seeing."

This schedule isn't working well. The children are increasingly restive as the afternoon wears on, and at six o'clock David returns like a triumphal hero. "It's as if they've just been let out of prison. They fly to his arms."

Worse, there is increasingly bitter rivalry between the children for David's affection. "They are always competing for a moment of his time, a look, a smile, anything. My daughter is definitely becoming a flirt. I recognize the little tricks she uses because in a less obvious way I used them with my father. The difference is that my father wasn't the center of my whole universe.

"She's even developed some of David's grown-up attitudes. She looks down on the kind of television programs her friends watch, for example, and prefers public television—the shows David likes to watch. They're sharing more and more interests. She's totally dependent on him. He's not only her father, he's her pal and her boyfriend all wrapped up into one. What she'd really like to do at this point is grow up to be his wife!"

The two-parent family in which the father is the homemaker is a small but growing part of our population. Not enough is yet known about the interactions that take place in such families, but there is striking evidence that social conditioning is more important in determining the status of a parent than classification by sex. There is apparently no biological definition for "mothering" and "fathering."

Another clue to the long-term effect of total fathering is in a letter I received from the forty-four-year-old typist who worked briefly on this manuscript. She wrote that "It still hurts me to have to think about my father who died a few years ago. My mother was too successful in business to spend much time as a mother, and my father had to look after my sister and me. He worked part time and raised us both. I always went to him if I was in trouble because he'd talk to me about my feelings. He always knew what I was going through. He was not only my Dad but my constant companion.

"Maybe you're right when you say that father's love demands a price from his daughter and that she has to fight to keep from going back to be his child again. And maybe you're right that we all have to grow up sooner or later.

"But as far as I'm concerned I'd give up all the so-called advantages of being a grown-up person if I could just be my father's little girl for as long as I live!"

THIRTEEN

ADOPTION

A woman who runs an adoption agency and has worked in the field for almost seventeen years tells about the changes she has noted during that time: "We used to take for granted that a father wanted to adopt a child who looked as much like himself as possible. It was part of the belief that the paternal instinct is frustrated when a man can't reproduce himself. So an adoption agency tried to match a child's coloring, hair and general appearance to the male parent. Such a child was easier for him to 'explain' to outsiders and would be more readily accepted by the parents.

"That picture has changed so drastically that the effort to 'match' children has just about vanished. There are so many more applicants who want a child than there are 'adoptable' children available that the rules of the game are different. Older children, handicapped children, emotionally maladjusted children, children of other races, are all considered 'adoptable' today. The lowering of racial barriers here in the United States and increased social 'mixing' have even made adoption across racial lines quite acceptable to childless parents. These children are not 'like their parents' in the old-fashioned sense."

The conscious, deliberate commitment to take care of a child is being made by an increasing number of parents. Even single men are adopting children. The state supervisor of adoption in Tennessee reports, "We still have many unanswered questions regarding one-parent adoptions, but we believe that having only one adoptive parent is better for the child and more helpful to his/her efforts to achieve a sense of identity than growing up in a series of foster homes."

We interviewed a single father, twenty-nine years old, who had adopted a nine-year-old girl three years previously. "I was a little dubious at first. It seemed to me I had only recently escaped from being a dependent myself. I had only begun making a living as a commercial artist. How did I know I could meet the responsibility of looking after anyone but myself? But I went to the adoption agency and met Teresa and all my anxieties about a new way of life were set to rest. I've never regretted my decision."

The paternal "instinct to reproduce oneself" is not an instinct but a learned response. Men who less than a generation ago would have insisted on a child "like themselves" are learning to father children totally "unlike" them. The urge to father is not necessarily the same as the urge to reproduce. An emotional bond can be formed without blood ties, feeling can be emancipated from biology, and a social commitment can be made firmly without benefit of genetic kinship.

Is the emotional bond different due to the lack of a shared genetic past? Can an adopted daughter be fully incorporated and placed in the line of ancestry as a true branch of the family tree, unchallenged as a descendant of her parents, her grandparents, and allied to aunts and uncles and cousins? Does adoption cause a dislocation in the basic bargain between a father and daughter— his support and care in return for her uncritical admiration and love?

We spoke on several occasions with the woman who runs an adoption agency, and she told us many firsthand stories of adoptive fathers and daughters. Toward the end of one long evening, she observed: "What still surprises me is the enormous variety and richness of parents' interrelationships with their adopted children. Not a single case is exactly the same as another. You can list as many as you like but you will never be able to draw parallels or similarities. The similarities, if there seem to be any, turn out to be superficial because people are as different as thumbprints or snowflakes."

A thirty-one-year-old commercial airline pilot, newly married, wanted to adopt a young Vietnamese girl. The girl had been badly scarred by napalm and needed extensive plastic surgery. His mother begged him not to go through with the adoption, and his young wife also seemed nervous about the idea. They were adopting because she could not have a child and had told her husband so before they were married. But she agreed with her mother-in-law that adopting the Vietnamese girl was too difficult an undertaking. His mother had suggested that they give the money to some charity for Vietnam orphans where it would do more good.

"What my mother doesn't understand," the airplane pilot said, "is that my wife and I really want this little girl. (He was unaware of her real feelings on the subject.) My mother is from the old school that only worries about how children will work out—as if they're living proof of they're having been good parents. It's how you look in the eyes of your friends or relatives or your social group. That attitude I have no use for. In this country we've got to 'win' at everything, even at being parents."

Well spoken. But until the adoption was finalized in court, a process which took months, he was legally free to change his mind. And, surprisingly, he did.

The woman who runs the adoption agency says, "I was surprised because he had already paid for the girl's plastic surgery and other medical expenses. He told me there was a discipline problem. He couldn't reach her or communicate with her. He thought she was hostile and that made him very uneasy. His attitude seemed to be: 'She owes me more than this after all I've done for her!'"

Neither the difficulty nor the expense fazed the father; it was the lack of appreciation. The unwritten contract between a father and daughter was breached. The final straw that broke the relationship was an argument about postoperative skin treatment that she was supposed to take every night at bedtime. The argument ran the gamut of "Why do I have to?" to "I won't!" to the unforgivable "You can't make me—I *hate* you!"

The father found this too much to put up with. He had tolerated her "rebelliousness" and "moodiness," but "I hate you" seemed to reveal a deep and intractable hostility.

"I pointed out that he had known there would be psychological problems," the woman from the agency told me. "Who could blame her after what she'd been through? There would be setbacks and times when he would wonder if he'd made the right decision. But he shouldn't have a timetable. He should keep on trying. He said he had tried his best but there was just no response, no warmth. He had sat up all the night before talking it over with his wife. His decision not to adopt her was final."

"You think he was wrong?"

"Yes. Even he had to admit there were some signs of progress. One time a small bird flew into their screen door at full speed. It was just lying on the ground, hardly breathing, and the young girl stood over it crying. When the bird's breathing stopped so did her crying. She never mentioned it again or seemed to care. She'd seen enough death to know that crying isn't any use. A lot of emotion was locked up in her. She had just learned not to show it."

I was happy to hear that the Vietnamese girl made a better adjustment at a new home. A couple had agreed to act as foster parents for a year. Their impulse in caring for the girl was charitable, but it soon became more than that. They decided to adopt her, despite the fact that they have five children of their own. A few weeks later her new parents found out she didn't know what legal adoption meant. At dinner one night she asked, "When are you going to send me back?"

"We're not ever going to send you back," she was told. "You're part of our family now. We're your *permanent* family."

An adopted daughter can feel a stronger sense of loyalty to her father than a biological daughter would. Even in later life she looks back on his decision to adopt her as altruistic and admirable, a testimonial of love that constitutes an unpayable debt.

One woman in New Jersey calls her adoptive father in Los Angeles every day, and once a month flies out to visit him for a weekend. Her adoptive mother died some years ago and all of her love and gratitude is now centered in her father. She is making installment payments on what she feels is an enormous emotional obligation to him.

Another woman's solicitousness toward her adoptive father led to quarrels with her husband. The husband complained that he had a "part-time wife" whose first duty was not to him. When her father had an accident, slipping on an icy pavement and breaking his hip, she went at once to his bedside to nurse him. After he left the hospital, she became his housekeeper-companion at home, ignoring her husband's pleas to return. Finally the husband delivered an ultimatum. Either she would return at once or she needn't bother to come at all. She wrote back to say she had decided her "place" was with her father. She never went back to her husband, and they were divorced some months later.

At Christmastime, a married woman with a family pleaded with her adoptive father to spend the holiday at her home. She went to great lengths to ensure that it would be a memorable occasion, enlisting her husband and children in making all the arrangements.

She reports: "It was the most difficult Christmas we ever had. My father smokes like a chimney and the house was full of cigar smoke. One of my children, a girl aged ten, is asthmatic and I had to practically lock her in her room with the fan going. We tried to play some of our favorite family games, such as charades and

Monopoly and Twenty Questions, but Father wasn't interested. His favorite game is poker. So we played poker every night, surrounded by a fog of cigar smoke. I had forgotten he didn't like turkey, so our Christmas dinner wasn't a big smash. And on Christmas Day we couldn't watch any of the special programs on television because my father is a football nut. He had the TV turned to football all day."

Donna, who conducted this interview, could not resist asking if the woman had thought of asking her father not to smoke rather than locking the ten-year-old in her room.

"Oh, no!" was the answer. "I wanted so badly for my father to have a good time. I wanted him to be comfortable!"

As you might suspect, her father had a most uncomfortable time. Later, he told her he had not slept well and at his age he "couldn't put up with" kids and pets running around. He had "stuck it out" for her sake but would have been far happier spending the holiday with his own friends!

Her reaction? "I wanted to make it such a happy Christmas for him and I messed it all up!"

A woman I know was abandoned by her real father when she was a child in Czechoslovakia during World War II. She and her mother were taken under the protection of a doctor, a strong capable man who later got them out of the country when the Germans moved in. Her mother later married the doctor, and he adopted her child.

"My mother never tired of telling me how much we owed him. I heard so much about the cruelties of the Germans that I can still tell you in detail about horrors I could not possibly have seen. They live in my memory because of the vivid way my mother related them. I grew up with the feeling that I could never have survived without my stepfather. He was a stern disciplinarian but it never occurred to me to question any of his rules. To me, he was a godlike figure.

"When I got to college I encountered a different world. That was the first time I ever realized, fully, that I could be a person in my own right—that I didn't actually need a male protector. I fell in love with a young man who was studying to be a doctor. I think the fact he wanted to be a doctor attracted me because it reminded me of my stepfather.

"Our marriage was not a success. My husband was so different from my stepfather. He was kind, gentle, rather timid, and I couldn't help but compare him unfavorably. I began to think of him as weak because he let me assert myself. Finally I began having an affair with a professor at the school where I was studying for my master's. One night my husband came home—a classic scene, complete with punches thrown and me flying to the baby's crib and snatching him up to protect him from his father.

"A divorce followed. I couldn't marry the professor because he was married. I think he was also some sort of symbol of my stepfather—being a foreigner and a 'strong' type as opposed to my husband."

Since then she got a master's degree and became a child psychologist. "I decided on that career because I wanted to be able to understand myself and my own childhood better. But it's all tied in somehow with the kind of man my stepfather is, and what I feel I owe him.

"I thought of getting married again about a year ago. My intended's family didn't have much money. I'd have had to help him through medical school. I asked my stepfather's opinion of what I should do. He didn't think I should get married again. I'm not sure why, maybe because of the way my first marriage turned out. Anyway, I didn't get married. To tell the truth, I don't think I will."

These are typical examples of the psychic payment extracted from a daughter as she tries to move into more adult roles as an independent person, career person, wife and mother. The payment is often higher for an adopted daughter. She is more obedient to her father's desire to keep her from "growing up and away."

FOURTEEN

SINGLE PARENTHOOD

In the Academy Award-winning motion picture *Kramer vs. Kramer*, Dustin Hoffman portrays a man whose wife leaves him and who must look after his young child.

This fictional predicament is being duplicated in life. According to the latest figures from the United States Bureau of the Census, since 1970 there has been a 70 percent increase in the number of single-parent families with children under eighteen. That works out to a total of nearly six million families. A growing proportion are families in which a father is the single parent.

A New York City employment agency specializing in obtaining part-time jobs reports an increasing number of men looking for positions that will enable them to spend more time with their families. The idea does not meet with much favor in the business community.

"To succeed these days," says John E. Lohnes, head of the nation's largest executive recruitment agency, "an executive cannot be one-dimensional: he has to know every aspect from procurement to public relations to personnel, from financing to the state of the general economy. The so-called Renaissance man had it easy compared to a modern business executive. The only way he can keep up is to put in a twenty-eight-hour day."

Many men willingly bear the emotional brunt of this kind of job. John Lohnes commutes over an hour to his office in Manhattan, arrives at his desk before seven-thirty, and is still there twelve hours later. In a typical year he travels well over a hundred thousand miles within the continental United States, wherever the job takes him. Luckily, his children are full grown so he doesn't have to meet the impossible demands of full-time fathering and a full-time career.

A Massachusetts firm conducted an experiment by offering working mothers shorter working shifts that fell within school hours so that mothers could still look after their children. But the positions offered are at the lower end of the pay scale. Executives are still required to work a "twenty-eight-hour day."

A computer expert answered an ad for someone with exactly his qualifications. He had an excellent work record, his training, background and skills were what the employer needed. Then came the cruncher. He was only willing to work until three o'clock in the afternoon.

"I have a daughter," he explained, "who gets home from school around three-thirty."

"There must be someone your daughter can go to after she leaves school."

"Sure there is. But I don't want anyone else taking care of her."

Needless to say, he did not get the job.

This man's approach to raising his daughter seems to him clear and consistent. In the absence of his wife, from whom he has been divorced for six years, caring for his daughter has top priority.

I spoke with the employer who did not hire him. He told me, "It isn't so much that he had to get off early. We could handle that. But we wouldn't feel right hiring a man who wants part-time work in order to look after his child."

"Would you feel the same way if a woman applied and made the same requirement?" I asked.

"At least that would be easier to understand. A man who isn't willing to put his career first has the wrong attitude. An executive has to go all out for his work and be aggressive in getting ahead. That's the kind of employee our business is looking for."

The *Wall Street Journal* editorializes about the need for corporate responsibility to prevent the "further disintegration of the American family," but relates the disintegration solely to working mothers, accepting without question the now questionable position that a woman is the only mainstay of the home and family. This merely demonstrates that an attitude of mind created by certain conditions persists long after the conditions cease to have validity. A father who puts his care-giving ahead of his career threatens the time-honored order of things, which is firmly rooted in the conviction that men are not suited physically or psychologically for the task of child rearing. If a man *is* suited to child rearing, it follows that he must be the kind not destined for success in business.

A single father who regards as his major responsibility the raising of his daughter is creating a dilemma not only for himself but for her. He is making himself the sole axis around which her days turn.

We spoke to a father who, after a two-year period of unemployment, had just found a job. During his unemployment he had been not only a father to his daughter, but a housekeeper, a confidant, a cook, a shopper, a tutor and adviser, as well as her telephone answering service and, in his words, "picker-upper-after and general organizer of her somewhat disorganized life." Now that he is working again his daughter continues to call him at the office about totally unimportant problems. Once she asked if he remembered where she had put her hair dryer because she had to do her hair for a party that night and "you always know where everything is." Another time she called to tell him, "Gee, I miss having you here. I just wanted to hear the sound of your voice."

This kind of closeness is attractive to a father who feels that it confirms his exclusive and irreplaceable value to his daughter. But adolescence is the only time a daughter has in which to clarify and strengthen her sense of identity, to integrate who she is with who she wants to be, and to establish methods by which she will be able to function later as a female adult. If she remains totally dependent on daddy, this precious time will be lost. A father who is solely responsible for his daughter's well-being can create in her the feeling that his rules are immutable and her survival depends on her obedience to them. Her typical response is to adapt and conform.

One young woman explained her decision to go to the college her single father had chosen. "I just didn't know it was possible to go against what my father wanted."

For two years a thirty-seven-year-old widower got up early and made breakfast for himself and his teenage daughter, then drove her to high school before driving himself to the train station and commuting to work. When she came home in the afternoon— on a school bus which she could have taken in the morning also— there were snacks and soda not only for her but for her friends. As soon as her father came home at night he prepared dinner, helped her with her homework, and then they usually watched television until her bedtime.

He has a complaint—not what you might expect.

"I found out she has a boyfriend. If I'd been home more I'd have known all about this boy. I regret when I can't be part of the things happening in her life. We used to have long discussions in which she'd confide everything. I didn't know how lucky I was.

"One evening about six months ago I got home and found her having a party with a lot of her friends. They had bought submarine sandwiches and other junk food and were drinking beer. Boys were in the group and I couldn't help wondering what had been going on. I thought about telling her not to have parties in the house when I wasn't home, but I knew what she'd think about that. Anyway, it didn't matter. Her friends don't come to the house anymore. At night they all go to their favorite hangout, a disco, where they can meet boys. I want to continue to have some part in raising her, but I'm scared. I can feel her drifting away."

Single fathers have greater difficulty accepting their daughters' progress to maturity than fathers in a two-parent family. They feel they are losing not only their "little girl" but often their chief companion, helpmate and Saturday-night date. For their daughters, the pain—and guilt—of "growing up and away" is also heightened.

A married woman with a year-old infant was driven to distraction by her single father's constant demands on her. In order to escape she persuaded her husband to accept a job offer in another city. But even that distance was too easily bridged by telephone. Her father called every day, usually with a plaintive, "When am I going to see you? I miss you so." This was accompanied by instructions on how to look after his grandchild, her house, her husband, and then a drumfire of questions about every detail of her day. In the end she got an unlisted telephone and refused to give him the number. "There just wasn't any other way," she said. "I know how I've hurt him, but if he kept on I'd have had to hurt him a lot more."

A woman lawyer of twenty-eight recalls her widowed father as "everything to me—as I was to him. Even today when I hear that Helen Reddy song 'You and Me Against the World,' I think of my father and me. I was always worried that if I lost him for any reason—death or remarriage or whatever—there was no telling what would happen to me. That feeling has affected my behavior with men. I'm not actually dependent, but the *feeling* of dependence is there.

"When I was married I said things to my husband that I never would have believed I'd say to anyone. Like: 'Promise you'll never leave me, no matter what happens.' I was a married woman but I was still a frightened little girl thinking if he leaves me I'll be lost. I'd find myself saying the very same words I used to say to my father, then bringing myself up short: 'Oh, my God!' In the end I left my husband and got a divorce. Part of the reason, I'm sure, is that I just didn't want to be afraid anymore."

A single father whose daughter is becoming an adult yearns to perpetuate the child who uncritically adores him. Once she outgrows him, he will be truly alone.

"My daughter wasn't doing well at school, particularly with reading," a father who is a single parent told me. "I went to talk to her teacher several times and had a session with the school psychologist. He told me that her problems stemmed from the fact that she lacked a 'parental nexus.' In other words, she came from a broken home. I told him I didn't like to use the term 'broken home,' because that implied there was something that needed fixing. I didn't want my daughter to get that idea in her head because it just doesn't reflect the truth. She's happy and loved and I certainly don't see how she'd have been better off if my wife and I had remained married. She'd have been in the eye of a hurricane, with fighting going on around her all the time. I could see I wasn't getting through to the psychologist. He kept coming back to the idea of her lacking a proper 'parental nexus.'

"You know what her trouble turned out to be? It was a mild case of dyslexia. I took her in for a physical exam and the doctor diagnosed it. A whole year of her education wasted because a stupid psychologist didn't understand her real problem. He had his mind made up there had to be something wrong in her home because she only had one parent. As if any child needs more than one good parent!"

As if any child needs more than one good parent. Until that remark I was ready to believe this was an example of the laxness and arrogance that afflicts many in the medical profession, particularly in the fields of psychology and psychiatry.

But that remark sent me to interview the school psychologist. He was casual, soft-spoken, an undoctrinaire man whose reason for thinking the daughter's problem was attributable to difficulty at home came from a very good source: the daughter herself.

"She is a well-mannered girl, but I noted from the first that she has a passive quality, an outward meekness that hides a good deal of inner anger. She told me many stories and gave many examples of how her father kept trying to run her life. She never argued or talked back to him, even though his attempt to completely dominate her was driving her to the brink of a nervous depression.

"I never used the words 'broken home' in my discussions either with the girl or with her father. That's his interpretation. I don't believe all single-parent children are neglected, nor that they are more likely to be delinquent or deficient in any way. A complete father-and-mother family in which authority is shared is usually better because there is some chance of appeal from one parent to the other. But this girl's passivity was her reaction to a single dominating and controlling parent against whom there was no real recourse.

"He had taken over her daily life almost completely. He told her what to think, and obediently she thought it. Time and again, I would ask a question and she would say, 'I don't know the answer to that. You'll have to ask my father.' She never challenged him about anything. 'Why bother?' was her attitude. 'He knows what is right for me to do. If I start asking him why, he will just get upset.'

"She didn't approve of girls her age who were beginning to talk and act as if their fathers weren't important, as if they didn't need their fathers at all and who even made fun of what their fathers said. She hadn't entered that first phase of separation in which a daughter begins to suspect her father doesn't know everything. She took her rules for living from him and never questioned them. She had to be rechanneled in a different direction if she was to have any hope of growing up into a young woman with a mind and personality of her own.

"For a while her personality problems seemed enough to explain her bad marks in school. When I tried to break through to her she would just sit there and say, 'Um, um, um'—no basic response. Then it began to happen. She began talking about her father. She was sure he acted only out of love for her. I explained that it was possible for a father to love his daughter very much but it could still be a rotten relationship if it didn't allow her to grow and become an individual. She appeared to be impressed, but it was superficial. She wasn't convinced.

"That summer she went to Yellowstone Park with her father and sent me a postcard with the words underlined, *I miss you and hope we can talk again.* When she returned that fall we did talk again, and she seemed changed, more willing to accept that her father might have been overcontrolling her. I urged her to try to enlarge her world and meet other people. At that point, however, I noted that her reading problem at school continued and began to suspect there might be a physical basis also."

It was he who recommended that she have the physical examination that led to the discovery of her dyslexia, a fact that her father conveniently, or deliberately, forgot to mention.

FIFTEEN

THE HANDICAPPED CHILD

Everyone knew Bernie was marked for success. By twenty-five he was a wunderkind in the garment business in Manhattan. "One good season can make you rich in this business," he said. "I'm going for twenty. I want to get more out of living than just older." He was headed for the promised land as directly as if he were running on railroad tracks. He derided men who were content with their lot and thought their highest purpose in life was to raise healthy, happy children. "The hubby-wubbies," he called them.

Bernie gave so much at the office that he had little to give at home. "Sure my wife was unhappy," he admits, "but I knew the way to keep her quiet was to give her a baby. So I gave her a baby. Something of her own. Not something of mine. Then everything changed. The bottom dropped out."

The infant girl was born with a badly twisted spine, and was diagnosed as an epileptic. In time they discovered she also suffered from mirror writing.

Describing the decision he had to make, Bernie says, "I never felt responsible for anybody but myself. Number one. But there was something about that little girl, so helpless and needing somebody. My wife and I were the only somebodies around."

Bernie was frightened by the tragedy of his daughter, but almost overnight he changed the direction of his life. Business took a backseat to fatherhood. He became attentive and protective. He bought a motorized wheelchair and had a special ramp built so his daughter could get easily in and out of their station wagon. When she was depressed and withdrawn he would tell her stories and play the kinds of games with her that were within her capacity. He never showed any exasperation at her helplessness.

At times his wife, confronted with the child's repeated failures to show improvement, would ask, "Why us?" Bernie's reply was simple. "Why not us? It had to happen to somebody." He saw no point in sending the child for training or treatment or enrolling her in special schools. "What's the point? It's not fair to expect anything of her. Let her be happy."

Nevertheless, when she was six years old he was persuaded to send the child to a special school. Just as he predicted, she was miserably unhappy. Her teacher kept urging her to try more activities despite her handicap, and once even scolded her for exaggerating the extent of her disability.

The girl went home that day in tears and Bernie promised that she would not have to go back. The next day he called the teacher to inform her of his decision. The teacher told Bernie that other children at school, some with equally severe physical handicaps, were making progress—playing games, acting in plays, working at hobbies, as well as learning. She said his daughter would do better if she was encouraged to try. Bernie said he would not have "that kind of pressure put on my daughter."

A few days later Bernie called to pick up his daughter's belongings at the school. The teacher told him a few of his daughter's friends had been asking about her absence. "Friends?" Bernie asked skeptically. The teacher took him to the class where he met the other children and discovered that his daughter really did have friends. And he saw for himself how these children were managing to adjust to their disabilities.

"I had a long talk with her teacher, who told me about disabled kids who had gone on to do worthwhile things. A famous television producer, a talk show hostess, a famous lawyer. Even Nelson Rockefeller, governor of New York and a vice-president of the United States, had coped with a learning disability. There were millions of handicapped persons making it in society.

"I went home and told my daughter I thought she'd better go back to school after all. You should have seen the way she carried on! She got so worked up and disturbed I could see it would do her more harm than good. The poor little kid has so little pleasure out of life I couldn't cause her any more grief. I talked it over with my wife. We really *talked* about how we'd feel if we sent her back. She might come to hate us. And we decided it would be best to keep her home where she'd be happier."

An overprotective father like Bernie can create a state of what is described as "conditioned helplessness" in a handicapped daughter. By keeping her under his protection, he convinces her that she will never be able to live independently.

Here are typical examples of conditioned helplessness:

- A thirteen-year-old girl did not think she could buy anything in a store if she did not have the exact change; she had never bought anything in her life.

- A sixteen-year-old girl could not sign her name because "my father never lets me sign anything. He says I don't need to; he'll do it for me."
- A young woman dining out at a friend's house for the first time waited patiently for someone to cut up her meat and butter her bread because her father had always done it for her.

Senator Robert Dole of Kansas says that such children acquire an "institutional mentality." By the time the parents die there is no place for the child to go except into an institution. Senator Dole describes a recent meeting in a large city where parents discussed with lay leaders and state officials the possible living arrangements for their disabled children in the event of the parents' death or some other emergency. "No one ever raised the possibility of a noninstitutional setting. The idea of increased self-sufficiency and independence in a private residential setting was foreign to them all."

John Gliedman and William Roth, authors of *The Unexpected Minority*, ask us to imagine two children in wheelchairs. When we see them at a distance our attitudes toward them are identical. As they come closer, we notice that one wears on her leg a plaster cast covered with autographs: a simple fracture. The other wears a steel brace: polio. One will be up and about in a few weeks; the other will be confined for life. How different our attitude toward them becomes at that moment!

The lives of disabled children may be stunted less by their afflictions than by the way the able-bodied behave toward them. It is not sentimentality that the handicapped require, nor false reassurance, but a realistic optimism. Others have been in their situation before, have survived and triumphed. No one should claim it will be easy—merely that it can be done.

At a winter resort in Colorado I witnessed a group of blind cross-country skiers following in the tracks of a sighted skier. One blind skier later took to the slopes in the company of a sighted skier who gave her directions by means of a light harness. Even amputees are learning to ski in this program (the Winter Park Handicap Recreation Program). Other disabled people have gone on mountain-climbing adventures, long canoe trips and wilderness expeditions, where they learn to cope with extremely demanding outdoor situations.

A clinical psychologist reports, "The benefits of this kind of experience in psychological terms are immeasurable. The disabled are happier, more energetic, more outgoing. That is what independence is all about."

Because the mother usually attends to a child's daily needs, a father is able for most of the day to deny the reality of her affliction. At night he may discuss her progress or lack of it with the mother, but the information he gets is secondhand and does little to enlighten him about the emotional truth of her situation. Often he does not want to know. Without motivation to learn, his daughter loses faith in her ability to improve and becomes truly helpless.

A physiotherapist told me this story of nine-year-old Christina, whose domineering father had accepted that she would never lead an independent life. Christina was diagnosed as having damage to the motor and speech areas of the brain. She spent most of her day in bed staring at the wall. When dolls and simple toys were offered to her she showed absolutely no interest. Her father thought her case was hopeless. "She really has no intelligence," he said. "I just have to love her for what she is, not what I'd like her to be."

The physiotherapist, a friend of the family, suggested Christina might be helped by a concentrated physical, occupational and speech therapy program. After two months his evaluation was that Christina's mental torpor was partly self-induced. She would not respond to questions and had a negative attitude toward her therapy, but there were signs of some mental endowment in her irregular answers to tests.

Finally he suggested to the father that she join an organized play therapy program with a group of other severely handicapped children. Here he found further signs of stimulation. When the other children were playing Christina would glance at them and smile a little as if she wanted to join.

After a while she began making peculiar throat noises, as if trying to communicate, and she got very upset when the other children didn't pay attention. Instead of turning away, however, she tried harder to make herself understood. One day she edged over to another girl who was playing with blocks. Christina picked up a block to put on top of the pile and knocked the pile over. She began to cry but the physiotherapist showed up instantly to assure her it didn't matter and to encourage her to try again.

When she finally succeeded in placing one block on top of the pile "she was so excited that she almost went wild. She beat her hands on the floor and began acting crazy. I let her celebrate her triumph, then we started with the blocks again.

"A month later I invited her father to observe what was happening. He watched her in the play room, saw her responding to the group, communicating, and how much interest she showed in the play. He was impressed when he saw her running a model truck around the floor. He had been convinced she was so clumsy she couldn't hold anything."

Christina will never attain normal speech nor compete physically on equal terms with normal children. But she is no longer a helpless, mindless child—merely a handicapped child. Perfection is not the only acceptable standard of performance; demanding too much of anyone is a covert form of rejection. What counts is being able to give a maximum performance considering our limitations.

A father who overprotects a handicapped daughter condemns her to a life of useless invalidism. His overprotectiveness may even represent an unconscious attempt to deny personal responsibility for her handicap. The effect is to deny her any chance of functioning on an independent level.

In many instances, as famed psychoanalyst Karen Horney declares, "love or any emotional bond is that which causes the greatest degree of dependence."

SIXTEEN

HOMOSEXUALITY

A father accepts a "tomboy" daughter far more readily than an "effeminate" son. One reason may be that tomboy tendencies bring a daughter closer to the "superior" male sex, while a son's effeminate behavior moves him in the other direction. Tomboy daughters also give the impression of knowing how to take care of themselves while an effeminate man does not. Most important, a tomboy daughter is not in danger of being seduced away from her father by another man.

No one knows the precise cause of homosexuality but we do know that homosexual tendencies exist in everyone. Very often the eventual choice is dictated by emotional patterns established in childhood. A father's seductiveness toward his daughter contributes to her sexual orientation. By stimulating her sexually, he may arouse desires that cannot be satisfied, and desires that cannot be satisfied seek another outlet.

One young woman told us that until the early years of her adolescence she bathed with her father in the same bathtub. He believed in being open about sex, and in satisfying a child's curiosity about sexual organs. He explained to her the function of his penis and once even allowed her to touch and fondle it. The resulting erection impressed and startled her. That night she prayed God would let her wake up in the morning with a penis of her own. God did not oblige. Next, she began to fantasize that she had been born a boy and her penis had somehow dropped off. By performing an emotional sex change on herself, she was transferring her sexual attraction toward her father into a yearning for a specific part of him: his penis.

Because she felt it was wrong to behave that way with her father, she transferred the "wrongness" from where it belonged—with her father's behavior—to the kind of sexual desire he aroused. Guilt about her secret desires eventually turned her away from heterosexuality. In her fifteenth year she had several homosexual experiences and began making it her way of life.

Some fathers try to offset a secret feeling that being the father of a girl is itself somewhat effeminate. Popular wisdom is that genuinely virile and masculine men breed sons.

Some years ago I was present at the home of a father whose fourteen-year-old daughter was dressed exactly like a boy. Her hair was cut short and she wore a tight bra to flatten and conceal her breasts. She talked exclusively about baseball and boxing, jumped up to spar with her father, who told me, "She has a really good left hook; if she hits you, you feel it." The young lady's gestures and mannerisms, even her voice level, were indistinguishable from those of a member of the male sex. The father said proudly, "She's a real tiger. We're all scared of her."

Today, at nineteen, his daughter works as a "repairman" for a large retail chain. In her short hair, shapeless mechanic's outfit, with her face and hair grimy, she could easily pass for a young man. She has held other "masculine" jobs—as house painter, bartender, karate instructor. Now she lives with an attractive young woman roommate and has served notice on her parents not to expect any grandchildren from her because "I'm not interested in marriage."

How does her father react? He boasts that his daughter is a "real broad who knows her own mind and won't let anybody push her around." Despite what she has told him of her attitude toward marriage and children, he still predicts that "she's going to be a handful for the right man—when he comes along."

Donna interviewed the young woman, who explained her sexual bias in this way: "My Dad had never made any bones about the fact that he wanted a son, somebody to carry on the family name and that sort of thing. He was so disappointed that he even gave me the name he intended to give to a son. When I was a little girl my mother, because she was anxious to please him, practically made me over into a son. She dressed me like a boy and kept my hair cut like a boy. Strangers never knew what sex I was. I grew up feeling I had let my father down by turning out to be a girl.

"I got the entirely wrong kind of training to be a woman. But I wanted to please my parents—especially Dad—and pretty soon I began to see certain advantages to it. If you wanted to get anyplace in life you had to be a man. I didn't like the role women had to play. My mother kowtowed to everything Dad said and all her women friends were so dependent on their husbands. One woman got divorced—her husband left her—and she sold the house and moved away because she was too ashamed to continue seeing her friends.

"When I was a young girl I took the 'husband' part in games played with girls, but mostly I preferred playing baseball and soccer with boys. I was good enough to do it. Once I got hit in the eye with a baseball and it became a real shiner. I told Dad I got it in a fight with a boy and he was pleased. Especially when I told him I won.

"He did everything he could to make me his pal. He taught me how to box. I went along on camping trips with him and his friends. After a while the men got used to it and treated me like one of them. They would talk about women just as if I weren't there.

"I got to be around fourteen-fifteen not liking men much. Not at all, really. I had a few dates with young men but they never worked out. We did some necking but it didn't excite me. I kept thinking something was wrong with them, that I hadn't found the right one for me yet. In my last year of high school I had a crush on a woman teacher; it was more intense than anything I'd felt for a man. But I still didn't think it meant anything.

"I got a kick out of looking at the nude women in the magazines that the men always had lying around. I'd look at some really beautiful naked girl and imagine myself running my hands over her and kissing her and get as sexually excited as any man. When I moved out of my parents' house I got a roommate. She's a well-built girl who likes to walk around in the nude. It made me hot. I could hardly keep my eyes off her, and I wanted to kiss her so bad I had to bite my lips. I'd force myself to read or look out the window, and I'd tell myself I'm not that way, I'm not, not *me!* Then one day I just walked up to her and started in. It turned out she'd been as hot for me as I was for her!"

There are no clear guidelines to homosexuality. Most homosexual women do not wear short hair, dress in mannish clothes, have deep voices, nor act like men. They are not usually attracted to occupations requiring physical strength and labor. In fact, few lesbian women can be distinguished from "straight" women. Marcel T. Saghir and Eli Robins, in their book *Male and Female Homosexuality*, say that lesbian women usually can't even spot others of their kind.

One might say the only thing different about lesbian women is that they are sexually attracted to their own sex. But even this statement is open to amendment.

According to Kinsey's research (compiled with the help of Wardell B. Pomeroy), only 2 percent of women are exclusively homosexual all of their adult lives. Women who have homosexual experiences are not necessarily "gay"; a great majority of lesbian women do not act in a "masculine" way, and there are no physical characteristics or mannerisms common to all. It has been estimated that only 5 percent of lesbians can be easily identified from their appearance. The other 95 percent appear to be no different from the rest of womankind.

"No matter what people would like you to believe," observes a contemporary historian, "homosexuality is not more 'popular' or 'open' than in previous eras. You have only to look at history to see the important role that great homosexuals, men and women, have played. The ancient Greeks and Romans considered homosexual behavior to be 'natural' in a way that is hard for us to imagine today. We have been incapable of being objective or dispassionate on the subject because our society is still largely controlled by a moral tradition which is basically against sexual gratification of any kind except for the purpose of procreation."

Currently, with the relaxation of the taboo on discussion of the topic, there has been an outpouring of personal detailed reporting that provides a new dimension to our understanding. Not even the most clearly written sociological summary or statistical report can equal the emotional impact of a book such as Katherine Brady's *Father's Days*, previously mentioned. After her incestuous relationship with her father, she continued to be sexually victimized by a husband who conducted their sexual relations with an absence of affection. Finally she began to link heterosexual lovemaking with feelings of exploitation, guilt and deception, and turned to lesbianism.

Katherine's experience illustrates another common misconception about the exclusive nature of female homosexuality. One out of three lesbians is married or has been married, and three out of four have had intercourse with men.

Most fathers willingly acknowledge that they have a powerful influence in helping to create a daughter's sexual identity, but they fiercely reject the notion that they could have had a part in influencing her lesbianism. This contradiction in logic has a simple emotional explanation: it is too painful to admit he may have been shaping his daughter's "defiant" behavior.

Rejection of personal responsibility is made easier by the fact that there is no single explanation for homosexuality. Theories about the cause of female homosexuality range from Freud's belief that the young girl becomes fixed in an early stage of psychological growth to explanations involving an inherent orientation to masculinity due to hormonal imbalance or heredity to the more fanciful concept of a "male soul" in a female body. The belief that emotional problems with parents are a strong contributing factor is merely one theory among many.

Jordan, a twenty-eight-year-old woman who told us she has "swung both ways," believed until a few years ago that female sexuality should only exist as a response to male sexuality. When she had her first lesbian encounter her reaction was surprise. "I didn't believe until I had that orgasm that a woman could have the means to satisfy my physical needs. I didn't understand how it would work.

"I knew how my dad would feel if he knew I was making love with a woman. He'd say I was diseased or sick in the head. I didn't let him know because I didn't want him to turn against me. Once I even dreamed he caught me in bed with her. In my dream I was trying to tell him, *She's lesbian, Daddy, I'm* not.

"I knew that sooner or later I was going to tell him, though, and that gave me a real sense of power. I kept imagining him having a heart attack or going crazy. I finally got to the point where there was nothing else to do. By then I had a really good woman friend and I wasn't going to keep her on the side to please my father. I made a decision that he would have to know. I went to visit at my parents' home, Mother cooked a great dinner, and later we sat in the living room talking. The conversation got around to a movie, a very romantic movie that my mother said was the kind to see only with a very special friend. She meant a man, of course, but suddenly I was telling them about myself and the woman I was living with. 'We're not just friends. It's the same as a marriage.'

"My father asked, 'What made you decide to tell us this?'

"I said, 'I thought you'd want to know. I love you both and I want to be able to share things with you. I don't want to keep any secrets.'

"My mother started to cry and Father took it as hard as I expected. He said, 'Well, you're grown up now and you can do as you please. But this isn't the way I thought you'd grow up.' He started begging me to think about what I was doing before I ruined my life. He said, 'I know you won't be happy unless you're a real woman. That kind of love isn't logical, it isn't right. You need a man's love and support.' I thought that was a foolish thing for him to say. All he did was make me realize that what was important to me was not being his daughter but being free to do what I want. He still expected to control how I live and love."

Sexual identity, of course, involves more than having certain types of sexual organs. It has to do with how a female feels about herself. It is biological but it is also culturally conditioned. Professor John Money of Johns Hopkins University says homosexuality is the long-term result of all the experiences a person has in early childhood acting upon her inborn tendencies, and Morton Hunt observes in his book *Gay: What You Should Know About Homosexuality,* "The same childhood experiences or parent-child troubles that make some children into sick homosexuals make others into apparently healthy homosexuals."

It might be argued that a homosexual who admits her sexual preference is healthier than one who tries to hide it. Let me quote from an anguished letter that Donna received from a sixteen-year-old girl: "I hide what I feel even at school. Most of the time I don't show any emotion at all, even to my best friends. They sit around and talk about their boyfriends, and it's hard not to feel a wall between us. I make up lies so they won't think I'm out of it.

"Sometimes I hate myself for not having courage. I've created this other person who stands between me and the world. I feel like an actress who can never take off her makeup. I have to lie and pretend, and it's like being in a torture chamber. I don't see any end to it."

What Freud called the internalized parent, or conscience, is what Margaret Mead described as "the capacity to feel guilt, to award oneself either in anticipation of an act not yet performed or retrospectively in terms of a past act, the type of suffering or reward once given by the parent." At some point, this punishment of self will destroy the ability to relate to others. The sufferer becomes locked in an emotional prison, unable to free herself or to survive within its walls. Her growth to maturity is stunted and the full range of her personality is inhibited as she continues to live a half life.

I will end by quoting from a letter written by a lesbian acquaintance after she read this chapter in manuscript:

"What I object to is the assumption that sex practices can be put into pigeonholes. Why is homosexuality any more of a problem for fathers than heterosexuality? Because heterosexuals are in the majority, that's why. If 51 percent of the population was homosexual, you'd have to write about the 'pathological problem' of heterosexuality. It's this attitude that made teachers a generation or two ago try to 'correct' people who wrote left-handed. We know now that being left-handed is perfectly 'normal,' but we don't seem to have arrived at the same realization about sexual preference.

"Believe it or not, lesbians don't have emotional problems of adjustment that are any worse than 'straights'.' Whatever our fathers may or may not have to do with it, we're perfectly happy as we are—if the straights would leave us alone."

Perhaps all one can say with reasonable certainty is that father plays an influential role in establishing a daughter's final sexual preference.

The danger is that his lesbian daughter may come to believe that there is a bad and a good side to her sexual nature. She becomes unwilling to take responsibility for her own actions: the "bad" persona isn't really her. This schizophrenic attitude hinders her passage to maturity. She continues to think of herself as an unworthy wicked child who *deserves* to be punished.

SEVENTEEN

INADEQUATE FATHERS

Until now we have examined daughter's relationship to a father who is a male authority figure. This is the prevailing relationship between fathers and daughters in our society. But what happens to the daughter who has, or perceives herself as having, an inadequate father? Isn't she deprived of an important role model?

We interviewed the daughter of a man who not only allowed himself to be abused by his wife and daughter but in all his relationships. The daughter, now thirty-two years old, told us, "He seemed to wear a sign that said *Please tread on me!* He took positive pleasure in talking about how much he suffered at the hands of others. About the only person who treated him with any respect was the manager of the appliance store where he worked. But Dad was about as unreliable and incompetent a worker as anybody could ask for, and finally the manager had to let him go. That brought on another complaint about the unjustified misfortunes always falling on his head. 'Why does everyone pick on me? I never do anyone any harm!' It was never his fault. It was always somebody else's."

Her mother called her husband a "loser," but the problem went deeper than that. Dr. C.B. Pollard explains the inner workings of masochism in his case: "He had to keep proving his unworthiness by inviting harsh treatment, much as a child indulges in deliberately provocative behavior until the punishment sought is obtained. That is why this man 'repaid' the manager of the store by being an incompetent worker. He invited his own trouble. Only then was his inner awareness of guilt and unworthiness temporarily assuaged."

The daughter was careful in our interview to make clear that she had in no way inherited her father's inclination to let everyone walk over him. But we learned of an interesting experience that casts a revealing light on her emotional legacy.

She hired a highly recommended contractor to insulate her house, got a good price and specified in the contract just what work was to be done with a proviso that no extra costs were to be tacked on. However, when the contractor sent in his bill she discovered there was an extra charge for insulating an open areaway in the wall above and behind the kitchen. The contractor had discovered a hole through which animals might get in. On a previous occasion a raccoon actually had gotten into the area. The contractor sealed off the hole and, while he was about it, insulated it. His bill included a charge for this extra work. On a total bill of over two thousand dollars this extra charge was only sixty-three dollars.

When the woman saw it she wrote him an angry letter informing him she had no intention of paying. When he called to explain she denounced him as a "cheap swindler" and vowed she would go to court rather than pay him a penny.

Unfortunately, the contractor's secretary was on a phone extension and heard the accusation. The next thing the woman knew she was sued for slander. The presence of a third party constitutes transmission of a slanderous accusation, and she ended up not only having to pay the bill in full but settling the slander suit out of court and paying for the contractor's legal fees.

Why, instead of protesting in a dignified way and allowing the contractor to explain, did she let the situation go to such an extreme? In Dr. Pollard's view: "The psychological underpinning of her anger was not a grown-up response to the real-life situation before her, but was based on her childish reaction to her father's weakness and inability to fight back when taken advantage of. In her own way she is carrying on the same kind of behavior for which her father was the prototype. She is inviting difficulties."

The ways in which a father's influence is passed on are as many and complicated as the genetic code that carries messages of heredity from one generation to the next.

"I always had a tremendous sense of disappointment in my father," a young woman told Donna. "I wanted a strong father I could look up to and fear a little. But he was basically a weak, shy man, undersized and frail, almost like a boy. His wrists were thinner than mine. He made little jokes about how poor he was at athletics at school, how he would watch other boys playing in the schoolyard and wish he could be like them.

"My mother was just the opposite, very sure of herself. When we had company to dinner my father was so shy that he stayed most of the time in the kitchen. Rather than make conversation, he would do all the preparing, serving and clearing away dishes. My mother jokingly called him her 'kitchen man.' What was sad was that no one missed him at the party. I felt sorry for him but I couldn't think of him as a real father like other girls had.

"During the war he took a job as a welder in a shipyard. The trouble was that he had terrible hay fever. Locked up inside his welder's helmet he was really miserable. He became desperate to quit but Mother wouldn't let him. He was making more money than he ever had, but he'd come home looking terrible, his face all swollen and red. One night when he was doing dishes in the kitchen he said to me, 'Your mother can be really mean sometimes.' It was all I could do to keep from screaming: 'Well, why don't you do something about it?'

"He never did. We used to drive up to see my grandparents—my mother's folks—every weekend in Wilton, Connecticut. Mother wouldn't let my father come along unless he was freshly bathed and shaved. She would sit beside the bathtub and soap him up and rinse him clean and even shampoo his hair. It was humiliating. I don't know why he stood for it. How can you respect a father like that?"

A father usually deals with his daughter on an adult-to-child basis. He can also deal with her as adult to adult, and one of the most effective, emotionally binding ways is to bring out the child in himself and deal with her on a child-to-child basis. What is never effective is for him to play the role of a child to his daughter's adult person. That is forsaking his natural role as a father; it causes a daughter to look upon him as an inadequate parent.

This same young woman is married to a not-too-successful store manager who works a long six-day week. Donna reports that during the interview the woman continually belittled him, saying his inability to better himself was due to the fact he never finished high school. Donna adds: "She also criticized the way he looks, behaves, called attention to his faults and failures, and questioned his competence. I couldn't help thinking that in her way she was repeating her mother's pattern. She had found a man like her father whom she could tyrannize."

Studies reveal that women who fail to develop into well-rounded, well-adjusted competent adults tend to blame inadequate fathering.

"I never got from him the kind of things a daughter has a right to expect," a recent divorcee says of her father. "He never made me feel that I was anyone special in my own right either. Other fathers made their daughters feel special, but not him.

"The real impression I wanted to make was on the opposite sex. I was trying to get a picture of myself as a woman and learn how to get along with men. That is where my father could have been a big help, but he wasn't. Without his support, I got a pretty negative picture of myself as a woman.

"My mother got hepatitis from a blood transfusion and lost a kidney. We couldn't affort dialysis, and when her second kidney started to go it was just a matter of time. Around then I met this good-looking man, a mindless type who used to pose for muscle magazines, and I figured I'd be less of a burden if I got married.

"I knew it was a mistake at the wedding ceremony. My husband's brother had flown in for our wedding and I met him for the first time. During the ceremony I kept thinking how much nicer it would be if I were going to bed with him that night. A year later I was living in a rural town in Florida where my husband was trying to make a living buying and selling fruit. My mother came down to visit me—she was dying then—and we sat talking. I was shredding a handkerchief into strips, I was so nervous and unhappy. She told me to get a divorce before it was too late—take my baby and go. She was afraid I'd follow her example and get stuck for life with a schnook.

"I got a job with an airplane rental firm. My boss was a man who knew what he wanted. He completely dominated me. After I'd worked for him two months we began having an affair. No physical affection, or holding or caressing or anything like that. I never had an orgasm. Actually, I've never had one to this day.

"But at least he was better than my husband. I didn't feel anything at all for him. After seven years we broke up. Since then I've had a number of affairs. It always goes the same way. Men's weaknesses are like hidden traps. You walk in thinking it's going to be okay and the next thing you know, spang! the trap springs on you."

Another woman, who is unhappily married at thirty-three, recalls: "My mother was the dominant figure in our household. My father was very sick, but we didn't know it then—and my mother had a barely disguised impatience with him. I grew up with a contempt for 'weak men.' I always looked for someone who would be the opposite of my father, strong, physically fit. I wasn't attracted to any other kind. But somehow I never worked out any satisfactory relationships."

"The lack of constructive interaction with a loving, attentive father," says a 1973 report quoted by Marshall Hamilton, "results in apprehension and inadequate skills in relating to males."

"Inadequacy" as a parent may result from many causes. A father may be too harassed by other problems to give his daughter the attention she needs. Or there may be personality differences that make communication difficult.

A writer I know, a distinctly antisocial type, has a bright, inquisitive, extremely talkative seven-year-old daughter. He retreats to his study rather than listen to her chatter.

One day the seven-year-old asked her mother, "Why doesn't Daddy talk to me? Doesn't he like me?"

Her mother tried to explain that her father's solitary personality did not mean he was rejecting her, or that he loved her less. She wasn't able to convince the little girl, and she has no hope that her husband will discuss his problem openly. "He doesn't believe he has a problem. He'd say it's just the way he is or it's part of being a creative artist. But his withdrawal is having a bad effect on our daughter. That I'm sure of."

Most men have difficulty admitting a psychological weakness because they are socially conditioned to be guardians and protectors. They are accustomed to being judged on the basis of achievement and to shun weakness as a confession of inadequacy.

One reason some fathers are uncomfortable in an intimate relationship is that in the business world relationships are impersonal and fact-centered. There is no attempt to bridge the emotional distance between coworkers, although many spend more time in each other's company than with their families. In the work environment there is little discussion of highly personal problems.

The controller for a large supermarket chain was disturbed about his daughter, who was having problems of social adjustment. She had few friends and was getting poor marks in school and her only date was a young high school dropout who openly smoked marijuana.

Unable to cope alone or to make his wife understand what he regarded as a serious situation, this man brought up the subject with his associates in business. They were sympathetic, but dealt with the problem in cool, factual terms. "They told me my daughter should make more of an effort to join clubs, invite friends to the house, get more involved in sports or activities at the YWCA. When I tried to explain that if she could do those things she wouldn't have a problem in the first place, they shrugged their shoulders and said something like 'Give it time; these things tend to work themselves out if you leave them alone.'"

Most of a father's life experience is gathered in this work world which values power, authority, logic, facts and coercive behavior. Experience is a highly portable commodity and what we have learned in one place is easily transferred to another. Not surprisingly, therefore, father carries his work experience home, and elements are embodied in his relationship with his daughter. This can have sorry consequences. A better way must be found for fathers to make the transition from the values and approaches of the world of work to the world of home and family.

A father sitting down to have a "man-to-man" talk with his son is a familiar scene. They will discuss seriously such problems as sex, school, physical and emotional health, money, friendships and future goals. The equivalent scene, in which a father sits down to have a "man-to-woman" talk with his daughter, is unfamiliar for the simple reason that it does not happen often. According to Ronald J. Burke and Tamara Weir, who conducted a study with 273 young women, "Unfortunately, it appears that the father-adolescent helping relationship often remains undeveloped or, at best, evolves haphazardly."

One result of this is reported by Dr. Henry Biller in his book *Paternal Deprivation*: divorces, separations and unhappy marriages are much higher in women who have had poor interactions with inadequate fathers.

FOUR

SEPARATION

EIGHTEEN

BREAKING AWAY

At a shower Donna gave for a friend some years ago, the women guests were all in their mid-twenties. The conversation turned to a discussion of fathers, and the general tone was amused exasperation. At one point Donna said, "You all seem to feel that your fathers in one way or another are a problem to you. Why should they be? You're no longer dependent on them. You have lives of your own. If they're a problem, why bother with them?"

Every woman present had a different answer. Only a few felt they had a really satisfactory relationship with their father. The group discussion seemed to bear out the comment by the celebrated wit Oscar Wilde: "Children begin by loving their parents. After a time they judge them. Rarely do they ever forgive them."

The majority of the group agreed with a young woman who was the mother of two children: "As a girl, I always used to think my father cared about me because he tried so hard to be understanding and knew me so well he could give me good advice. He was practical and down-to-earth, and he saw things with a perspective I found very helpful because he'd lived longer than I had. I don't mean he wasn't a pest at times, because he was. But there was no one I'd turn to sooner if I was in trouble.

"Now it's all become glib and superficial. He only wants to hear that I'm well and happy. If I complain, he shrugs and says, 'Well, that's life.' He worries more about the children than about me. I'm not his daughter anymore; *they're* his children. He'd like to be a father to them, but he can't because my husband won't let him.

"I thought when I was grown up we could meet on an equal basis, but that isn't how he wants it to be."

However, the group discussion did arrive at a sort of consensus. In Donna's words: "We agreed that a father stands for an alternative life-style, and a daughter bounces against it. If she didn't have him to bounce against, she would have to invent someone just like him. She has to be against something in order to know what she's for."

In order to know if she is making an autonomous decision or merely acting in accordance with her father's wishes, a daughter can use a simple litmus test: Is her choice or decision reversible?

The case history of a young woman of nineteen who discovered she had a medical problem provides an apt illustration. For a while she passed off occasional dizzy spells as nothing important, either stress or hypochondria. She had been studying hard for exams at the end of her sophomore year at Cornell, which could have accounted for the stress. Her mother had for years suffered from a long series of imaginary afflictions, and this supported the case for a diagnosis of inherited hypochondria.

Nevertheless, the young woman's dizziness persisted, and one morning in the mirror she noticed a pulsing at the corner of her mouth. Shortly thereafter another pulse began beating visibly in her temple. She called her father. "I don't want to worry you," she began, feeling as she spoke the words something very close to terror. Her father was authoritative. "I want you on the first train you can get out of there. Don't drive under any circumstances. I'll call our doctor and he'll have a look at you."

When the doctor examined her he did not think there was a serious condition, but he suggested she undergo a more thorough examination by a neurologist. By the time the neurologist examined her, she had a new symptom. The entire front of her head felt ice-cold and she had trouble coordinating her arm and leg movement. The neurologist gave a tentative diagnosis of a brain tumor. He suggested exploratory surgery, which he could schedule for the following week.

They went home, terribly shaken and depressed. Her mother was adamantly opposed to an operation. She did not believe her daughter had anything seriously wrong with her. "How could she? She's so young!" Anyway, who was this neurologist? What did they know about him? Their doctor had recommended him, but what did he know?

They agreed to seek a second opinion. She was not to worry, her father told her, he would handle this problem for her. She was relieved to have the decision taken out of her hands.

They got a second opinion from a kindly older surgeon who tried to calm her fears which were almost as palpable as the pulsing at her mouth corner and temple. He told her that if there were a brain tumor, it was most unlikely to be malignant. The operation would be simple, a penetration far enough to remove the lump and then a biopsy. Yes, there would be a scar but her hair would cover that.

Meanwhile, she had done a lot of reading on her own and had talked again with the family doctor. He was opposed to surgery except in a case of absolute necessity. There were dangers involved in general anesthesia and in complications from surgery. He told her, "A real emergency hasn't been established. Your symptoms haven't gone away but they haven't gotten worse either. And neither surgeon seems quite sure what the trouble is."

She carefully weighed the risks against the gains, and decided to postpone the operation. Her father exploded. She wasn't old enough to know what she was doing. Two eminent surgeons had agreed an operation was needed. He would not allow her to risk her life by ignoring what they told her. At one point, he actually told her, "That's enough! You're going to do it *my* way!"

She refused to have an operation. She was willing to challenge her father's authority because on her side was her family doctor, whom she trusted, the fact that no one had a clear idea of what her condition was and her own intuition that her ailment was not that serious.

She went off to New Hampshire to a lakeside resort where there was nothing much for her to do but relax and read. One morning she woke up and the dizzy spells had gone; so had the pulsing at her mouth corner and temple and the other symptoms. The problem, her family doctor assured her, must have been stress or some unknown malady—possibly a virus—that had run its course.

If she had been a daddy's girl who accepted what he told her in order not to offend, the ending would have been less happy. Because she was able to defy his disapproval, because she was capable of *reversing* herself, she was spared an unpleasant episode. Even if the eventual outcome had been that surgery *was* needed, she would have had the comfort of knowing it was her decision to submit to the risks.

I have watched with interest the struggles of young women to break free of paternal authority. Several months ago Donna sat up with a friend who was packing to move from her father's home to a small apartment in Cazenovia, New York, not far from Syracuse. The friend told Donna that her father, with whom she had been living for six years since her mother's death, was very disturbed at her departure.

"All the time I've been packing, he's been taking old stuff out of the attic and basement for me to take. Stuffed animals and picture books and a toy phonograph that plays stories and songs from *Mother Goose.* I know what he's doing. He's reminding me that I'm his little girl.

"Life hasn't been very happy at home for the last year. We're always arguing over trifles. I see him steadily losing patience with me. Why won't I *listen* anymore? My God, I've listened to him for twenty-four years! Isn't it time to listen to myself?

"He isn't prepared to let go, not yet. He reminds me how much he's given up for my happiness—how he's always given me priority over his work, his interests, not only paid my bills but even washed and ironed my clothes. It's true, but what can I do about it? When he says, 'All I want is for you to be happy,' I want to say, 'That's all I want too!'

"There's another side he doesn't mention. I don't want to hurt him by bringing it up. He's always after me about something—pushing, prodding, nagging, ridiculing—always telling me what to do. There is so much conflict between us. I go into the bathroom sometimes and put my face in a basinful of water so I can scream out my anger. I go around with clenched teeth, muttering under my breath, *'For God's sake, leave me alone!'* During the last year everything has been heavy between us. I've already left him. Moving out is just the final act."

After several months I asked Donna to interview her again to find out how the separation from her father is working. The interview took place in a small apartment which she now shares with a roommate. A framed photograph of her mother was on the table, and for the first hour she talked only about her late mother.

"I have such good memories of her. She was one of those dedicated women—president of the PTA, a big fund raiser for charity, even a five-handicap golfer. I don't understand how she had time to be a mother. But somehow she did."

"How are you getting along with your father?" Donna asked.

"When he isn't being indifferent he's hostile. I can't talk to him. When we meet it's just be quiet, listen to him, the big authority. If he says so, that's it. My birthday went by without a card or a gift. Our phone calls are only a few minutes long. I was thinking about him the other night and it's hard to believe we were ever close. I try to remember things about him that I loved but bad memories keep coming up. I'm doing better on my own. He's an empty space in my life."

Separations often acquire a momentum of their own and go on to a stage of true alienation.

A middle-aged father's story illustrates what happens when the desire for separation becomes too intense. "When my daughter was growing up she was very affectionate to me and her mother. Her mother wasn't a well woman and my daughter did everything to help around the house and be a nurse to her also. Then my wife died. That's when I began having trouble. I was trying to look after a daughter who was sixteen and hold down a full-time job. My daughter wasn't any help to me at all. Just the opposite. She let the house get as dirty as a pigpen and began to run around with a wild bunch. I tried to put my foot down to stop the way she was carrying on, but she just laughed at me.

"Her mother had brought her up with a decent set of morals, but she was changing into somebody I couldn't recognize. I tried everything to discipline her, but she just got worse. 'Off my back,' she'd warn me. 'I've got my own life to live.' Finally she took off and went to Chicago. I found out later she was doing nude modeling for art classes. She got her nude picture in *Playboy* magazine.

"Around that time the doctor told me I had to quit my job. It was too strenuous for my bad heart. I didn't have any money saved—my wife's illness had wiped me out—and I was in bad shape. I hadn't heard from my daughter in months, no letters, no phone calls. She never gave me her unlisted phone number. I wrote her, telling her I could use help. Weeks went by and I got a short little note saying she was sorry but she wasn't able to do anything for me. Then I got a bad attack and spent a while in the hospital. I asked the doctor to let her know how bad off I was. He wrote to her and she called him up and yelled at him for interfering in her life.

"When I got out of the hospital I had nothing but welfare to keep me going. They evicted me from my apartment and sold off the furniture for debts. I was desperate. Finally I got her unlisted number and called. It was late at night and I heard some kind of party going on. I pleaded with her to give me a stake, enough money so I could get to a better climate and build up my strength. She told me she didn't believe in children hanging on to their parents or vice versa. I begged her. Then she got mad. 'I don't care if you drop dead in the street and they cart you away with the rubbish. I don't want to hear from you anymore, and I'm not sending you any money. Find somebody else to leech on!'

"I don't understand what happened. I never was bad to her that I can remember. She treats me like I was her worst enemy. I don't think she has any feeling for her own father!"

I tried to interview the young woman to get her side of this story, but she threatened to sue if we used her name or described her in a way that she could be identified. I changed a few details of her father's background and her own, although the essentials of the narrative remain.

Without knowing her motivation one is left with only the father's version, in which she appears to have acted in an uncaring, even vicious manner. It would be easy to let this stand as an example of a daughter's desire to separate that went beyond permissible parameters and became an act of revenge against her father. But there is a note of self-pity in the father's account that makes one question how much of a "leech" he may have been.

For the purposes of example, however, this true case history illustrates how a daughter's intense need for separation can vanquish normal feeling toward a loving parent.

Anger also shows itself in unexpected ways, in actions that appear unfathomable to those who don't know the history of the relationship.

A well-known magazine writer worked hard, writing articles by day and laboring on his books at night. He was determined to write books that would give him a "little piece of immortality," an obsession that left him no time for his family.

When his daughter grew up she became interested in the business side of publishing. She worked herself into a high administrative position at the publishing firm that published her father's books, his "little pieces of immortality." By now he was retired, comfortably off, writing only occasional essays for erudite journals. His years of "achievement" were over, but he felt he had done well; there was an audience that remembered him.

A decision came up at the publishing firm about whether his older, slow-selling books should be kept in print. The editorial board decided that two or three of the books should be "retired" from their list. To their surprise, his daughter argued in favor of letting all his books go out of print. In the end that is what happened. This has been cited as proof of what a hardheaded young businesswoman she is. There is, however, another explanation: she was declaring her neglectful father to be obsolete.

A young woman whose father was flagrantly adulterous uses this as an excuse for her own promiscuity. "What would you expect from the daughter of a father like that?" is her attitude. A therapist suggested that her real motive is to punish her father. Having watched her over some years, I am convinced her therapist is right. Her problem is not with imitating her father, but with trying to punish him.

The daughter of a talented musician who is a nearly hopeless alcoholic also became a heavy drinker. She believed she was reliving her father's pattern. What she was actually doing was making him suffer by "proving" she had inherited his addiction. The drinking problem was hers, and could only be cured by her. I am happy to say that for the past three years she has been a member of Alcoholics Anonymous and is no longer drinking. She has recognized that her father's self-destructive behavior does not have to influence her adult behavior. The vengeful child in her who wanted to pay her father back is no longer in control.

Dr. Stella Chase quotes a woman: "My father refused to take me seriously. It made me doubt myself for a long time. And any time I saw myself getting into the clutches of some guy, I was scared to death he would destroy me too. For ten years after I left home, whenever I began to feel serious about a boy, I ran like hell. I was terrified of getting into that bind again."

In interviewing thirty women about life with father, Dr. Chase discovered that the majority did not remember their fathers with "unqualified affection and joy." Most recalled themselves as little girls adoring fathers whose attention and love they were never sure of having.

Almost without exception, however, fathers remember the early years with their daughters as a magical time. In a few instances I encountered a father who had become estranged from his daughter (in two cases the daughter had taken the mother's side in divorce hearings), but he held fast to the conviction that all had been idyllic when his daughter was younger. A recurrent theme was that daughter's leaving home directly resulted in an increase in marital problems. "As long as she was there I felt my marriage was worth fighting for. When she left it all changed for the worse. Looking back, I'd have to say she was all that my wife and I still had in common."

Edith Wharton, in her brilliant story "The Mission of Jane," tells of a clever cynical man married to a not very bright woman. After years of shallow marital existence, his wife decides to adopt a baby girl. Mrs. Wharton traces what follows with the unsparing, knowing eye of the true artist. At first, the husband finds his wife so occupied with the new baby girl that "he perceived that she no longer saw him, that he had become as invisible to her as she had been to him." When their daughter reaches childhood he becomes the one who "was to educate Jane." The more Jane learns, the more she is estranged from her not very bright mother. And the father comes to dislike Jane's sharp and shrewish ways. After a time she acquires a suitor, marries and leaves the home. The husband and wife share an immense feeling of relief. "Jane had fulfilled her mission after all; she had drawn them together at last."

Mrs. Wharton anticipated the discoveries of social scientists, first in the baby's attachment to mother, second in the child's attachment to father, then his role in educating her in the ways of the world and, last, in her portrayal of the final stages of separation.

A forty-nine-year-old man sheds a revealing light on separation from a father's point of view: "I really was crazy about all my kids and especially my little girl. I was a sucker for her. She was the youngest and everything she did was okay, just fine. She didn't get marks in school, that was all right, marks didn't matter. She didn't want to help her mother with the housework, okay too. She was my little queen. It was like that all her life. Then she went off and married this jerk she has to do everything for and treats her just like anybody. And she's crazy about him. I never hear from her. When she had a baby all I got was a postcard."

Donna's interview with the daughter is equally revealing: "Dad fussed over me a lot but I never got any attention. I mean he never saw me as a person. To him, I was a charming little doll he liked to play with. Part of the decoration of the house. I don't remember ever having a discussion with him about anything important. If it was up to him, I'd still be living like I was eight years old."

The contrasting viewpoints of father and daughter reminds one of the movie *Rashomon* in which an episode is related by several different principals, each of whom sees it in an entirely different way. Who is telling the truth? Is there any definite, ascertainable truth?

The variance in testimony resolves itself into a question of interpretation. For example, what is the meaning of a comparatively simple term such as "affection"? The father who professes himself to be "crazy" about his daughter and a "sucker for her" thinks he is proving his affection by giving her "anything she wanted." She was his "little queen," and he cannot understand why she would jilt him in the end for a man who "treats her just like anybody."

For his daughter, however, real affection would be better demonstrated by his treating her not as a "charming little doll" or "part of the decoration of the house." She did not want to play the role he assigned to her. In the process of rejecting the role, she rejected her father also.

"What she wanted was to stand on my own two feet," a successful businessman remarked about his twenty-two-year-old daughter. "She wanted me to give her a job when she got out of college, but I've got a rule in my business: no relatives, no friends, are hired. That's the rule. I couldn't go out of my way to make an exception for her. She had to do for herself. I gave her a fine education and supported her for more than twenty years. It was time to call quits."

True separation implies freedom from obligation, and that applies equally to a father. The end of nurturing frees the nurturer too. However, most fathers do not think in terms of reducing their commitment to a daughter after separation. They still feel they owe her the kind of paternal looking after that fostered her childhood dependency.

A young research scientist in Purdue, Indiana, concerned about the skyrocketing costs of college tuition, gave up a well-paying job with an industrial firm to accept a much lower paying position as a college instructor. Why? Because the position with the college entitled his three daughters to nearly free college educations.

His income as a teacher will never reach the level of his income working in industry, nor will he have the same challenge or opportunity for advancement. This may not bother him now because being relieved of the financial burden of paying for three college educations makes up the difference. But how will he feel later when his daughters have completed their education and left home? Will he regret sacrificing his own prospects in order to give them a start in life?

A college education for children is often regarded as a proof of paternal power. "My father thought he had to get all his kids through to a bachelor degree at least," says a woman who is the eldest of three children. "He was like all the other middle and upper class fathers in the town in Ohio where we grew up. He never asked the important questions, like would we benefit from a college education. Or did we have any real aptitude for learning. It so happens I did have, but my brother didn't. He wanted to join the Navy. He went to college but didn't benefit from it. In a way it detoured him. Now he works in a shipyard. My sister, the youngest, is in her junior year at college. She was going steady with a nice young man. I think she'd have been happier marrying him and settling down to raise a family. Now her young man claims that she's getting 'snobby' because she's in college and he's not. I don't know if they will get married. I'd feel easier if Dad had allowed her to make her own choice.

"Dad expects us to be grateful for the sacrifices he made to send us to college. But what he did wasn't for us, it was for him. Well and good, but I don't think it's right for him to use his 'sacrifice' as a way to make us do everything he wants."

At the point where true dependency diminishes, a daughter can maintain the illusion of dependency only by a sacrifice of her integrity. The goals she wishes to pursue, the quality of her performance, even her ability to acquire valuable new contacts, must be trimmed, altered and reduced if she maintains a tie to her father based on an increasingly false premise.

"All I want is for you to be happy," father says, pretending to accept the inevitable. He lies. What he wants is for his daughter to continue making *him* happy.

I recall when Donna left home for college. One day she was a little girl leaping up and running to me for a hug and a kiss, spilling over with the "faery power of unreflecting love." Suddenly that little girl was nowhere to be found except in memory and old photographs. There is no salve a father can put on that wound.

How is a father to behave when his daughter goes, not only out of his house but out of his life, out of everything but his heart?

Whenever I thought about Donna getting married it was an event in the undefinable future, nothing to worry about now: something like death. She dated several different young men in college and I was pleased that she was popular, especially since she had had to endure four years in the boyless society of an all-girls high school. If someone had asked me to describe the sort of man she would eventually marry, he would have turned out to be my clone.

I was only vaguely aware of her first significant interest in a young man. Usually we discussed such epochal events at length, but I was several thousand miles away when the affair underwent its first crisis. "Where were you?" Donna cried over the telephone.

I knew that romance would come to a bad end. He didn't appreciate her; her sweetness was wasted on his desert air. I didn't even resent him, because his failings so obviously emphasized my virtues. He did not have, nor could he have, my special communication with Donna.

Shortly after, Donna moved to Los Angeles to study for her master's degree at the University of California at Los Angeles. My wife and I followed. Donna and I began to see each other frequently. She came to dinner at our apartment, we went to parties in her Westwood cubicle. We lunched alone at her favorite hangouts—the pizza place that showed old movies for free, the attractive little Swedish place with mezzanine and grilled railing that served delicious cheese fondues. I heard about the young men who came and went in her life. I tolerated them; I defended them indulgently against the shortcomings Donna perceived. Only fathers are perfect.

Donna went to New York for the Christmas holidays to visit her mother. The return flight to Los Angeles was delayed until three o'clock in the morning, Pacific coast time. Nevertheless, we met the plane. In the hurly-burly of getting her luggage in the milling crowd, she introduced me to a young man she had met on the plane. Pleasant, spectacled, blond. Not her type. As we drove back to her Westwood apartment, she told us her mother had brashly singled the young man out and asked him to look after her on the plane flight. Tsk. *Mother.*

The pleasant young blond man tracked her down, although he knew only her first name and the school she was attending. I should have guessed from that. Persistence wins fair lady. When they began dating we made a convivial foursome—Donna and Richard, Joanna and me. Not for a moment did I feel I was losing her. I had accepted her independence, her right to exist apart from me, and I did not foresee that there was a further step in separation: another man would usurp my position and priority.

When they began living together Donna did not discuss the pros and cons with me. (She interjects that she certainly did discuss it with me. "You *forget*," she says.)

Perhaps the reason I don't remember is that I still did not take seriously Richard's intrusion into our special relationship. I clearly remember the afternoon when she told me she was sure Richard would propose to her that evening. It was the first anniversary of their meeting, he had made reservations for dinner at their favorite restaurant, and "You know how romantic he is." For the first time, the prospect of her marrying began to take on reality for me.

A telephone call came the next day and Richard formally asked for my daughter's hand in marriage. We both laughed at the formality, but I think Richard chose this method of signaling a return to old-fashioned virtue. Donna told me later that Richard thought I took the news in stride: "Really unflappable," he said.

Not so; I was flapping. Would Donna still seek my counsel and support, would I still get from her the assurances of admiration and love that had for so many years fed my self-esteem? Would meeting her from now on as a married woman be as much fun, or would it unbind us, would there be a drifting apart? Her husband, capable of passing judgment on me, might begin to make his influence felt. The power to judge is the power to destroy.

My fears have not been realized, although I am aware that she needs me less; but I still need her to need me.

My wife is younger than I by twenty-three years, young enough to be my daughter. When anyone tells me how beautiful she is—and she is—I glow with as much fatherly as uxorial pride.

My real daughter is married. I can no longer accept compliments for her.

NINETEEN

PARTING

When my father entered his sixties I began to notice he wasn't aging well," says a married woman with two children. "Nothing ailed him, but he looked a lot older. I couldn't bear to watch the change in him. His gums had shrunk and he wouldn't go to a dentist about the fact that his dentures had worked loose. He became terribly cranky, sent back food in restaurants two or three times. In company he told unfunny jokes and people pretended to laugh, but they were really laughing at him. I wanted to sink through the floor with embarrassment."

An aging father can be a burden. There are also unexpected feelings of desertion: the hidden emotional dialogue that contributed so much to a daughter's growing-up years is no longer available. The aging father is no longer to be resisted, he is merely to be cared for. Hard choices loom ahead, particularly if father is the surviving parent. Should he be allowed to live alone? Can a daughter make a place for him in her home without causing problems for her husband and children? Can she persuade him to join a retirement home, a senior community, even a nursing home? Who will pay for the extra expense?

"When I was a child I had no clear idea of how old my parents were," says a twenty-seven-year-old woman. "To a child, everyone over thirty seems old and the difference between thirty and forty, or even fifty, is not apparent. When I was a teenager my parents seemed about the same as everyone else's. By the time I was twenty-five I knew the difference, because my father was at least ten years older than any other parent I knew.

"Once I had to take him to a hospital for an examination and the nurses thought he was my grandfather, not my father. My mother had died and there was no one else to look after him. I had to check home every day to see if he was eating or sleeping enough; he grew dependent on me for everything. I resented it, because at the same time I had to deal with the concerns of my job and my husband and small son, aged three. It was pretty time-consuming. I had no time to be a parent to my father. I wondered why he couldn't have had me earlier. Why did he wait until he was in his mid-forties? There wasn't enough time between my growing up and his becoming dependent on me."

A woman executive says, "I usually go to quite fashionable restaurants, where I am well known. When my father, a widower who lives in another state, visited me I took him to one of my favorite places. During dinner he used his napkin to wipe off the silverware. When I asked him what he thought he was doing he replied, 'You can't be too careful when you're eating out.' I gave him money to pay the bill because I didn't want to embarrass him. He undertipped terribly. I saw how the waiter looked. Not only that, he took an ashtray from the restaurant for a souvenir. I'll never be able to go back to that place again!

"Later I took him on a shopping tour to get him some badly needed clothing. At every stop he struck up a conversation with the salesclerk about what an important woman I was, what an important job I had. Then he would supply a little of our family history. I pleaded with him to cut out the personal talk, but he wouldn't. At each store he'd launch into the same tiresome routine. Those people couldn't care less! It made me feel foolish!"

The inversion of the roles of dependent and protector has a special poignance. During her adolescence he gave her rules to live by; now she must impose rules on him. He tried to keep her close to him by refusing to let her grow up; now she has to grow up in a hurry and become his protector.

She becomes alert to any symptom that might portend something alarming. If he complains of indigestion or has a pain under his breastbone, is it gallbladder or something worse? She nags him about his diet and about getting enough exercise and rest. One forty-year-old woman even took up golf so she could get her sixty-four-year-old father to play with her!

A daughter who sees the "strong man" reduced to a point where he cannot perform his usual functions may find herself in conflict with a mother who does not play a meaningful enough role in this sad scenario.

"When my father lost his job because he was getting old he became very depressed and my mother wasn't too sympathetic," a young woman recounts. "Basically she seemed to feel that Dad ought to 'buck up' and 'pull himself together' and 'make a new start.' She couldn't stand the idea that he was willing to accept old age. It was almost as if that reflected discredit on her. Maybe she was worried old age would overtake her too, because of the way he was acting."

Donna and I talked with young women whose fathers had become dependent because of a physical affliction (a stroke), a debilitating disease (nephritis), an accident resulting in an amputation of a leg, and a nervous breakdown that resulted in what the daughter referred to as a "psychic collapse." In addition, we interviewed two daughters whose father had suffered what was euphemistically called a "personality disorder," involving addiction to alcohol and to heroin. In all instances, the daughter's first task was to break off connections with anyone who might be contributing to his inability to cope. This included separating him from sources of tension and anxiety, such as other members of the family and friends and associates who might be adding to his emotional instability. Daughter functioned as either a persecutor or a rescuer, often alternating these roles with her mother. Their former competition for dad's affection was subordinated to the necessities of the immediate crisis.

One wife and daughter who were caring for a father (the victim of nephritis) went so far as to ban any contact with the rest of his family, including his mother, sister and brother. The daughter explained to them that their visits and phone calls were "having a bad effect," and that "Dad doesn't really need anyone but us." When her decision was challenged she persuaded her stricken father to give them the same message.

The daughter who described her father as having a "psychic collapse" blamed job-related anxieties. She prohibited visits from business associates who insisted on talking about what was "going on at the office," even though the reports were humorous and intended to keep her father's mind off his troubles. She felt they might be a conduit back to the source of his anxiety.

Somewhat similar was the problem of the young daughter who was trying to deal with an alcoholic father. "I got him to join A.A., but his friends were always inviting him to have a drink. They either didn't believe he had a sickness or didn't care. I put him on a strict allowance but he continued to cadge drinks from friends who thought they were being good guys by staking him. When everything dried up he borrowed from his brother, my uncle. I found out what was happening and went to my uncle and asked him to stop. He told me he couldn't, 'I can't say no to him. When we were kids, he never said no to me.'

"After that I realized I couldn't rely on anyone else to help. Looking after Dad became my responsibility."

A woman of twenty-four, who is married and has a young son, took her father in to live with her. He is fifty-eight years old and ailing with Parkinson's disease. She says, "After the way he looked after me, this is the least I can do for him." Her mother was institutionalized when the daughter was only ten years old. "Dad could have sent me away to a boarding school but he never did. He wasn't a big earner but he made sure I had nice clothes and a nice place to live. Whenever I wanted anything he dug deep in his pocket to come up with his last pennies. I didn't find out until a few years ago that he put off a needed hernia operation so I could have braces. I wore them until I was eleven, God knows how he paid for them and for the regular examinations by the orthodontist.

"It was a proud day of my life when I could afford to help him. I thought of it as a little down payment on what I owe him. Then he got this terrible disease; it's progressive and he can't get better. I want him with me. My husband understands how I feel. Dad isn't going to recover and this arrangement isn't forever. When I think of how much my dad did for me, what I'm doing is little enough. He had two jobs at one time. Worked practically day and night to support his family. Never a day off. But I never lacked for anything. I'll never turn my back on that man."

This new phase of the relationship between father and daughter requires major adjustments. For daughter, there is a heightened sense of how little time she and he will continue to share.

"Since my mother died, all Dad wants to do is reminisce," a novelist tells us. "At the end Mother had begun to look like a small bird, with a beaked nose and wisps of gray hair. But Dad remembers her as she looked in the photograph of their wedding he keeps in a prominent place on the mantel. He tells me endless stories about how they met, their courtship and marriage, how my brother was born during a snowstorm when the roads were blocked and the doctor couldn't come.

"He speaks about my brother as though he were alive, although he was killed in Vietnam. He's alive in my father's memory just as Mother is. He has no one else to tell his stories to, so I listen although I've heard them dozens of times.

"He used to come and stay in our spare room for a weekend. Now the spare room is rarely empty. He moves into it and stays for a month or more. He isn't aware that he is interrupting lives in progress. He wants to sit and talk. He comes to the kitchen early in the morning when I'm still getting the children off to school. His hair is rumpled and he looks distraught; the nights are bad because when the memories come he has no one to tell them to.

"I try to help him plan for the future, but he can't. Oh, he says he will, but tonight—tonight the spare room is waiting. He goes to sleep with a small portable television set on, and I sneak into his room and tune the set down so the noise won't wake the children.

"There was always a spare room in my parents' house when I was a child. It used to be my room as a child. My brother's bedroom was long since converted into a storeroom for old magazines and pattern books, and it's where Mother kept her sewing machine. My parents liked it when I came to stay in my old room during college vacations.

"It is easier for me to think of myself as an adult than to behave like one when I'm around him. Father brings out the little girl in me. When I'm with him I still have long curls and bows in my hair. It's hard to accept the image that looks back at me from the mirror. I am my father's daughter, but the father who sleeps in my spare room is a stranger to me.

"He is seventy-three. I wish my husband and children could have known him as he was when I was a child. He knew how to make me laugh and to make my tears go away. When a pet turtle died he took an empty cigar box and lined it with felt and laid out the poor dead thing in it. We had a proper funeral in our back yard. Only the funeral didn't go quite as expected. In the middle of it, the turtle came to life and started crawling out of the cigar box.

"He can't bend over to tie his shoes anymore and I have to tie them for him. He is stiff with arthritis and doesn't loosen up until past noon. His recreation is walking in the neighborhood, looking at familiar landmarks being torn down or replaced.

"Yesterday I was baking a pie when he wandered into the kitchen. 'I love that smell,' he said. 'It reminds me of home. Don't you miss home?' He isn't aware that this is my home. He is a visitor whose former life is more real to him than the one he is living now.

"Tonight he will sleep restlessly in the bed in our spare room. And tomorrow? He will come into the kitchen at some inconvenient time wanting to talk. He will pull up a chair close to where I am working and start telling me a story I've heard many times before. And I will try to be patient, for he is not only my father, he is a child in my house."

When a father becomes dependent the process of separation, which is founded in emotion and not in physical proximity, continues apace. His daughter cannot regard him as her guardian and protector, and she is more consciously aware that she lives a separate life.

In any situation involving living persons the variety of possible interactions is beyond description. We can identify certain kinds of "childlike" and "adult" behavior, discern certain social tendencies, but we cannot confine individuals within a category. A daughter does not have a single identity as "daughter," nor does her father as "father." Neither is caught in a freeze frame of gesture and response; they live within a continual flux and shifting where individuals keep on making new and unexpected connections. To pretend that they are inert specimens on a laboratory table is as foolish as trying to take a fish out of water to discover how it swims.

The final reckoning comes with death. "After my father died I couldn't sleep alone," says a twenty-two-year-old woman. "If I wasn't spending the night with anyone, I'd sit up as late as I could, watching television, playing solitaire, doing anything until I was tired enough to go to sleep. I tried pills, but they made me dopey the whole next day. I always kept a lamp on in the bedroom and a light in the hallway. I imagined all sorts of terrible things lurking in the darkness, just as I did when I was a little girl and Daddy came in to comfort me and assure me that the phantoms weren't real. Sometimes I would wake up in the middle of the night with an overwhelming feeling of being in a dark void, cut off from everyone, unable to make contact, just drifting away into a terrible blackness."

F. Scott Fitzgerald called that feeling the "dark midnight of the soul," and it is an emotion closely associated with death, either one's own or that of a loved one.

"I had hardly seen my father for two years before his death," a woman remarked to Donna during an interview. "But somehow I always knew he was there, that I could pick up a telephone and call him. I didn't see him as much because he had married another woman after he divorced my mother, and our lives went in different directions. But when he died the knowledge that there was nowhere, absolutely nowhere on earth that I could go to find him was devastating. A week after he died I became engaged to a man I'd only been dating a few weeks. I don't think I'd have done that if Dad had still been alive. I felt so rudderless, so alone..."

The inner voice of the dependent child is still speaking through the lips of a grown woman.

A woman who visited her father's home shortly after his death wrote this moving account: "I came to the little room he used as his library, his hiding place where he could go to read. How mysterious this room seemed to me then! It was like some secret spring from which he drew all the marvelous energy that made him the center of my world. The room had his presence, the album that held his stamp collection, a book he had been reading with a leather bookmark dividing the pages. On the walls were family pictures; himself as a younger man with his growing family (seven of us altogether), the shelves lined with books, the record player with the stacks of his favorite albums nearby. Over there was his battered green recliner beneath the huge ancient floor lamp with the enormous shade. Looking at these things I wondered if he ever knew how much we all loved him, his generous sweet nature, his humor, his honesty, his freedom from jealousy or from anything cruel or mean. The only times I saw him angry were when someone was trying to take advantage of the weak and helpless. With a pang I realized how much I would miss him. I'll never be able to relate to any man the way I did to my father."

"I was always a little ashamed of my father," a young woman confessed. "He was definitely of the 'lower class,' and my mother never tired of saying she had married beneath her. She met my father on a trip to the old Freedomland amusement park in New York. He was employed with the maintenance crew.

"Mother always said she was attracted to him because he was the brawny muscular type and a contrast to her father, who was a cripple. From the time I was five or six, I already knew I was supposed to look down at my father. He read tabloid newspapers and girlie magazines. He smoked cheap cigars and drank beer and had a poker night and a bowling night. He watched the kind of television shows that were in the top twenty, and he especially liked westerns and cop shows that were popular then. He had poor table manners.

"I guess he tried to be a good father. I remember him bare-chested and hairy at the beach carrying me on his shoulders into the water while I squealed with delight. He was very physical, very strong. I never thought of him as die-able. He was killed in an accident with a high tension wire. Electrocuted.

"I went with my mother to the hospital and we attended to all the details of the funeral. I felt a heavy numbness, not grief exactly. A year later, when my mother remarried, I became fond of my stepfather, a very nice man. I would have told anyone that I had made a good adjustment to my father's death. I could no longer get a clear image of what he looked like. Only scattered memories, like his lifting me in his arms or carrying me on his shoulders at the beach.

"When I was nineteen I went into a bad depression and had to see a shrink. He became interested in the fact that I couldn't remember anything about my father. He said I couldn't forget my father so quickly. He asked, 'Did he love you?' All of a sudden I couldn't see, my eyes were so full of tears. I don't remember anything else that he said. I suffered a real emotional blackout. The next thing I knew I was in Santa Monica, near the pier, almost four miles from his office. I was walking on the beach. I hadn't the faintest idea how I got there. I called the shrink the next day and told him I couldn't see him anymore. He told me that would be a bad mistake, I had real emotional problems to work through, and he wanted to help me find the answers. Finally I promised to go back if he wouldn't talk about my father. That was one closet I didn't want to open because I couldn't cope with what might come out.

"But I brought up the subject myself. I told him all I remembered about my father and asked if he thought someone like that could be a good father. He said it was wrong to label anyone 'good' or 'bad,' that my father was a human being with contradictory qualities like all of us have.

"I began to realize I'd been making a judgment about my father based on only a few things that were not really important. What was important was that he loved me and tried his best to be good to me. There must have been many times I hurt his feelings, but he never showed it.

"Memories started coming back. My father continually smoked at meals and my mother couldn't stand it. She worked up a scheme with me and told me exactly what I should say. The next time he lit up a cigar at the table and the battle started, Mother said he was setting a bad example for me, that I hated it but was afraid to tell him so. I told him I couldn't stand the smell of his cigar smoke. "Well, then, what we've got is a case of whose rights take first place,' he said. "The fair thing is for me to give up smoking at dinner and for you to stand it at other times. Does that sound fair?' That was no stupid man. He had respect for his own rights as well as ours and didn't insist on having his way.

"Then I remembered that other people—including my mother's brother—always spoke of my father as solid and steady-going. I used to think that meant he wasn't too bright—at least not bright enough for Mother. But that couldn't have been what they meant. Because I remember my mother's brother telling her that men like my father didn't have 'thinking quickness,' but that didn't mean they weren't intelligent or couldn't make good sound judgments.

"Other things came back. I remembered as a snippety young girl telling him off for something he'd done. He didn't resent it as he had a right to do. He just listened to me treating him like a fool, and finally a slow smile spread over his face. He said, 'Well, I guess the trouble is you haven't stood where I have.'

"And there was the time Mother sent me to my room as punishment at the end of an argument. I remember stamping my feet, sobbing, 'I hate you. I hate you all!' I sat in the bedroom promising myself never, never to make up with anyone who lived in the house again. Suddenly a paper airplane sailed into the room. I picked it up and my father had printed on it in crude letters, *Nobody here hates you*. It was signed, *Love, Dad*.

"I was telling the shrink some of these things and how I had never cried for my father after he was dead, never shared the grief of others who had less reason to care. I asked him why that was, and he said, 'I think you loved him and it was too hard for you to think about his being dead.'

"I cried for my father then. It was too late for tears to do any good but, oh, how I cried."

What is notable in these true stories is that the daughter was not granted an opportunity to complete the full transition to independence within her father's lifetime. She was suspended in quasifreedom, unable to be dependent on a father who was dead and unable to be free of him. In the Orthodox Jewish religion, the shoes of the departed are cut up and thrown into the sea so the soul will not wander endlessly. But it is more likely to be the survivor whose soul wanders endlessly in search of emotional release.

The problem is more complicated when death is sudden. Edwin Shneidman, professor of thanatology at the University of California at Los Angeles, says: "Unexpected death of the beloved, whether due to heart attack, assassination, suicide, automobile or airplane accident, catches people with their psyches down."

Sudden death deprives a daughter of the time she needs to disengage her feelings. "In the midst of life we are in death," warns the Bible, but the Holy Book provides no guidelines on how a survivor should deal with the shock. In self-defense the psyche reacts by denying the tragedy. The usual reaction is to say, "Tell me it isn't true!"

"Denial becomes your chief mechanism at this point," says Anne Rosberger, executive director of Manhattan's Bereavement and Loss Center. Denial is needed to carry the survivor across the unbearable, overwhelming, abrupt transition into the "psychic numbness" which is the next stage of mourning.

The period of psychic numbness lasts from two to six months, during which a defensive pattern is erected against the destructive impact of grief. Then begins a process of healing that takes a different course for each individual. The full period of mourning is said to last about two years, although the schedule obviously varies with circumstances. Emotions born of loss, premature separation, guilt, anger, loneliness and pain are slowly absorbed into the daughter's life history.

In a rare instance, a daughter may become locked into one of the earlier stages of recuperation. The result is an inability to form deep emotional attachments, bouts of irrationality, a tendency toward combativeness and even violence. The most common reaction of all is a deep continuing depression which cannot be treated with the drugs effective in combatting other forms of depression.

"I wait by the window sometimes and look out. We live near a subway station and it's busy at rush hour. There's a lot of people rushing by. I just look at them. My mother came to me while I was sitting at the window and said, "He won't come back, dear. He can't.' That's the first time I knew who I was looking for."

The speaker is a depressed 16-year-old girl whose father died of cancer six months earlier.

Dr. David V. Forrest, who, as a combat psychiatrist in Vietnam, treated many cases of "survivor guilt" among soldiers who lost their friends in action, says, "Most sedatives and minor tranquilizers interfere with the working through of the normal mourning process. Although it's terribly painful, a person needs his or her full emotional and intellectual resources and bodily health to go through that process."

Naomi, a young woman of sixteen, encountered so much difficulty in accepting her father's death that she had to be sent to an institution for disturbed adolescent girls. At the institution she was kept under close psychiatric observation because her record included three attempts at suicide.

A disruptive family background preceded her father's sudden violent death. (He was a restaurant manager killed during a holdup attempt.) Shortly after the tragedy, her mother moved in with another man who wanted no responsibility for looking after Naomi. For a time she joined a youthful gang of petty thieves and shoplifters. She was arrested and paroled in her mother's custody, but again her mother's lover refused the responsibility. Naomi moved out and began living with a young man who had been a leader of the youthful gang of which she had been a member. She continued to give her address at school as her mother's house. When the deception was discovered she told the parole officer she had moved out because her mother was a "phony" who didn't really care for her.

Naomi was turned over to a foster family, to whom she became very antagonistic. At this point she appeared incapable of real feeling for anyone. She lacked ambition or direction. Under psychiatric care at the institution, her emotional problem was traced back to the death of her father, who, because of her erratic mother, had provided the only love and guidance she had known.

Finding this out was only the first step. Naomi still had to learn more responsible ways to behave. Her psychiatrist assumed a new role, holding her strictly responsible for her behavior lapses. He evaluated her on a daily basis and informed her regularly of how she was being "rated." He set high standards but maintained discipline without punishment. Naomi began showing steady improvement. When she tested him by breaking a rule he showed that he was ready to forgive and forget and start over again. He never showed his power by punishing her for an infraction.

After an emotional scene with other girls in which she was accused of stealing, she became semihysterical, shouting that everyone hated her and they had a right to hate her because she was no good and no one could help her. At the next session with the psychiatrist, she again threatened suicide. He replied calmly, "I won't be able to help you if you kill yourself. And I want to help you because I think you're really a good person and I care about you."

At their next session Naomi was in better spirits. She asked how long she would have to stay in the institution, and the psychiatrist responded that it was up to her to decide when she was ready to leave. She admitted that she felt ill prepared to return to a living situation in which she would lack his close supervision. On subsequent visits they discussed her future and how she would be able to support herself. She could not go back to a mother who did not want her. Finally she decided she was willing to try another foster home. "But can I come back to see you sometime, just to talk?" she asked. The psychiatrist assured her, "Anytime you like." She left the institution the next week and has not returned.

The psychiatrist who told us Naomi's story says: "She suffered from a feeling that she was not, in her words, 'much good for anything.' Her problem entered a critical stage with the death of her father and could be solved only by restoring some of the stability she had lost with his death. Being rejected by her mother confirmed her poor estimate of herself. Until she learned to accept herself, she could not accept her father's passing. The remedy was to show her she was worthy of respect, to offer her care and concern, and to become involved with her problems. I had to place her in discipline and be firm when needed, and when she was ready let her find her own way. That was an act of trust. At the same time I continued to show interest in her development."

In other words, he acted as a substitute father.

"I didn't really appreciate Dad when he was alive," a young woman confesses. "To him, I was just one of three girls. There was nothing special about our relationship. I would say we had an average relationship, nothing very different. It's weird, how much more important it seems to me now. I think of Dad as someone very special. It's as if we began having a romance after his death. Time and time again I keep remembering things about him. I can't stop myself from doing it."

Judged in a new perspective after he is gone, a father's image looms larger. If the act of separation was not completed, if the symbiotic tie was not broken, the daughter remains plugged into a person who no longer exists. From the grave, father's influence continues to be strongly felt. If he were alive she might exert her will against him, but now any resistance to him appears almost an act of blasphemy. It is difficult to imagine a more frustrating situation.

The psychic trauma caused by a father's death has lately become the subject of extensive research. A British study, conducted among girls under treatment for psychological problems, reveals that many still have fantasies about their fathers. They talk of a dead father as if he were alive, unable to accept the fact of his death. One girl of eleven told her interviewer: "My daddy is coming to see me today. He told me so. He's going to take me home. He came to me last night and sat on my bed and talked to me for a long while. He said he was sorry he'd been away so long and promised he wouldn't ever leave me again." When she was told gently for the hundredth time that her father was dead and could not have talked to her, she replied, "Oh, he told me you'd say that, but not to pay attention. He will come and we will be together forever." Afterward, when her father did not appear, she grew very reluctant to discuss him, saying, "He won't come while everyone keeps talking about him being dead."

The researcher concluded that her persistent affectionate relationship with a dead father helped her to cope with inarticulable feelings about his death. This psychological dependence can, in certain circumstances, be malignant and dangerous, as with another young girl under treatment for suicidal impulses who told of hearing her father's voice telling her to kill herself.

"But why would your father want you to kill yourself?" she was asked.

"He wants us to be together. I want that too."

I have saved for last an interview with a thirty-five-year-old woman who expressed her feelings about her father's final illness: "When he first got sick I didn't do everything for him that I should have done. At the time I resented him being sick in my home. He was taking valuable time, and I was busy and worked hard and had little enough time for myself. I never took seriously about him being in danger.

"I kept ignoring the signs. He coughed terribly at night, but I was only anxious that he would wake the baby. He couldn't keep food down and he couldn't sleep. He hardly spoke. Most of the day he spent in bed propped up on a pillow. He'd become so thin. How could I not have known? I didn't want to. That last night I patted his hand on the coverlet and asked if there was anything he wanted. I knew he wanted me to stay with him awhile and talk to him. His eyes were bright with fever. He was too weak to have said much but I could have talked to him. I might have comforted him. I think he was frightened. The truth is, I was frightened too but I couldn't admit fear. If only I could have said, 'I'm frightened too,' it might have helped. That kind of honesty is better than giving impersonal care, like a nurse.

"But I was tired, and I left the room and went to bed. If I had stayed it might have been different. It happened sometime during the night. As soon as I looked at him I knew it was hopeless. He was gone. I'll never forgive myself for letting him go like that, for not fighting harder to keep him.

"The aftermath is worse than the dying itself. My feelings were on hold. I couldn't respond to anything. My husband tried to console me, but he was like a stranger. I was closed off from him and from my children. All I had in my thoughts were memories of my father. I wanted to live the rest of his life for him—the part God had refused him.

"I felt helpless not being able to change things. It was the kind of predicament from which only one person could rescue me—and he was gone. Inside myself I was crying, 'I don't know how to go on anymore. Please listen to me somebody. Please help me.' My husband at one point told me to stop keeping my grief to myself, to let it out. But I couldn't.

"It was not until the funeral was over and we were walking back to our car through the cemetery—all those headstones of people who had been loved and had also died—that I could accept the fact of his death. There with my son and daughter beside me, I felt like a little child. I wanted to put out my hand and take my father's hand and let him guide me down the path."

One could hardly ask for a clearer expression of the feelings of someone who had never achieved true emotional separation from her father.

TWENTY

THE SUMMING-UP

When Donna was nine years old her mother and I arranged for her to spend the summer at camp while we took a long yearned-for vacation in Europe.

We were in Rome when we got a postcard from Donna saying she had been chosen for a leading role as a juror in *Twelve Angry Women*—an adaptation of the famed *Twelve Angry Men* play and film by Reginald Rose. In the same mail we received a letter from her counselor saying Donna was suffering from a virus and fever, but that she would probably be all right in time for the play.

We made an overseas telephone call to Donna. Her mother told her she must not attempt to appear in the play, that we were returning home right away to be with her even though this meant cutting short our European holiday by several weeks. When I got on the phone I asked Donna if she was all right. Assured that she was feeling better already and wanted very much to appear in the play, I told her to go ahead. Her mother and I would stay in Europe.

"On the night of the play I was still feeling a little rocky," Donna tells me now, "and pretty unsure of myself. All the other girls had their parents there, and I was the only one who didn't have anyone. But I went on and got the most applause, and everyone came around to congratulate me. I'll never forget how proud I felt of myself. I did it alone. What a triumph!"

A friend of mine has two daughters who left home, one to be married, the other to work in a nearby city. He describes his new relationship with them: "I'm a parent plus friend, but it's a very special friendship because we have a history that covers all her life and a good part of mine."

A few months ago the daughter who left home to take a job wrote him that she was miserable, the job wasn't as nice as she expected, she didn't like her boss, and she hated the tiny dark furnished room that was all she could afford. "It's exactly the size of a sarcophagus," she told him.

"My first impulse was to say come home right away," my friend said. "She could live with us until she found a more

199

suitable arrangement. The prospect of getting her back was enough to make me feel years younger. But I knew this wasn't what she really wanted. I was now a 'parent plus friend'—and the friendship, the very special friendship, had to come first. I couldn't play protective father any longer. I couldn't fall back on my long-rehearsed routines. If I did, she would end up with a conditioned reflex: when in trouble go to Daddy. As a child, she had expected me to come up with workable solutions. As a young woman, my job was to resist pressing my solutions on her."

In subsequent phone calls and letters he discussed the situation with her and urged her to "stick it out" for a while longer. As time passed she became acclimated, made new friends, even got improved working conditions. She was promoted to quality-control inspector at a better salary. The extra money enabled her to buy bright curtains and slipcovers to make her apartment more cheery.

"She's on her way now," her father says. "Neither my life nor hers depend on each other anymore. I can love her but I still have to let her be what she wants and do what she feels is right."

His daughter's reaction: "I love Dad because he is somebody I can tell my problems to. He isn't always bugging me about what I do wrong. He just sits there and listens. There aren't too many fathers who do that."

She is right. Not too many fathers do. They are far too intent on maintaining their authority to recognize that a dispute offers a chance for them to display understanding and sympathy for a daughter's point of view and to reinforce her sense of having a separate identity.

Another example: When Donna was a small girl I refused permission for her to stay up and watch a television show. She uttered the familiar whine of the helpless offended child: "That isn't faaaaiirrr!" I might have accepted this as a challenge and insisted that she must do as I told her. But I tried to forgo the crude delights of mastery and, instead, explained my reasons: she had homework to do, school in the morning, and needed her sleep.

In turn, she informed me that she had done her homework and she promised to take a nap after school the next afternoon. Our dispute was settled in reasonable compromise, by her getting into pajamas and going promptly to bed at the end of the show.

What was important about this minor incident is that she was allowed to state her case, discuss options, reckon costs and benefits and even (hallelujah!) carry the day. Maybe it cost me a tad of infallibility, but it increased her faith in her power to influence some decisions. There is always more going on under the surface of a relationship than is apparent to the participants.

Let us take another very minor incident, the type likely to occur any day in any household. Daughter is petulant, fretful, restless. Father reprimands her. She apologizes but tells him she is bored. He suggests that she watch a television program, listen to music, read a book, call a friend; or he may devise some game they can enjoy together.

What he transmits to her, more important than the intrinsic worth of anything he says (his suggestions are no better than she could think up on her own), is a somewhat clearer idea of what the adult world considers remedies for boredom. This represents a widening of her experience; she learns more of what the adult world is like.

A daughter's symbiotic attachment to her father does not eliminate conflict. As an authority figure he still tries to exercise authority, and as a challenger she still wishes to explore new horizons of challenge. She opposes his inhibitive power instinctively, almost as a way of testing herself.

Recently I had lunch with a man I have known for many years. When he discovered the subject of this book he launched into a discussion of his problems with his daughter.

He was deeply troubled: "My daughter and I were always buddies. Lately that's changed. She's been going off in strange directions and we've lost touch. She even considered moving out and living in a commune. She only eats organic food and refuses dinner at our house. She's into hand-painting silk scarves that she tries to sell for fifty to a hundred dollars each—*scarves!*—and of course she doesn't sell many. When I give her advice about anything she looks blank. It's what she calls 'tuning out.'

"She's always had lots of boyfriends, three or four different guys around all the time. I didn't mind. I felt it was natural. She was too young to have a serious relationship and none of her young men amounted to much.

"Suddenly one young man began coming around a lot, hanging around the house, eating organic food with her in the kitchen while we were having dinner in the dining room. He said he was going to be a lawyer and work for consumer rights. I found out he had dropped out of high school because he had poor grades. He wasn't going to be any kind of a lawyer.

"When I told my daughter she didn't get angry at him for lying to her. She got angry at me. She said I was trying to break them up. She didn't want to hear anything bad about him. We had a big argument about that. I want her to at least go out with other fellows. She says I'm just trying to make her forget her friend and that it won't work. She said, 'Daddy, you keep this up and I'll just move out and live with him.'"

This father can't understand why his daughter flouts his parental "wisdom." It is hard for him to recognize that what he considers self-destructive behavior is nothing more than a desire to solve her own problems and make decisions her own way. "Why, O Lord, did this happen to me?" is the worst possible parental reaction.

If his attempt to help is met with a rebuff, if daughter says, in effect, "I can't talk to you," a father can always reply, "That's all right, dear. I can talk to you!"

The communion between daughter and father is largely determined by the *reliability* of the response each offers to the other. An extreme example will make the point. Suppose during a discussion a father rebuked his young daughter for being fresh. He would expect the acceptable range of response to vary from an apologetic "Gee, I'm sorry, I didn't mean to be fresh" to an accusatory "You're always picking on me!" If her response went beyond those parameters, if, for example, she burst into tears and went stomping out of the room, or took up a knife and threatened to cut her wrists, clearly there would be a serious problem. Such a reaction is outside normal experience and expectation.

In turn, a daughter depends on an expectable performance from father. The contract, though unwritten, cannot be breached. If, for example, a young daughter had been fresh and instead of rebuking her her father threw her out of the house and warned her never to return, she would be justified in considering this an exaggerated response.

This kind of extreme behavior rarely occurs, of course, but every day even in ordinary interchanges, father and daughter gain insights into each other's responses that enables them to make the continual small adjustments that sustain their closeness.

Human nature being what it is, neither father nor daughter will get all they expect. The embarrassing questions remain: What do you *really* mean? How much are you willing to compromise? How far can I resist before I am punished?

If one had to choose the kind of father most likely to have a good long-term relationship with his daughter, the odds would favor the so-called permissive parent. The word permissive has acquired unfavorable connotations, but for the wrong reasons. Permissiveness is a long way from indulgent, almost as far as from strict. What does the word really mean? It signifies that a father will "permit" his daughter to seek out her own experiences and make her own mistakes.

A "strict" father deprives his daughter of the ability to make her own judgments because he substitutes a value system complete with prohibitions and commandments. She cannot challenge on grounds of unfairness and she has no hope of winning an appeal. Everything must move along predictable lines to a foregone conclusion. If she attempts to speak in her defense, she stands warned that her testimony must follow narrow rules of procedure: she cannot be rude or loud (even if that is the only way to express indignation); she may not openly contradict him without calling down upon her head the dread "Are you calling me a liar?" The most she can hope for is that consideration be given to her before sentence is passed, whereupon she must accept it in the proper spirit, which is to say, meekly.

The "strict" dad invariably suffers some degree of estrangement from his daughter.

The indulgent father, on the other hand, is unprepared to accept any cooling in daughter's filial piety. He sincerely believes that by giving in to his daughter's wishes, sometimes anticipating her wishes, he is binding her closer. The message he conveys, without realizing it, is that her wishes are made to be granted.

The usual term for children who come to believe this is "spoiled." That is not a felicitous term if by spoiled we wish to connote overripeness. Underripe is nearer the truth. This kind of daughter is not "ripe" enough to go out into the world where rejection, refusal and denial are ordinary events. She is not ready to accept that what she gets must bear some relation to what she earns.

Without such commonplace wisdom she remains a child— simply because she was never allowed to grow up.

Let us examine each of three different fathers, Indulgent, Strict and Permissive, in an identical situation. Ellen, on the eve of an important exam in school, announces she is feeling too sick to go to school. She has a headache and a bad stomach and is sure she is coming down with flu. Indulgent Father asks if she has a fever. She doesn't know but says it doesn't matter because she feels too rotten to go to school. Indulgent Father may suspect her real reason but he says all right, she doesn't have to go. He may insist that she go right to bed, or he may not.

At this moment Diane, her classmate (who is part of the childish conspiracy to avoid taking the exam), announces to her Strict Father that she is having symptoms of illness. Strict Father takes her temperature, which is normal. He tells her she must go to school to take her exam. If she pleads that she is not prepared for it, he will insist she go because he won't allow a daughter of his to sham her way out of difficulty. He adds that if she flunks the exam, "that will teach you to study harder the next time."

The third girl, Mary (also involved in the plot) tells the same story to Permissive Father. He takes her temperature and although it is normal, he volunteers to call the doctor "if she really feels that rotten." Divining as did the other fathers that her real reason is not to take the exam, he tells her, "You can stay out of school if that is what you're after, but I don't think you'll be proud of yourself later. Whatever you decide, though, do it for the real reason and don't try to fool either yourself or me."

Three different households, three identical situations, three varying resolutions. The last answer is best for daughter and for her all-important relationship with her father. Treated "permissively," the episode becomes part of an ongoing educational process. Daughter learns 1) something about the meaning of social obligations, 2) something about her own probable reactions if she fails to meet the social obligation and 3) something about her father and the nature of deception. The lessons are subliminally learned but will have an effect on judging what options are available to her in the next similar situation she encounters.

However, any of these three paternal responses is better than inconsistency. Some fathers exhibit indulgent, stern or permissive behavior entirely at their caprice and whim.

A woman at a group therapy session conducted by Dr. Pollard told about an incident with her father that happened when she was eight years old.

"One night we were having company and my father brought me in to be introduced to everybody. They all made a fuss about me and my father looked pleased when everyone told him what a nice daughter he had. He asked me to play a tune on the piano to show everyone how accomplished I was. When I finished he said, 'Come and give your daddy a kiss.' That night I went to bed on Cloud Nine, flushed and happy.

"The next night there was company again. I went in after dinner expecting another happy occasion. My father was smoking a cigar and talking with a man at the head of the table. He just stared at me and said, 'You ought to be in bed. What are you doing up this late?' I told him I'd come in to kiss him goodnight. 'Sure, sure,' he said, and kissed me on the cheek. As he did he whispered fiercely in my ear, 'I want you out of here and in bed— fast!'

"I held back tears until I got to my room. After a while Father came to my room. I was sure he had come to apologize or at least to explain what I had done wrong. Without sitting down, standing a few feet away, he said, 'I want you to get something straight once and for all. You're *never* to interrupt me again like that when I'm with company. You hear?'

"Later I found out that the people we had to dinner that second night were important business people and Father was trying to make a good impression. But that didn't explain anything to me. He had turned against me, and I never felt safe with him again."

"Inconsistency," Dr. Pollard says, "is one of the worst problems in any authority relationship. A daughter responds to love received from father with her own love. When love is not forthcoming or is denied for any reason, she responds, as one might expect, with bewilderment and confusion."

Competitiveness is one method by which a daughter's skills can be developed, but a father often fails to understand this. He does not realize that his function is not to shield but to assist her in coping so that she will learn to manage her own affairs.

Anita, at seven years old, was doing so well as a student in her Bible class at church that the teachers said she was ready to move up. Anita, however, did not want to go to an unfamiliar class. She went to her father, who told her that if she felt strongly about it there was no reason she had to be promoted. (Obviously an indulgent father)

Her teacher protested that Anita would be wasting her time staying in his class because she was already far ahead of the other children in comprehension and reading. "You don't get the point," her father replied. "It doesn't matter whether she gets promoted. All I want her to be is happy."

"She won't be happy if she isn't allowed to perform at her natural level," the teacher replied. "She'll know in her heart that she failed to meet a challenge."

The teacher suggested a compromise in which Anita would stay in his class for two weeks longer while he introduced her to some of the advanced work she would be doing in her new class. He also suggested that her father read and study Bible passages aloud with her at night.

At the end of the two weeks, Anita herself asked to be promoted.

By getting her ready to meet competition, this understanding teacher counteracted Anita's fear of failure. She no longer felt overwhelmed by the prospect of the challenge. In the process, her self-respect and self-confidence were significantly enhanced.

This does not mean that a father should abandon his daughter to sink or swim in the maelstrom. A young girl's psychic state is unformed and precarious. If she encounters unfair competition, or finds herself in a situation in which she is not allowed to compete on equal terms, she may need help.

A fifty-three-year-old woman recalls her father fondly: "We were the only Jewish family in the small town in central Long Island where I grew up. Those were the days right after Hitler and World War II when anti-Semitism of the active kind was going out of fashion. But a quiet verbal kind was still much in practice. In school I was called Mary Matzohs by my classmates, and every day at roll call the teacher seemed to have difficulty pronouncing my name, causing the students to break up. I stood it as long as I could, and one day I told my father I didn't want to go back to school anymore. He found out why and said, 'I can't move out of town or change your school, but I can make sure you're treated like everyone else.'

"The next morning he visited the school principal, who called in my teacher. At the principal's request my father pronounced our name. The teacher was asked to repeat it several times. 'You won't forget it now, will you?' the principal asked politely. The teacher said she would not. My father smiled, thanked the teacher and the principal, shook hands with them and left. From then on the teacher never failed to pronounce my name correctly. As if that were some kind of signal, my classmates stopped calling me Mary Matzohs too."

That father did not try to shield his daughter from the knowledge of bigotry—an impossible task—but he did what he could to be sure she did not suffer from its effects. He taught her a valuable lesson in how much can be accomplished by standing up against injustice. As a wise man said, all that is required for the triumph of evil is for good men to do nothing.

Donna writes: "A father should let his daughter know what he feels and thinks. If he makes it clear that he has confidence in her judgment once she has all the facts, he can proceed to fill her in on what he knows. Then he should listen to her point of view with great respect. He must not try to ride her down or trample her under or in any way intimidate her. The old saying is true: 'Someone convinced against his will is of the same opinion still.'

"If they can't reach agreement, he can console himself that at least he started her thinking about it and she may come around to his point of view later. If she doesn't, so be it. He will never be able to cram his viewpoint down her throat. She'll simply gag on it.

"The fourteen-year-old daughter of a neighbor told me recently, 'My father took me to a movie that was in French with subtitles. I can't stand reading words off a screen. He was really hot for it and couldn't understand why I didn't go for it the same way. He started making cracks about me and about my favorite TV shows like *Saturday Night Live* and *Laverne and Shirley*. I think they're the funniest shows in the world, but he thinks anybody who watches them is an idiot.'

"What presumption! Because a daughter is a generation younger, she cannot value the things her father does in the same way. He can't force her to accept his views on politics, morality, religion, literature, movies—or anything else!"

As a daughter passes out of girlhood into independence a father should become less her protector and more her mentor. Mentor was the friend of Ulysses to whom he entrusted his household and the care and education of his son. The dictionary now defines a mentor as "a wise and trusted counselor." He is a little like a movie director. A director can indicate to an actor the general direction he expects him to go, but the actor has a unique and separate function. The director can't perform for him. He must let the actor find his way on his own. The test of a good mentor is like the test of a good director: knowing when to keep hands off.

Finally, no father can be all the father that his daughter needs. He cannot be all-wise, all-protecting, always loving. He has no magic lamp to summon up a genie who will solve all her problems. That particular genie isn't answering anymore.

At one time my daughter had no fear of the world as long as I was in it. She knows now that the world is a dangerous place and that I am powerless. Understanding that as well as she does, she is still able to love me. That is a gift beyond my deserts.

We don't have the oneness I envisioned when she was a child, but I was a child myself to have envisioned it.

A DAUGHTER'S POSTSCRIPT

My father is a man of formidable charm. Even casual aquaintances are moved by it and close friends agree that, if he wished, he could "talk a shark out of his skin."

I've always been a sucker for that charm. Even as a little girl, I remember how easily my father could manipulate me. One of my favorite games was when he'd lift me up slowly towards the ceiling in stages, all the while demanding in mock outrage that I stop going up: "Where do you think you're going? Stop right now, do you hear me?" The pretense of disobeying only made it all the more delightful to be held and lifted up so high.

My father could always get me out of any mood, even crying from pain, by "punishing" the offending object that had hurt me. He'd swat it, saying, "That'll teach you to hurt my little girl!" If I hurt a finger, he'd "swallow" it and "take the pain away." The pain did not go away, of course, but I enjoyed the game so much that I was usually willing to go along. And the attention and love I was getting did have a therapeutic effect.

As I grew older, our interplay evolved into slightly more complicated forms of manipulation. Dad might say, "I'd ask you to be absolutely quiet for ten minutes, but I know you couldn't do it without bursting wide open." Then, of course, I *had* to be quiet for the full ten minutes just to prove I could. Or really, to win a greater reward: the delighted amazement he would register at my having performed such a stupendous feat.

When I was fourteen I got sick while at our beach cottage and had to stay in bed. I was terribly bored and my father commiserated with me because there was nothing in the house for him to read to me except J. D. Salinger's tales, which were much "too complicated" for "a girl your age." Then he went on to say one story in particular, "For Esmée with Love and Squalor," he would like me to read in a few years when I was "ready for it." By then wild horses could not have kept me from hearing that story. But still Dad held out, pointing out such difficulties as a change in viewpoint midway in which you have to figure out that the third-person and first-person narrators are the same person, and that the

209

understated references to the brutality of war are really more effective than saying so outright, and that the character of the girl in the story was one of the very few instances in literature that he knew of (Tolstoy's Natasha in *War and Peace* was the other) in which an author who set out to portray a girl as charming succeeded in doing so. This added the piquancy of discovering what Dad thought was charming in a girl—a discovery whose importance to me could hardly be overestimated. Needless to say, Dad's reading that story that afternoon in our beach cottage was one of the most memorable events of my childhood. "For Esmée with Love and Squalor" is still, as far as I'm concerned, one of the monuments of our literature.

As I look back, I'm sure I was aware of how I was being gotten around. But I didn't mind; I loved my father, loved his protectiveness and concern, even loved having someone understand me so intimately that he *could* manipulate me.

To ensure my father's continuing love and protection, I tried hard to be a "good girl"—which usually meant being appreciative and compliant. This was very important to me. I remember sometimes in the privacy of my room reflecting with pleasure on how "good" I really was—only to stop and sharply reprimand myself for my lack of humility (pride was *not* something I considered a characteristic of a "good girl"). When I did something bad I was thoroughly miserable, as though some horrible inner secret about me had been revealed.

Once, when I was about ten, I broke some minor house rule. It must have been a bad day for my father, for though he had never spanked me, he did that day. I was terribly upset, not so much because my behind smarted—which it did—but because I had so clearly fallen from favor. A friend was visiting me at the time and when I came back to her, sobbing, she advised, "Don't speak to him at all. Just look angry and hurt and you'll make him feel bad and then he'll apologize. That's what my dad always does." I thought about it; I *was* angry because the punishment seemed out of proportion to the crime. But I couldn't bear the thought of being in disfavor one minute longer. So I went back to my father (who was indeed feeling very guilty and rotten), told him what my friend had said and added, still weeping, "But I d-don't want to do that. I just want to be *f-f-friends!*" My father took me in his arms then and we made up. All thought of what was right or wrong, just or not, vanished from my mind. I was so happy to be redeemed, to be once again Daddy's little girl.

My father was always a marvel to me—so sensitive, witty, wise, powerful—and, of course, *always* right in his opinions on everything from Marx to premarital sex. I suppose that if someone had suggested it to me in so many words, I would have denied it, but it truly never occurred to me that my father could actually be wrong. If I enjoyed a movie and later found out that my father thought it was bad, my reaction was, "Whoops! I guessed wrong about that one!" If he expressed approval of a particular political figure or economic policy, I believed that his statement represented the views of all right-thinking people—and I felt utter contempt and scorn for those who disagreed (even though I very often had no real understanding of the issues at all). My father's ideas on women, fashion, beauty, were invariably correct. His wife Joanna recently reminded me of one incident that occurred when I was seventeen. I had discovered a new kind of face foundation that I liked very much. All my friends liked it too: one friend was so pleased with it she went right out and bought a jar for herself. But this night I had applied it a bit inexpertly, and looking at me under some bright lights my father commented, "What's that funny-looking line along your chin? It looks like your face is disconnected from your neck." I never wore that makeup again.

It's uncomfortable for me to admit that these feelings persisted well into my adult life. I remember in particular one occasion just before my marriage. I had been dating Richard, my husband-to-be, for over a year and had lived with him for six months, so I knew and loved him well. Indeed, there was no doubt that he was the best, sanest, kindest, most loving man I'd ever known. We had often gone out as a foursome with my father and Joanna, and everyone got along very well. There was no reason in the world for me to doubt the wisdom of the step I was taking.

Yet one week before the wedding I panicked. *Was* Richard really right for me? I wondered. He was so different from my father, more low-key and deliberative, shyer, lacking Dad's easy charm and grace—*and* his ability to manipulate me. The thought worried me. Was I making a mistake? It occurred to me that I had never actually asked my father what *he* thought about my marrying Richard. Suddenly I knew I had to call him. He would, after all, know the "right" answer to this terrible question. How foolish of me not to have thought of asking him before! So I ended up, twenty-five years old asking my father over the phone, "Do you think Richard's the right man for me, Dad? Do you like him? Am I doing the right thing?"

To my father's credit, he refused to play Big Daddy to my childlike request for reassurance, replying in somewhat surprised tones that he liked—even loved—Richard very much but that marrying him was a decision whose wisdom I would have to determine for myself. Despite the manifest good sense of his response, I felt let down. The oracle had refused to "ope his lips." and I was adrift on an uncertain sea with no clear voice to guide me. Except my own. And I had not yet learned to trust it.

That crisis passed and three days later I married Richard, which turned out to be the smartest thing I've ever done, as I should have known. Not long after, I decided to explore the reasons why I was so reluctant to make difficult decisions, to confront people, to stand up for myself. I wanted to learn why I was still trying to win approval through compliance and appeasement. So I consulted a therapist, in the "short course" of ten weeks.

I remember the exact moment when the message finally got through to me. The therapist asked me, "Do you like everybody you meet, Donna?" "Why, no," I replied, wondering what she was getting at. "Then why do you feel that everybody must like *you?*" she asked. Click! I understood the essential irrationality of my behavior. Over the course of the next few months I finally began to learn how to say no, how to stop apologizing for everyone and everything, how to express anger, how to take an unpopular position and stick to it—in short, how to be a grownup. Today I can even pass that ultimate test—being able to close the door in the face of an overly persistent vacuum cleaner salesman!

My dearest hope is that my daughter Emily will be able to do these things *without* the need of therapy. In this brave new world of changing family relationships, her chances are good, I think. Just the other day I heard Richard trying to instruct her on the correct way to skip (she does something more resembling a gallop). Emily listened patiently and then resumed exactly what she had been doing. "Daddy," she said, "you skip your way and I'll skip mine!" I can think nothing I wish more for her than that she skip her own way.

Today, partly as a result of writing this book together, my father tells me he has discovered many things he did wrong as a parent. But I'm not sure he realizes how much he did right. I'd like him to know some of the things he did that meant—and still mean—a great deal to me:

My father was always *there* when I needed someone to talk to. Even when I was very small, he treated my problems with seriousness and respect. I never looked to him for help and found him looking elsewhere. Once, in the middle of explaining to him how upset I was about an unfair distribution of favors at a birthday party, I had a moment of insight and commented, "This must seem awfully silly to you compared to your problems with your work and everything." My father replied, "The size of the problem is determined by the feelings of the person who's got it. Your problem is every bit as important to you and you feel every bit as strongly about it as I do about mine. That's what counts." I knew then that I could talk to my father about anything. I knew that no matter what the problem I wouldn't be lectured at or talked down to. Indeed, I don't think my father ever had any fixed idea about what I as a child ought to do at any given time, except a vague feeling that I should do whatever I thought was best. We would sit down and reason together, and I don't think he had any better idea of the answer we'd come up with than I did. The knowledge that I could have a sympathetic and noninterfering listener anytime I needed him helped me through some difficult times.

My father helped me to understand those inexplicable creatures called boys. I remember one time when a boy I'd had a real crush on—and who I thought liked me too—was deliberately rude and insulting to me. I was very unhappy and confused, and didn't know how to respond. Then my father told me how once, when he was seventeen, he had done the same thing to a girl he liked. He had a terrible crush on a girl at school, but he never had the courage even to speak to her and he confined his courtship to staring at her back adoringly during math class. One day he and a group of kids began playing a game in which the boys concocted elaborate marriage proposals to the girls of their choice. My father, who had a reputation as class poet, was paired off with his secret flame. "C'mon, Bill," his friends encouraged him. "Give her a really beautiful proposal." Embarrassed and desperate to mask his true feelings lest he be laid open to ridicule, my father waved the girl off, saying, "Sorry. There's not sufficient inspiration."

Recounting that story to me years later, my father winced

at the memory of his own clumsiness and vulnerability. Another father would probably have laughed at my sad story of puppy love. So many adults—I'm an adult myself now but I still don't understand it—think that the throes of adolescent love are a fit subject for hilarity. "He jests at scars that never felt a wound," Romeo says. It's not that most fathers never felt a wound. They just can't find the scar tissue anymore. My father was willing to put his finger right on his wound in order to tell me how it felt.

My father has always respected me as a person—my feelings, my opinions, my privacy. A good example is an incident that occurred when I was eighteen. My mother accompanied me to Philadelphia, where I was to be interviewed for admission to the University of Pennsylvania. On the train ride, my mother and I playfully began to invent statements that would horrify the interviewer: "I'm interested in Penn because it has a ratio of eleven men to one woman, and after six years at an all-girls high school I want a little action!" "I'm into the hard stuff and I've really got a good connection here in Philadelphia." As we thought up more outrageous reasons, laughing, my mother jotted them down on the inside cover of a paperback book she was carrying.

A few months later my uncle Ralph was visiting us and, browsing through our library, he found that book. He approached my father solemnly, warning him that his sweet daughter was not all she seemed to be and if he wished to learn more about what I was *really* like, he should read the inside cover of such-and-such a book located on the third shelf of the library. Though he must have been curious, my father did not seize this apparent opportunity to spy on my inner thoughts. Instead, he simply told me what Uncle Ralph had said and suggested that I might want to look into it and perhaps remove the book from the shelf. I found the book and, relieved to find it harmless (who knew what my uncle might have accidently stumbled upon?), showed it to my father, who was amused (it was so ridiculously exaggerated— and not even my own handwriting!). But I have always been grateful to him for the opportunity he gave me to protect my own privacy—at the expense of his own curiosity. It takes a certain largeness of soul to do that.

My father was always very patient with me. I have only

discovered, with my own daughter, how much patience is required with a small child. Sometimes, with the pressures of a full-time job, a home and book writing, I have felt stretched to the limit, convinced that I have absolutely no more to give her. But somehow I manage to reach down into myself for more. I think I know where that extra measure comes from. It comes from half-remembered childhood moments with my father and from the tolerance and love he showed me. I have rediscovered my father's love in my own child and, to pay him the ultimate compliment, I know I could not be so happy a mother had I not been so fathered.

In the course of writing this book, my father and I have had to explore our relationship in ways that have sometimes been painful. I know he feels guilty about the times (particularly during the breakup of his marriage to my mother) when he misused the enormous power he had over me. What he does not know, and what I have never told him, is that I was a coconspirator in those times—conspiring with him to keep myself from growing up and away. My cooperation was unconscious and never verbalized, powered by my own reluctance to take on the incalculable burdens associated with maturity. The unknown, the darkness at the top of the stairs, was my most vivid terror.

I have climbed those stairs now and penetrated the darkness, and found it not without comfort and companionship. Sometimes I still wish to be protected and coddled, to have someone take away the worry and the pain of adult life. My husband will never "swallow" my hurt and make it go away as my father did. No one will ever do that for me again. But I know now the rewards of being an independent, fully functioning adult woman. There may still be moments when I wish I could be Daddy's Little Girl again, but most of the time I am glad I am not.

DONNA WOOLFOLK CROSS

INDEX